THE ASSAULT ON INTERNATIONAL LAW

THE
ASSAULT ON
INTERNATIONAL
LAW

JENS DAVID OHLIN

OXFORD
UNIVERSITY PRESS

OXFORD
UNIVERSITY PRESS

Oxford University Press is a department of the University of
Oxford. It furthers the University's objective of excellence in research,
scholarship, and education by publishing worldwide.

Oxford   New York
Auckland   Cape Town   Dar es Salaam   Hong Kong   Karachi
Kuala Lumpur   Madrid   Melbourne   Mexico City   Nairobi
New Delhi   Shanghai   Taipei   Toronto

With offices in
Argentina   Austria   Brazil   Chile   Czech Republic   France   Greece
Guatemala   Hungary   Italy   Japan   Poland   Portugal   Singapore
South Korea   Switzerland   Thailand   Turkey   Ukraine   Vietnam

Oxford is a registered trademark of Oxford University Press
in the UK and certain other countries.

Published in the United States of America by
Oxford University Press
198 Madison Avenue, New York, NY 10016

Library of Congress Cataloging-in-Publication Data
Ohlin, Jens David, author.
The assault on international law / Jens David Ohlin.
   pages cm
ISBN   978-0-19-998740-5 (hardback)
1. International and municipal law—United States.   2. International law—United
States.   I. Title.
KF4581.O35 2015
340.90973—dc23
2014023293

9 8 7 6 5 4 3 2 1
Printed in the United States of America
on acid-free paper

For Nancy, Christopher, and Clara

CONTENTS

PREFACE

Like many writing projects, this book quickly fell behind schedule. Although I had long since mapped out the core of its argument, in May 2013, I was hopelessly behind schedule, delayed by other writing commitments and distracted by the quotidian aspects of professorial life.

Then, in June 2013, came a remarkable period of productivity. I took a brief vacation to Cape Cod with my wife Nancy and my daughter Clara. I awoke early each morning at 5:00 a.m., while my family slept; I fixed a pot of coffee and would start writing at a furious pace. In the space of seven inspired days, I wrote the crucial first stage of the book (chapter 4) that lays out the nuts and bolts of the philosophical argument upon which the entire project rests. Little did I know that during that week, amidst my bolt of creativity, something in my body was terribly amiss; I was in the process of getting very sick.

Back in Ithaca the following week, I put the finishing touches on chapter 4. I was pleased with the result, but I also felt exhausted. I couldn't climb a flight of stairs without becoming so short of breath that I wanted to collapse into bed. On Sunday morning, while fixing my daughter breakfast, I actually did collapse, losing consciousness and falling to the floor. Thankfully, my wife rushed me to the Emergency Room.

Upon my arrival at the ER entrance, the nurses slapped an EKG on my chest and read the results. A doctor appeared and told me that there was something seriously wrong with my heart. I was in third-degree heart block, so the signals from the atria were getting lost before they could reach the ventricle and trigger a normal heartbeat. The doctors couldn't get my heart to beat faster than 29 beats per minute. "Why am I in heart block?" I asked my doctor. "I'm 39 years old and in perfect health."

"We have no idea," he said, "but you need a pacemaker and you need it now. We're prepping an OR and we're paging the implant team. If all of them call in, then we're a go for surgery in an hour." By lunchtime, I awoke from surgery with the latest pacemaker technology in my chest.

After a few days, they sent me home. I was wearing a sling because the doctors wanted my arm immobilized, and they didn't want me to move around too much. A pacemaker is implanted right above the heart with two wires that are jammed directly into the heart muscle. There isn't much to hold the wires into the heart, other than tiny surgical screws, and the doctors don't want the wires to get dislodged while scar tissue develops and solidifies the connection. So I sat on the couch and complied with their instructions to stay still.

With little to do, I wrote on my laptop. This began a period of immense productivity for the next two months. I proceeded quickly through the remaining chapters of the book, writing with speed, intensity, and inspiration. My writing provided a welcome distraction from my own health as well as from anxiety and fear about my condition. It was easier to think about the foundations of international law rather than the machine that was connected to my heart.

It was during this writing spasm that I received a call from one of my doctors, an infectious disease specialist who was consulting on my case. He told me that I had Lyme Disease. "The bad news is that you have Lyme Disease," he said. "The good news is that we can cure it with an antibiotic. And your heart abnormality was caused by the Lyme Disease. Once your Lyme is cured, we have every reason to believe that your heart will return to normal." Sure enough, over the next six weeks, my heart continued to improve. I slowly became less and less pacemaker-dependent. Eventually, I reached the point where my heart wasn't using the pacemaker at all. It was just sitting there.

At the beginning of October 2013, I finished the manuscript and sent it to my editor at Oxford, Dave McBride. The following morning, I drove to the hospital for a second surgery—this time to have the pacemaker removed. This ended the most productive summer of my scholarly career, though it is one that I'm not eager to repeat.

Ithaca, NY
October 2013

ACKNOWLEDGMENTS

I received helpful comments from faculty at Vanderbilt University, William & Mary Law School, and Cornell Law School during workshop presentations. Cornell Law School provided generous summer research support that allowed me to complete this book.

I attended several conferences at the Center for Ethics and the Rule of Law (CERL) at University of Pennsylvania Law School, where Claire Finkelstein, Christopher Morris, Duncan MacIntosh, and David Gauthier deepened my understanding of rational choice theory. I also benefited from conversations on rational choice with my colleague Emily Sherwin, and from conversations on international legal theory with Lea Brilmayer.

Brad Wendel, Sid Tarrow, and Matt Evangelista read the entire manuscript and gave detailed reactions and suggestions that improved the book immensely. I am also grateful for the editorial stewardship of David McBride at Oxford University Press, Sarah Rosenthal, and my agent Jeff Gerecke.

Portions of chapter 3 were originally published as *Nash Equilibrium and International Law*, 96 CORNELL LAW REVIEW 869 (2011), later reprinted in shorter form in 23 EUROPEAN JOURNAL OF INTERNATIONAL LAW 915 (2012). All other material in the book is original.

Introduction

DRAMATIS PERSONAE

When the hijacked airplanes hit the World Trade Towers on 9/11, John Yoo was working in his Justice Department office in Washington, DC. At the time, he was assigned to one of the most crucial legal departments in the federal government, the Office of Legal Counsel (OLC). Although he was an important lawyer in the administration of President Bush, Yoo himself was not well known outside of a close circle of Washington bureaucrats and policy wonks. He wasn't famous. But all of that would change very quickly.

Yoo had taken a leave of absence from Berkeley Law School to work for the Bush administration. His academic work had focused on constitutional law and foreign affairs, and he had earned a reputation for being a strong supporter of presidential war powers. According to Yoo, the president of the United States has virtually unlimited power as the constitutionally appointed commander in chief of the armed forces. Although Congress can play some role in times of war, Yoo had insisted in a series of law review articles that this role was secondary at best.[1] In times of crisis, presidential power always trumps congressional deliberation.

Before 9/11, Yoo's views were mostly of academic interest. His writings had attracted some skepticism among his law school colleagues, but prior to 9/11, his views were hardly part of the wider political discourse. All of that changed dramatically after the planes hit.

1. The Office of Legal Counsel

Within days, the White House was asking the OLC to answer a whole set of crucial legal questions: Could the president order the bombing of al-Qaeda training camps in Afghanistan? What type of congressional authorization was required before the president could use military force? Could the president use preemptive force to stop future terrorist attacks? Could the United States attack not just terrorist organizations but also the foreign states that harbored them? After the OLC answered yes to each of these questions, and President Bush ordered military attacks against al-Qaeda and the Taliban, a second round of no-less important questions were raised about the conduct of the war. Could terrorists be detained by the military, and did the Geneva Conventions apply to them? Could interrogators torture detainees to extract life-saving information about future terrorist attacks?

It was this last question that made Yoo famous. Yoo quickly researched the issue and concluded that it was both legally and morally permissible for interrogators to use coercive interrogation measures—and even outright torture—to induce a detainee to spill information that might save American lives. He drafted a memo that was sent to his superior who was then running the OLC, Jay Bybee, who signed the memo and delivered it to White House Counsel Alberto Gonzalez.[2] The memo was long and extensive and filled with scholarly looking footnotes, but the analysis was troubling and controversial. First, Yoo concluded that although the federal anti-torture statute did not define "severe pain," a definition might be gleaned from a Medicare provision that allowed emergency medical services for cases of severe pain "capable of producing organ failure or death." So, according to Yoo, interrogators could inflict as much pain as they wanted on a detainee, so long as it did not cause organ failure or death, and it would not be classified as torture under federal law.[3]

Yoo also argued in another memo that the Geneva Conventions, which prohibit torture during wartime, did not apply to al-Qaeda or Taliban fighters, so long as the president determined that neither group respected the laws of war. This determination was plausible for al-Qaeda but was much more suspect with regard to the Taliban, and in any event, it was unclear why the president could unilaterally make this decision by fiat. Yoo also argued that the United States was not required to follow the Geneva Conventions because Afghanistan was a "failed state"—a legal nonentity under international law.[4] According to Yoo's argument, the Geneva Conventions embody reciprocal promises between nation-states. Since Afghanistan did not exist anymore, the Conventions were no longer in force between the United States and Afghanistan. With it went the legal protections afford by the Conventions. Or so claimed John Yoo.

After the infamous "torture memo," more legal research followed. The OLC concluded that al-Qaeda and Taliban fighters could be held indefinitely as enemy combatants and did not deserve POW status.[5] The OLC concluded that the president alone could order captured fighters prosecuted before military commissions and that they could be denied access to federal courts to contest the lawfulness of their detention.[6] Targeted killings, or what critics call assassinations, were approved. The National Security Agency was given the green light to eavesdrop on wiretapped conversations between American citizens and foreigners—even without a warrant—despite the fact that Congress had explicitly passed a law limiting this wiretapping to foreigners.[7]

Much of this legal strategy was hammered out by an informal group of lawyers, nicknamed the "War Council," who met in the White House. In addition to Yoo, the group included White House Counsel Alberto Gonzalez, who reported directly to Bush, as well as David Addington, the top lawyer for Vice President Dick Cheney, and Defense Department General Counsel William Haynes.[8] The group had no formal status, and its membership was not appointed by President Bush. Its authority stemmed only from the fact that Bush relied heavily on the advice of Gonzalez and Cheney, who were trusted confidants, especially on war matters. Cheney relied on Addington for legal analysis, and Addington listened to Yoo. By most accounts, the legal foundation for the War on Terror was developed by the War Council.[9] Attorney General Ashcroft was noticeably absent from this group, and he apparently resented Yoo's influence in the War Council.[10] After all, Yoo worked at the Justice

Department and was supposed to report to him, not to Gonzalez or Addington.

In 2003, the top position at the OLC opened up after Bybee was nominated for a federal judgeship, and the War Council wanted Yoo promoted to lead the office. But Ashcroft objected and torpedoed the idea, fearing that the OLC, which was ostensibly located in the Justice Department, would effectively now report to Gonzalez and Addington.[11] Ashcroft claimed that Yoo was incompetent, and without Ashcroft's support, Yoo's candidacy went nowhere.[12]

So who would lead the OLC? Yoo suggested that his old friend Jack Goldsmith would be perfect for the job.[13] Goldsmith, a young law school professor at the University of Chicago, had been working as a top legal adviser to Haynes at the Pentagon. Goldsmith and Yoo were friends and traveled in similar circles. In the relatively liberal crowd of law school professors, conservative lawyers provide mutual support for their endeavors. They join the Federalist Society in law school, clerk for the same Supreme Court justices (Rehnquist, Scalia, Thomas), and read drafts of each other's articles. Goldsmith and Yoo were no exception.

Yoo left the Justice Department to return to academia just as Goldsmith was taking over the helm at the OLC in 2003. The controversy surrounding Yoo's work there was only just beginning, because most of the memos written by Yoo were still confidential or classified.

Goldsmith enjoys an encyclopedic knowledge of constitutional law and its relationship with international law; while plenty of liberals disagree with his scholarship, everyone agrees that he has an impressive command of the law. But when Goldsmith got to the OLC, he was horrified by what he saw. Now that he was on the inside, he suddenly had access to all of the OLC memos written by Yoo and his colleagues since 9/11, only some of which he had seen during his time at the Pentagon. Goldsmith read the entire stack of memos and found them riddled with errors, unsupported conclusions of law, exaggerations, and fallacious arguments.[14] He called the arguments cursory, one-sided, and legally flawed.[15]

What he would do next would ruin his friendship with John Yoo. Goldsmith went to his boss, Attorney General John Ashcroft, and told him that the Yoo torture memo needed to be withdrawn. Although it sounds like a minor bureaucratic change, in fact, it represented a massive rejection of John Yoo and his tenure in government service. And it was also unprecedented. Not only had the OLC never withdrawn such a significant memo during the same administration, but they had never even done it after a *change* in administrations, when a new political party inevitably brings a new cohort of lawyers with a different ideological perspective on crucial questions of international law.[16] Even then, the culture at the OLC was to respect precedent and the prior work of the department on matters of great significance.

Goldsmith's withdrawal of the Yoo memo was also something that could not be done quietly. Ashcroft had to inform the White House and every department in the executive branch that they could no longer rely on the legal advice in the torture memo. That meant informing everyone in the Pentagon and the CIA and deployed forces overseas. It meant Ashcroft admitting that the Justice Department had gotten it wrong, something that does not happen often in government. All of this made John Yoo look politically inept at best, legally incompetent at worst. Yoo would later write in his memoirs that Goldsmith and the new OLC lawyers were "too worried about the public perceptions of its work" and that they had caved to political pressure.[17] Addington was furious that Goldsmith was undoing countless hours of legal strategy decided by the War Council.[18]

The next task was to actually rewrite the flawed memos. The new "torture memo" refused to define "severe pain and suffering" and declined to make the ridiculous analogy to the Medicare provision dealing with emergency medical services. Goldsmith also made sure to withdraw John Yoo's unsupported statements that the president could violate both international law and congressional mandates because the Constitution designates him commander in chief of the armed forces.[19] All of it was gone. What was left was a far more cautious, and subtle, work of legal analysis.

Goldsmith had ruffled so many powerful feathers in his quest to reverse the Yoo mess that he decided to quit and return to teaching law school.[20] He had lasted only nine months as head of OLC and didn't even have time to finish the new memos. But he set the revision process in motion and, in so doing, stood up to the worst excesses of the Bush administration and its shadowy War Council. He set the law back on track.

This is the standard story of what happened from 2001 to 2004, a crucial time in our nation's history when the government was formulating its response to terrorism and its posture toward international law. The United States had been attacked and had fought back, but in so doing, the nation's commitment to the rule of law was severely compromised. However, principled men and women like Goldsmith pulled us back from our darkest impulses; they saved the law itself.

This story, like all good stories, has a hero and a villain and a narrative arc that ties them together. Jack Goldsmith, still reliably conservative, comes across as careful, smart, and courageous for reversing the excesses of the first years of the Bush administration. And his actions were heroic because he sacrificed his relationship with John Yoo and annoyed many in the Justice Department and the White House to do it.[21] Addington practically shook his fists in rage when he learned that Goldsmith was unwilling to issue a ruling that would back up a key anti-terrorism initiative. "The blood of the hundred thousand people who die in the next attack will be on your hands," Addington reportedly yelled at Goldsmith.[22]

After less than a year, with the important work of righting the ship accomplished, Goldsmith left government service for the ivory towers of academia. Instead of returning to the University of Chicago Law School, he was offered a chair at Harvard Law School, a far more liberal academic environment than Chicago. Although his hiring was controversial and garnered some opposition by Harvard faculty, his supporters defended him on the grounds that Goldsmith was one of the "good guys."[23] He had gone in to a seriously dysfunctional OLC and cleaned up a legal and ethical mess. He was on the right side.

While Goldsmith was settling into his new office in Cambridge, things were not going so well for Yoo, who was back at Berkeley and readjusting to academic life. But his work in Washington was still haunting him. Ashcroft had agreed to launch an ethics investigation into the torture memos, which was led by a separate division of the Justice Department responsible for investigating the conduct of government lawyers. Liberal critics of the administration were clamoring for Yoo and Bybee to be disbarred, and protestors were lining up outside of Yoo's lectures at Berkeley calling him a war criminal for being complicit in torture. Yoo was furious that Ashcroft was now pretending that he hadn't been involved in every step of the process, and Yoo was also bitter that Goldsmith had sold him out. "By refusing to defend its own logic, and pretending to distance himself from it," according to Yoo, "the administration only succeeded in eroding public support for the war against al Qaeda."[24]

So the story has all of the essential characters. One villain, one hero, and a critical moment that defines each of them. Yoo learns about the planes crashing into the Towers and instantly resolves to provide the president with the legal superstructure to fight the War on Terror. An idealistic Mr. Goldsmith goes to Washington and confronts the cynical reality that law is polluted by politics. But in the end, idealism wins. The rule of law had been threatened by a Justice Department that was all-too-willing to sacrifice our most cherished values in order to vanquish our enemy; at the last moment, principled individuals stood up for the Law. And, in the end, Goldsmith and others like him saved us from our heart of darkness.

It is a great story, one that has been told in Goldsmith's memoirs and repeated in hallways across the country from DC to California. The only problem is that the story is fundamentally wrong. Not wrong in the sense of being a lie, but wrong in the sense that it paints a completely distorted picture of how the United States drifted so far from international law, and its institutions, since 9/11.

The ballad of Goldsmith and Yoo—hero and villain—focuses our attention on an intramural dispute between two central characters and, in so doing, diverts our attention from the bigger picture. The real story here is not the dispute and the fallout between Goldsmith and Yoo that almost cost Yoo his career, certainly cost the two men their friendship, but allowed Goldsmith to escape DC with his honor and reputation intact. The Goldsmith-Yoo story avoids the larger backdrop that unites both Goldsmith and Yoo and their fellow travelers in a common cause—the devaluing of international law. The debate about torture floats on the surface, but beneath the water lies a much deeper and far more consequential movement to which both Goldsmith and Yoo contributed.

2. The Emergence of the New Realists

International law is under attack in the United States. Although most lawyers—and certainly most law school professors—consider international law to be a central and profoundly important element of our legal system, many conservative lawyers are deeply suspicious of international law and the infringement of American sovereignty that it represents. They want U.S. affairs to be dictated by the American political system and the laws that it produces, not the international legal norms that flow from faraway European cities like Brussels, Geneva, and The Hague.

This book tells the story of how a small group of legal scholars—and by small, I mean fewer than six—have earned a completely outsized influence on the legal discourse in this country. Like the Federalist Society, the conservative group that has wielded outsized influence on American constitutional law, a handful of skeptics about international law have completely upended academic research on international law.

Although many academic arguments have little to no impact on our daily lives, the new skepticism about international law has directly changed American foreign relations since 9/11. That is because these arguments do not stay in the abstract confines of the Ivory Tower. They influence how the State Department conducts diplomacy, how the Defense Department conducts the War on Terror, how the CIA and the NSA spy on foreigners and citizens alike, and how judges craft their opinions. And all of this from just a handful of individuals armed with skeptical arguments about the very *idea* of international law.

What unites this group is a shared hostility toward international law, a preference for presidential power in the face of global crisis, and a recommendation that the United States withdraw and remain isolated from international legal institutions. Both Yoo and Goldsmith are part of this very small club. To tell the story with them as antagonists against each other is to completely distort the picture. The fact of the matter is that Goldsmith and Yoo are fellow travelers in a crusade against the growing impact of international law on our lives.

To understand this new skepticism about international law, a new character must be introduced into the story: Eric Posner, a prolific professor at the University of Chicago Law School who wrote or cowrote no fewer than five books between 2007 and 2013, in addition to the numerous law review articles and book chapters that make up the rest of his publication list.[25] He also has a reputation for being exceedingly generous with his time, reading drafts for colleagues and offering helpful suggestions and criticisms, a personal characteristic that unfortunately is becoming all too rare among today's busy professoriate. By all accounts, it is difficult to get the better of Posner when he lectures or debates in public. He speaks in carefully rendered paragraphs that communicate well-worked-out positions with great precision; he is never vague or indecisive. No one has ever accused him of being a lightweight.

Posner's books all share a common refrain: an underlying skepticism about the scope and legitimacy of international law. Because these theories attack the very foundation of international law, they are far more important—and consequential—than the superficial arguments Yoo made at the OLC and Berkeley. So Posner is, in many respects, the modern father of the new skepticism about international law. The media attention given to Yoo has completely obscured the fact that Posner's arguments provide the theoretical foundation for the entire movement.

Although he had published books on other subjects, Posner burst onto the international law scene in 2005 when he published *The Limits of International Law* with Jack Goldsmith. The book articulated a restatement of Posner and Goldsmith's view of international law (which they had published in law review articles prior to 9/11), and it created a ruckus. The insight of *Limits* was pretty succinct: the world community is full of states that act in their own self-interest and essentially ignore international law. When states *appear* to be following international law, in most instances, their actions are really motivated by self-interest, not by the idea that international law *needs* to be followed. Much of international law is therefore illusory—it is just self-interested state behavior. And when self-interest conflicts with international law, states have no moral obligation to follow it. They should do what is best for them—the international rules be damned. In many ways, *Limits* was an intellectual manifesto expressing much of the sentiment—and policy—of the Bush administration.

Limits was only the beginning. What followed was a new wave of scholarship expressing skepticism about international legal institutions such as the United Nations, a position that was articulated quite forcefully in Eric Posner's 2009 book, *The Perils of Global Legalism*. Posner also teamed up with Adrian Vermeule in *Terror in the Balance* to defend the administration's aggressive response to the specter of terrorism, including torture.[26] At the same time, other books argued that the president should have virtually unfettered authority to fight the War on Terror and should ignore Congress—and international law—if necessary. John Yoo published the *Powers of War and Peace: The Constitution and Foreign Affairs after 9/11*, while Posner and Vermeule published *The Executive Unbound: After the Madisonian Republic*, which both argued, among other things, that only the executive branch has the flexibility to meet the changes of modern security threats like terrorism and Islamic extremism.[27] Posner and Vermeule argued that we now live in a permanent state of exigency.[28]

If it seems as though the same names keep popping up, that is because a very small list of *dramatis personae* is driving this scholarship. But the characters are having a tremendous influence among Washington elites.

One can immediately see why *Limits* was important, not just for academics but for politicians and policy wonks too. *Limits* articulated a broader theory that expressed the Bush administration's hostility toward international law that was being exposed by Addington, Yoo, Goldsmith, and Gonzalez. When Yoo argues that the president can ignore Congress, he cites his own articles; when Yoo argues that international law cannot constrain the president, he cites articles written by Goldsmith, Posner, or Vermeule.[29] When Addington and Gonzalez argued that the president needs all available tools to interrogate terrorists, including torture, they did so comforted by the knowledge that scholars like Posner and Vermeule were laying the intellectual foundation for these policies.[30] And when the Bush administration derided international law as a quaint relic of a previous era, they did so out of a belief that states did not have a moral obligation to follow international law when it conflicted with their state interest, a position that was artfully defended by Posner and Goldsmith in their book.[31]

When it comes to law, ideas really matter. Of course, some law school professors write esoteric articles for an expert audience. But academic arguments questioning the validity and scope of international law affect how the U.S. government conducts its business. This is so because these professors do more than just write articles; they also serve as lawyers working for the State Department, the Justice Department's Office of Legal Counsel, the White House Counsel's Office, the Defense Department, and the CIA. And even when their arguments are not having this direct effect, their arguments are indirectly influencing policymakers, lawyers, and federal judges who deal with international law. The assault on international law is far broader than John Yoo and a few memos on torture. This multipronged attack influences how the president fights the War on Terror, whether federal judges can "interfere" with the detention or killing of suspected terrorists, and whether victims of human rights abuses can file lawsuits in federal courts. It determines whether international treaties can be enforced in U.S. courts and whether foreigners on death row should have access to consular assistance, just as an international treaty promises. And that is just the tip of the iceberg. When President Bush ordered the creation of CIA black sites in Eastern Europe, he did it because government attorneys said he could. When President Obama ordered the targeted killing of an American citizen in Yemen, he did so only after the Justice Department said it was legal. In short, arguments about international law implicate every corner of our foreign relations, and it is hard to imagine an area of the law with more practical consequences.

The impact of Goldsmith and Posner's academic arguments in *Limits* explains why the Yoo-as-villain and Goldsmith-as-hero story is a distraction. True, Goldsmith came into the OLC and withdrew the poorly reasoned memos. But when you zoom out and look at the entire spectrum, you see that Yoo and Goldsmith are on the same side, both committed to an intellectual project whose central foundation is executive branch aggrandizement and international law deflation. The movement was incredibly successful between 2000 and 2008, and it permanently transformed the political rhetoric regarding international law in this country. In the United States, compliance with international law needs to be politically defended and explained to the electorate, whereas in Europe, compliance with international law is assumed, and politicians must justify their *departure* from international law.

Zooming out in this way also demonstrates that the media and the public have been wrong to focus their attention and ire on John Yoo. His return to Berkeley after serving with the OLC was met with unrelenting hysteria. But in reality, Yoo is a bit player whose ideas are having a secondary impact on this debate. It is Posner and Goldsmith—and, to a lesser extent, Vermeule—whose ideas are the driving force behind this movement. They are the ones crafting the ideas that devalue international law and suggest that states can reject it. That is the intellectual foundation upon which Yoo's more specific policy and legal arguments rest. Unfortunately, the mainstream media (and hence the broader public) has focused its attention on Yoo and has missed the real story. The complex truth is often obscured when sensationalism and slogans get in the way. This book is meant as a corrective, to explain the real story of why international law is under attack in the United States. And while Yoo is a character in this story, the real protagonists are Posner and Goldsmith. Their ideas matter.

Taken together, these lawyers are best described as the New Realists. They are realists about international law because they have infused their understanding of international law with a dose of *realpolitik*. They are more concerned with how states behave and less concerned with how states ought to behave, and they are skeptical that international law ever forces a state to change its behavior. The first wave of realism came in the 1950s when political scientists who studied international relations expressed a similar skepticism and focused almost exclusively on self-interest and bald power. Some of these realists even used rational choice—the building block of economics—to develop quasi-mathematical models of how states interact with each other.[32] A second wave called neo-realism emerged in 1979 and explained state behavior by appealing to the structural constraints of the mostly anarchic world order.[33] Law was not a big part of either story because it was assumed that there was no world government that could force states to follow international law.

Yoo, Goldsmith, Posner, and Vermeule, as well their kindred spirits in government like Addington, follow in this realist tradition. They believe the study of international law, just like the study of international relations a generation ago, needs to be sprinkled with a heavy dose of realism about the capacity of law to change state behavior. To them, international law has little impact once you divorce it from what states have already decided to do based on their own self-interests. For the New Realists, then, international law isn't really a distinct field of inquiry at all—it is just a special branch of diplomacy as political scientists understand it. There isn't anything especially *normative* about international law.

The New Realism has influenced not only our theoretical understanding of international law but more importantly the actual *practice* of the U.S. government. That is why I think we ignore this movement at our own peril. The same scholars who invented the New Realism have also applied it and made it come true through their work in the Justice Department, the Pentagon, and the White House. They have influenced policy and policymakers. They changed the way the War on Terror was fought and how the United States interacts with international institutions on a wide number of issues ranging from climate change to the International Criminal Court.

It bears mentioning that I am not arguing that the New Realists have *caused* the United States to be skeptical toward international law or invented the movement out of whole cloth. The origin of the movement is a much broader and more complex question—one that implicates a deep current of isolationism and exceptionalism at various moments in our nation's history. There are many reasons for this isolationism and preoccupation with "sovereignty"—all of which are independent of (or at the very least pre-date) the arrival of the New Realists.

So what am I claiming? The New Realists have provided the intellectual foundation for a new skepticism about international law, and they have also succeeded in turning that intellectual vision into a strategic reality, by access to key positions in the U.S. government. They have dressed up the old realisms about international relations (both classical realism and neo-realism) with new clothing—this time, the economic language of rational choice, self-interest, and game theory, and applied it specifically to international law. They have resurrected a distinctively American attitude about international institutions that had their heyday in the 1950s after Hans Morgenthau published *Politics Among Nations*, a manifesto that gave birth to the doctrine of political realism and its emphasis on power politics. By becoming the heirs to that tradition, the New Realists have accomplished two things. First, they have imported Morgenthau's vision—originally about international relations— into the domain of law, which was always supposed to be normative, that is, a field about the way we *ought* to behave. Second, they took Morgenthau into the political mainstream and audaciously installed his worldview right in the building that ought to be most hostile to it: the Justice Department's Robert F. Kennedy Building in Washington, D.C.

1 :: Gaming the Federal Courts

At roughly the same time that Eric Posner and Jack Goldsmith were attacking the status of international law in *The Limits of International Law*, Goldsmith was collaborating with another law professor, Curt Bradley, in attacking customary international law as *American law*. Customary international law is the collection of *unwritten* legal norms that govern the interaction between states. What distinguishes customary international law from "mere custom" is that customary international law is performed with a sense of legal obligation, that is, states believe that the custom has ripened into law. Since *Paquete Habana*, a prize case decided in 1900, it has been widely settled that customary international law is incorporated into the American legal system as part of the common law—the legal tradition of case precedent that courts apply when deciding legal cases.[1] Specifically, the Supreme Court in *Paquete Habana* stated that "[i]nternational law is part of our law. . . ."[2] In light of that decision, courts and scholars have long assumed that international law is enforceable in U.S. courts.

The well-settled nature of international law as American law was so obvious that even Bradley and Goldsmith conceded that they were swimming upstream. Here is the opening to their famous 1997 *Harvard Law Review* article on the subject:

The proposition that customary international law ("CIL") is part of this country's post-*Erie* federal common law has become a well-entrenched component of U.S. foreign relations law. In this Article, we refer to this proposition as the "modern position." During the last twenty years, almost every federal court that has considered the modern position has endorsed it. Indeed, several courts have referred to it as "settled." The modern position also has the overwhelming approval of the academy.[3]

Bradley and Goldsmith's self-described project was to disrupt that well-settled understanding and convince scholars and judges that everything that had happened in human rights litigation in the last twenty-five years had been a complete mistake. They half succeeded.

1.1 The Erie Doctrine 2.0

In a nutshell, their argument was as follows. In 1938, the Supreme Court decided *Erie v. Tompkins*—one of the most famous American cases of all time and one that many students learn in the first month (or first week) of law school.[4] Until *Erie*, federal judges were developing and applying their own "common law," in essence slowly building an independent corpus of law that governed tort and contract cases that would be resolved by judges. The *Erie* case proclaimed that this was a mistake and held that federal judges had no authority to generate their own common law. The "rule of decision" for such cases, the Supreme Court declared, was *state* common law:

> Except in matters governed by the Federal Constitution or by acts of Congress, the law to be applied in any case is the law of the state. And whether the law of the state shall be declared by its Legislature in a statute or by its highest court in a decision is not a matter of federal concern. There is no federal general common law. Congress has no power to declare substantive rules of common law applicable in a state whether they be local in their nature or "general," be they commercial law or a part of the law of torts.[5]

The practical consequence of the *Erie* decision was that federal judges deciding a dispute in, say, New York, would now apply the precedents developed by New York state courts, rather than the precedents developed by other federal judges. The "federal common law" was essentially dead, except in specialized areas where federal law remained supreme. The era of state common law was born.

Bradley and Goldsmith argued in their *Harvard Law Review* article that the rule from *Paquete Habana*—that customary international law was incorporated into federal common law—did not survive the Supreme Court's ruling in *Erie*.[6] If the federal common law was dead, then customary international law had died along with it, and federal courts were no longer bound by it.

However, legal scholars long ago considered the possibility that *Erie* might disrupt the status of international law in the American legal system; Bradley and Goldsmith were not the first to raise the question. Indeed, as Bradley and Goldsmith noted, the influential international jurist Philip Jessup had raised the question only a year after *Erie* was decided.[7] Writing in the *American Journal of International Law*, Jessup acknowledged that *Erie* could be read to dislodge international law from its privileged position in the American legal system because it had been introduced through a door—the federal common law—that had now closed. According to Jessup, "[i]f the dictum of Mr. Justice Brandeis in the *Tompkins* case is to be applied broadly, it would follow that hereafter a state court's determination of a rule of international law would be a finding regarding the law of the state and would not be reviewed by the Supreme Court of the United States."[8]

Ultimately, though, Jessup flatly rejected this argument: "Any question of applying international law in our courts involves the foreign relations of the United States and can thus be brought within a federal power."[9] If international law were excluded from federal power, each state would have authority to decide for itself the content of international law. Can you imagine fifty states interpreting international law in fifty different ways? While different interpretations of domestic tort or contract law are messy, they are by no means fatal to the administration of a coherent system of justice. In contrast, a nation-state cannot be run with fifty different conceptions of international law depending on the state jurisdiction. How would the state conduct its foreign relations? A consistent national conception of international law is a necessary predicate for the state's outward-looking foreign relations power. Justice Kennedy once wrote that the Founding Fathers, in their wisdom, split the atom of sovereignty.[10] For purposes of domestic affairs, the individual states retain their individual sovereignty; for all outward-looking functions, the federal government is sovereign and state authority is subordinated. This explains why the *Erie* doctrine could not be extended to international law, and Phillip Jessup understood this. If there was a specialized area of federal law where the federal common law persisted, international law was it.

For many years, the Supreme Court never confronted this question. Then, in 1964, the court decided *Sabbatino*, a case that directly dealt with the status of customary international law in the federal system.[11] That case involved the Cuban national bank, which was demanding money from an American company's sale of sugar—an industry that had recently been nationalized (through expropriation) by the Cuban government. The Cuban bank argued that the expropriation was an "act of state" by the Cuban government and that U.S. federal courts could not pass judgment on the acts of a foreign government—a well-known doctrine in courts all over the world.[12] The American company, on the other hand, wanted the court to invalidate the expropriation on the grounds that it violated customary international law. This framing of the dispute put the status of customary international law squarely within the Court's focus.

The Supreme Court ultimately decided that the act of state doctrine was controlling and that it was irrelevant whether the expropriation violated customary international law.[13] But that did not nullify the question of customary international law; in fact, it only heightened the underlying question. The Court concluded that the act of state doctrine itself was a rule from customary international law that had been incorporated into the federal common law and was therefore binding in courts of the United States.[14] What then of the *Erie* doctrine and its evisceration of the federal common law? The court concluded:

However, we are constrained to make it clear that an issue concerned with a basic choice regarding the competence and function of the Judiciary and the National Executive in ordering our relationships with other members of the international community must be treated exclusively as an aspect of federal law. It seems fair to assume that the Court did not have rules like the act of state doctrine in mind when it decided *Erie R. Co. v. Tompkins*. Soon thereafter, Professor Philip C. Jessup, now a judge of the International Court of Justice, recognized the potential dangers were Erie extended to legal problems affecting international relations. He cautioned that rules of international law should not be left to divergent and perhaps parochial state interpretations. His basic rationale is equally applicable to the act of state doctrine.[15]

In fact, the Court even cited Jessup's 1939 law review article on the subject. It seemed that customary international law was safe from *Erie*'s grasp.

Bradley and Goldsmith were undeterred by *Sabbatino* and its seemingly unambiguous support for international law's status as federal law, concluding in their essay that "[n]either *Sabbatino* nor *Belmont* addressed the domestic legal status of CIL."[16] Given the decision in *Sabbatino*, this is an odd statement. What else was the Supreme Court doing, other than agreeing with Jessup and rejecting the application of the *Erie* doctrine to international law? The answer is that Bradley and Goldsmith read *Sabbatino* narrowly. They argue that the Supreme Court decided that the act of state doctrine was immune from the *Erie* doctrine, but the court did not say that *all* of customary international law was immune from *Erie*. Scholars may have viewed the latter conclusion as implicit in the *Sabbatino* decision, but Bradley and Goldsmith concluded that an implicit understanding and an explicit endorsement were two different things.[17]

To complete the Bradley and Goldsmith story, it is important to restate the full scope of their account of the "modern position" regarding customary international law. In essence, they argue that customary international law was historically understood as part of the general common law—the unwritten law that was common to all English-speaking legal cultures that traced their origins back to England.[18] *Erie v. Pennsylvania Railroad* changed that when it rejected the idea that there was a federal common law for judges to apply.[19] Instead, common law was to be determined at the state level, and the federal common law vanished overnight. For Bradley and Goldsmith, customary international law as federal law vanished with it. The Rules of Decision Act stated that "[t]he laws of the several States, except where the Constitution, treaties, or statutes of the United States otherwise require or provide, shall be regarded as rules of decision in trials at common law, in the courts of the United States, in cases where they apply."[20] According to the Supreme Court in *Erie*, the phrase "laws of the Several States" included not just state statutes but also the common law precedents decided by state judges. Consequently, a federal court sitting in New York, for example, was required to apply the common law as it had been interpreted by New York state judges.

But the *Erie* case was about more than just the interpretation of a single statute—the Rules of Decision Act. It was also a decision steeped in legal philosophy, and Bradley and Goldsmith seized on these philosophical principles in an attempt to banish customary international law from the federal courts.[21] The *Erie* Court made two principal arguments for why federal judges should not be in the business of exercising their own judgment about the common law. First, the Court's decision was heavily influenced by legal positivism, or the idea that a law's validity stems from its enactment by a legitimate source, a point of view that Justice Holmes had advocated in the past. In fact, the Court quoted something Holmes had written in a prior case:

> [L]aw in the sense in which courts speak of it today does not exist without some definite authority behind it. The common law so far as it is enforced in a State, whether called common law or not, is not the common law generally, but the law of that State existing by the authority of that State without regard to what it may have been in England or anywhere else . . . the authority and only authority is the State, and, if that be so, the voice adopted by the State as its own [whether it be of its Legislature or of its Supreme Court] should utter the last word.[22]

According to Bradley and Goldsmith, "this strand of *Erie* requires federal courts to identify the sovereign source for every rule of decision. Because the appropriate 'sovereigns' under the U.S. Constitution are the federal government and the states, *all* law by federal courts must be either federal law or state law."[23] Under this view, there is no room for international law in this equation because it does not emanate from a *sovereign* source.

So customary international law's banishment from the federal courts is actually directly related to the previous set of arguments pursued by Posner and Goldsmith, which sought to label much of customary international law as either exaggerated or downright illusory. The same reasons suggest that it cannot be applied in federal court because it is not *real* law in the way that legal positivists understand real law. As Bradley and Goldsmith put the point sharply, "even if CIL is 'real law,' *Erie* still requires a domestic source of authority (the federal government or a state government) . . . CIL no more applies in federal courts in the absence of domestic authorization than does the law of France or Mars."[24] Apparently, the application of international custom in federal courts is no more justified than the application of Martian law.

The second argument stemmed from legal realism, or the idea that when judges decide cases, they are making law, not finding law. Justice Holmes had famously written that the common law is not a "brooding omnipresence in the sky" that federal judges could "find" in the same way that scientific laws could be found through rational thought or empirical evidence.[25] Rather, the power of common law judges was the right to engage in decision-making, to decide or say what the law is. And *Erie* very much embodied this view of legal realism. Because of constitutional concerns about equal protection and federalism, it was a mistake to give federal judges this discretion; it belonged only to state judges. Bradley and Goldsmith concluded that the legal realist "critique" applied just as much to international law as it did to other aspects of federal common law.[26] Federal judges applying customary international law are not "finding" international law; they are deciding what constitutes international law—a highly objectionable result since they have no authority to do so. All of this depends, of course, on the previous line of thinking: that international law is vague and indeterminate, not emanating from a real sovereign with the power and authority to enforce its obligations—that is, it is not law in any conventional sense.

What can be said of these two critiques? First, the legal positivism underlying the *Erie* decision represents a brand of legal positivism that ought to be rejected or at least severely cabined.[27] It relies on the notion of law as the commands of the sovereign backed up by threats or sanctions. This was the definition of law proposed by the British philosopher J. L. Austin, and it was indeed influential.[28] But its influence has waned, and there are far more subtle flavors of legal positivism. For example, the Oxford philosopher H. L. A. Hart argued that a legal system involved the unification of primary and secondary rules.[29] Primary rules are usually addressed to the population and govern conduct: the rules say what individuals can and cannot do.[30] Secondary rules, in contrast, are often addressed to government officials and detail how the primary rules should be interpreted, applied, created, and enforced.[31] They are rules about how the primary rules should be handled. For Hart, the most important secondary rule is the "rule of recognition," a rule in a legal system that allows individuals to select rules that qualify as legal rules.[32] A rule of recognition is a set of criteria that govern what counts as a valid law in a particular judicial system. In most cases, these are procedural criteria that demonstrate that the law can be traced back to a particular source, such as a legislative, judicial or executive official.[33] A final element is that the rule is generally observed by social practice, that is, that individuals in the system generally recognize the rule of recognition as one that picks out valid laws.[34]

Hart was well aware of the anxiety regarding the status of international law, and he devoted a whole chapter to the question in his pathbreaking THE CONCEPT OF LAW.[35] While recognizing that the international legal system was quite different from its municipal counterparts, he cautioned against evaluating it based on a standard set by the domestic context.[36] International law does not look like domestic law, but that is not the point. The question is whether it is generally observed and whether it has a rule of recognition. Article 38 of the International Court of Justice Statute lists the legal sources that the world court may consider (including treaties, custom, and general principles of law) and in so doing, embodies a customary norm regarding what counts as the correct sources of law—an international rule of recognition. In fact, article 38 might be the closest thing one could find in any legal system—domestic or international—to a pure rule of recognition. In terms of a direct statement about the sources of law that are valid in the U.S. legal system, you will not find anything of this sort. As for enforceability, the lack of an international sovereign to "enforce" international legal norms was not a fatal defect, from Hart's perspective, because that conclusion emanates from Austin's false portrait of law as the commands of a sovereign backed by threats and sanctions.[37]

In any event, it is too facile to suggest that international law is never enforced. As will be discussed in subsequent chapters, international law is full of enforcement mechanisms, though they do not resemble domestic enforcement models. In addition to sanctions imposed by the United Nations Security Council and sanctions imposed by ad hoc tribunals as well as the International Court of Justice, there are also informal sanctions imposed by the world community, a process that scholars have termed "out-casting," that is, denying cooperative benefits to states that fail to live up to their international obligations.[38]

Furthermore, it is not quite correct to say that there is no "sovereign" where international law is concerned. First of all, Bradley and Goldsmith are too quick to note that *Erie* adopted Holmes's view that the common law was only valid if it came from a sovereign.[39] Here is the full quote from Holmes when he originally coined his famous "brooding omnipresence" turn-of-phrase: "The common law is not a brooding omnipresence in the sky, but the articulate voice of some sovereign or *quasi sovereign* that can be identified."[40] And if ever there were a quasi-sovereign, the international community would qualify as it. Why is the international community of nations, which decides the content and enforcement of legal norms, not a sovereign? The only answer can be that it does not *look* like a domestic sovereign—but that is begging the question.[41] Indeed, Rousseau's conception of the sovereign represents the "general will" of the people, and the international community embodies it: the general will of the *world's* peoples, mediated through the decision-making procedure of each state as it participates in the formation of international legal rules.[42]

1.2 The *Filartiga* Era: Enforcing International Law at Home

Bradley and Goldsmith's assault on customary international law was, in many ways, directed against a single man more than any other: Louis Henkin.[43] Professor Henkin, one of the founding fathers of the modern human rights movement, was the chief reporter for the Restatement Third on Foreign Relations Law—a codification project that summarized the current intersection of U.S. and international law. The Restatement is often cited for the proposition that customary international law is part of federal law.[44] Bradley and Goldsmith flat out accused Henkin of bootstrapping his way into the modern position that customary international is part of federal law because Henkin's first draft cited no case for this proposition of law.[45] Instead, the Restatement cited one of Henkin's own law review articles that concluded that international law was incorporated into federal law.[46] Was this a case of scholarly bootstrapping?

After the first draft was released, the Second Circuit decided *Filartiga*, a human rights case filed against a Peruvian police official for torture committed abroad.[47] In allowing the case to proceed under the Alien Tort Statute, even though the conduct had occurred abroad, the court also adopted the Henkin approach, though it cited neither the Second Restatement nor Henkin's article.[48] It rested its opinion on *Sabbatino* and the Supreme Court's rejection of the *Erie* argument as applied to the act of state doctrine. *Filartiga* was a watershed moment and paved the way for dozens of other human rights cases to be filed in federal courts. When it came time to release the final version of the Restatement, *Filartiga* was then a solid precedent for the proposition that customary international law was incorporated into federal law. Although the final version of the Restatement did not cite *Filartiga*, the case was so well known for the proposition that international law had a place in the federal courts that the Restatement's final version was met with broad support by academics. But according to Bradley and Goldsmith, the result was viciously circular because Henkin used his two projects to provide support for each other (the article and the Restatement), with nothing external to prop either one up.[49] Henkin had bootstrapped his way into giving international law a privileged place within our domestic legal system. *Clever.*

This is an uncharitable reading of both the Restatement process and the Second Circuit's decision in *Filartiga*. Both were based on a close reading of the Supreme Court's decision in *Sabbatino*, and both concluded that the Supreme Court had sided with Judge Jessup: specialized islands of federal common law had survived *Erie*, and customary international law was one of them.[50] It was intolerable to allow each state to be the arbiter of international law through the process of creating fifty different state common law doctrines of international law. And that points to the greatest weakness in the Bradley and Goldsmith argument: the inability to articulate a coherent alternative. What would the world look like if customary international law had not survived *Erie*?[51] The results would be far more significant than simply the end of human rights litigation in federal courts. That litigation would be unloaded into the state court system, with international law being incorporated into state common law adjudication, pushing in fifty different and incoherent directions. For state contract and tort law, the result is complex and centrifugal, but by no means catastrophic.[52] But for international relations, the result is intolerable. How is the United States supposed to engage in foreign relations with other countries when each state engages in separate—and potentially conflicting—interpretations of these legal obligations? That is exactly what Jessup was afraid of and is why the Supreme Court rejected the *Erie* argument in *Sabbatino*.

Furthermore, the Bradley and Goldsmith argument misunderstands the concept of federalism that underlies the *Erie* decision. They are correct, of course, that *Erie* is about federalism, and about the relative powers of the state judiciaries and the federal bench. The state governments are sovereign, and the laws of the individual states shall apply in diversity cases in federal court. At least one argument in *Erie* was that litigants should not receive different justice depending on whether they have the luxury of suing in federal court or state court.[53] All of this is true. In the federal system, though, sovereignty is complicated because the Founding Fathers split the atom of sovereignty.[54] For inward-looking matters, the states retain their sovereignty despite their joining the Union, but for outward-looking matters pertaining to foreign relations, sovereignty resides with the federal government. For governmental matters affecting intercourse with the outside world—treaties, war-making, trade—the individual states are not sovereign. So there is a difference between internal and external sovereignty. Under this system of divided sovereignty, it is clear why customary international law within the U.S. courts survived the *Erie* decision.[55] *Erie* was a federalism case, but generally speaking, the individual states—including their judiciaries—are not the final arbiters of our nation's rights and obligations under international law. To suggest otherwise is to open up the biggest potential equal protection can of worms, far greater than the one animating *Erie*. Imagine a New York state court interpreting the content of human rights in one way and Pennsylvania courts interpreting it in another.

1.3 *Filartiga's* Demise, Parochialism's Rise

The Supreme Court substantially curtailed the growing wave of Alien Tort Statute litigation when it decided *Sosa v. Alvarez-Machain* in 2004.[56] The case represented the second time that Humberto Alvarez-Machain, a Mexican physician, made his way to the U.S. Supreme Court. He was wanted by U.S. federal agents for the killing of a DEA agent, but he was living in Mexico at the time of his arrest.[57] Instead of seeking formal extradition through the Mexican judicial system, federal agents paid intermediaries to kidnap him in Mexico and bring him to the United States, where he was promptly arrested and placed on trial for killing the federal agent.[58] Alvarez-Machain challenged his arrest, calling it a kidnapping in violation of the bilateral extradition treaty between the United States and Mexico. The Supreme Court rejected the argument and also held in a related case that the Fourth Amendment did not apply to government conduct in Mexico.[59] As for the extradition treaty, the Court concluded that extradition was not the sole and exclusive method of obtaining a suspect—other avenues were possible. In today's anti-terrorism parlance, this would have been described as an extraordinary rendition. As for the Fourth Amendment claim, the Court concluded that the amendment did not apply extraterritorially, and criminal defendants brought to the United States could not invoke its protections.[60] Having lost his constitutional case, Alvarez-Machain proceeded to trial where, in an ironic twist, a federal district court acquitted him of murdering the federal agent. Unable to convince the Supreme Court of his constitutional claims, he apparently was nonetheless successful in convincing a trial judge that the government presented insufficient evidence of his guilt.

Having escaped a conviction, Alvarez-Machain then sought a judicial remedy for his unorthodox transfer from Mexico to the United States. Where would he find one? The Alien Tort Statute (ATS) provided just such an avenue, and he filed suit, in federal court, against Mexican nationals, including Mr. Sosa, who participated in the kidnapping, accusing them of violating established principles of international human rights law.[61] (He also filed suit against the U.S. government officials under another statute, the Federal Tort Claims Act.). The U.S. Supreme Court heard an appeal in this case and took the opportunity to severely restrict the access that foreign litigants would have to U.S. courts.

In his majority opinion in *Sosa v. Alvarez-Machain*, Justice Souter concluded that ATS cases could proceed only if the alleged violations had sufficient precision and universality under international law.[62] In particular, Justice Souter argued that the standard was set by the three international offenses that eighteenth-century English jurist William Blackstone had identified as requiring a remedy in domestic courts in England: violation of safe conducts, infringement of the rights of ambassadors, and piracy.[63] An ATS case could proceed in a U.S. court only if it alleged a violation of a norm that was as equally well settled as the original Blackstonian norms. Applying this standard to Alvarez-Machain, the Court concluded that his kidnapping did not violate a sufficiently precise or universal legal norm, though a claim of genocide or torture might be different.[64]

In *Sosa*, the Supreme Court could have taken the opportunity to declare that customary international law was not part of federal law, but it explicitly declined to do so. Writing for the majority, Souter noted that

> *Erie* did not in terms bar any judicial recognition of new substantive rules, no matter what the circumstances, and post-*Erie* understanding has identified limited enclaves in which federal courts may derive some substantive law in a common law way. For two centuries we have affirmed that the domestic law of the United States recognizes the law of nations . . . It would take some explaining to say now that federal courts must avert their gaze entirely from any international norm intended to protect individuals.[65]

Citing both *Sabbatino* and Jessup's article in a footnote, the Court concluded that customary international law's status as federal law was appropriate in cases dealing with matters of concern to foreign relations.[66]

The Court also took note of the issue of legal realism and the philosophical debates surrounding the status of international law. Taking a page from Scalia's playbook (original intent of the framers of a particular statute or constitutional provision), Souter's opinion rhetorically asked what the intent of Congress was when it passed the Judiciary Act of 1789, which included the ATS provision. The Court found it implausible that the meaning of the Act should change drastically once the philosophical position on the common law and international law (i.e., legal realism) gained traction in modern debates about the nature of law. "We think it would be unreasonable to assume," Souter wrote, "that the First Congress would have expected federal courts to lose all capacity to recognize enforceable international norms simply because the common law might lose some metaphysical cachet on the road to modern realism."[67]

In the end, the *Sosa* case severely curtailed the nature and scope of Alien Tort Statute claims that could be heard in federal courts. Going forward, new claims were restricted to universally recognized legal norms whose content could be defined with the same level of precision as the norms identified by Blackstone as giving rise to a domestic remedy. However, *Sosa* also *reaffirmed*, in unambiguous language, the status of customary international law as federal law.

Undaunted by this development, Bradley and Goldsmith concluded in a second *Harvard Law Review* article that *Sosa*, far from endorsing the so-called "modern" position regarding customary international law's incorporation into federal law, was in fact consistent with the Bradley and Goldsmith critique of the modern position.[68] However, this conclusion was only possible after a significant amount of neck twisting. Although they conceded that the Court agreed that customary international law survived *Erie*, Bradley and Goldsmith nonetheless argued that this statement was "inconsistent" with Souter's reasoning regarding the status of international law as general common law prior to the *Erie* case.[69] Nonetheless, whether there is an inconsistency here or not, the Court clearly concluded that international law survived *Erie*.

In fact, Scalia, in a separate opinion, railed against the majority's holding in this regard and, citing Bradley and Goldsmith's original *Harvard Law Review* article, concluded that customary international law did not survive the *Erie* decision. "Because post-*Erie* federal common law is made, not discovered," Scalia wrote, "federal courts must possess some federal common-law-making authority before undertaking to craft it."[70] No such authority exists where international law is concerned. In Scalia's pithy rendering: "In Benthamite terms, creating a federal command (federal common law) out of international norms, and then constructing a cause of action to enforce that command through the purely jurisdictional grant of the ATS, is nonsense upon stilts."[71] Bradley and Goldsmith's argument clearly swayed Scalia but not the majority of the Court. Although *Sosa*, by tightening the standards for ATS cases, closed the door of the federal courthouse for many human rights victims, it nonetheless left the door slightly ajar. The status of international law as part of the American judicial system was safe (at least for now).

Lower federal courts were tasked with applying the *Sosa* standard and determining which ATS allegations were based on sufficiently precise and universal norms to be acceptable to the Supreme

Court. One notable category of cases proliferated and dominated in this post-*Sosa* period, and they involved suits against corporations accused of complicity in foreign human rights abuses.[72] Typically, the corporate defendant was involved in business dealings with foreign governments that engaged in atrocities or human rights violations against its own citizens. According to plaintiffs' attorneys, the corporate behavior made them complicit in the human rights violations and therefore responsible under the Alien Tort Statute.[73]

Corporate attorneys immediately noticed two major problems with this theory and pressed both problems with appellate courts in the Second Circuit and the D.C. Circuit.[74] First, they argued, it is unclear if corporations can be sued under international law, since corporate liability is not explicitly provided for in international criminal law. No corporation was prosecuted *as a corporation* at Nuremberg, and neither the ad hoc tribunals for Yugoslavia nor Rwanda have jurisdiction over corporations.[75] When the Statute of the permanent International Criminal Court was adopted at Rome in 1998, the drafters excluded corporations from the court's jurisdictions.[76] Since corporations could not be prosecuted at these tribunals, defense attorneys argued that corporations were not persons under international law and could not be sued under the Alien Tort Statute.[77]

This argument is problematic. Just because a corporation cannot be a defendant at a *criminal* tribunal does not say much about whether corporations can be civilly sued. Furthermore, the fact that international criminal tribunals have no jurisdiction over corporations does not indicate whether corporations are capable of violating international law. The criminal tribunals have no jurisdiction over *states* either, but states are clearly subjects of international law and are capable of violating it. State responsibility is a bedrock principle in public international law.

The second argument involved the legal standard against which corporations would be judged for their actions. In criminal law, accomplices are usually judged under one of two standards, depending on the jurisdiction. Under the first approach, accomplices are guilty only if they provide assistance to the principal perpetrator with the *purpose* of facilitating the crime.[78] The competing approach permits an accomplice conviction even if the accomplice only provides assistance with *knowledge* that his assistance will help the principal complete the crime.[79] Needless to say, corporate attorneys in ATS cases argued in favor of the more demanding purpose standard. When appellate courts concluded that the corporate aiding and abetting should be governed by the purpose standard, the corporations usually won and the cases were dismissed.[80] In most cases, corporations could argue that their conduct was motivated by a desire for financial profit, not by a pure desire to help a foreign government violate international law by abusing their own citizens. In these cases, corporate greed was actually a good defense.

The *Kiobel* case raised both of these scenarios. Nigerian defendants sued a subsidiary of the Royal Dutch Petroleum Company, accusing the company of complicity in a campaign of torture, extrajudicial killings, and other human rights abuses by the Nigerian government.[81] Lawyers for the company argued before the Second Circuit that it could not be sued under international law; alternatively, if it could be sued, its conduct should be evaluated under the more demanding purpose standard for corporate complicity. A closely divided Second Circuit Court of Appeals largely agreed with the lawyers and threw out the case.[82]

The Supreme Court granted certiorari and agreed to take the case as a way of providing more guidance to questions about ATS liability. At the oral argument in February 2012, lawyers for both sides argued over corporate liability and standards for complicity.[83] However, the oral argument took a surreal turn when it became clear that at least some of the Justices wanted to resolve the case on simpler—albeit more aggressive—grounds. Skeptical questions from Justices Kennedy and Alito suggested that the case lacked a nexus with the territory of the United States since the conduct occurred in foreign territory by foreign corporations against foreign plaintiffs (so-called foreign-cubed cases). There was not a sufficient connection to the sovereign territory of the United States. None of the attorneys were sufficiently prepared to discuss this issue, which was not briefed in the case, so the Supreme Court took the unusual step of re-calendaring the case for reargument based on this alternative theory of the case.

Why the radical change in posture by the Justices? Although previous Republican presidents, including George W. Bush, had taken the position that the Alien Tort Statute did not apply to human rights abuses committed abroad, there was little way to predict that it would sway the Supreme Court at this point in time, especially after years of ATS litigation in the lower courts, seeming approval in *Sosa v. Alvarez-Machain*, and wide support among law professors for *Filartiga*-style cases.

What changed? Goldsmith filed an influential amicus brief in the case on behalf of Chevron, Dole Food, Dow Chemical, Ford Motor Company, GlaxoSmithKline, and Proctor & Gamble, which nicely teed up the territoriality argument for the Court.[84] Goldsmith argued that the proliferation of ATS cases based on foreign abuses violated international law principles of jurisdiction that generally constrain when and how a sovereign government can exercise jurisdiction over foreign conduct. He correctly noted that these international principles are designed to minimize potential international conflicts caused by overlapping claims of jurisdiction.[85]

The amicus brief starts off by describing conceptual errors. First, Goldsmith distinguishes the ATS from universal criminal jurisdiction—the right (or even responsibility) of any government to prosecute serious international crimes, such as genocide, even if the conduct did not occur within its sovereign territory.[86] Under a universal jurisdiction scheme, a state must extradite or criminally prosecute the offender because impunity for gross violations of international law is intolerable. Goldsmith contrasts this with the universal *civil* jurisdiction of the Alien Tort Statute, which is based on private lawsuits. The difference, according to Goldsmith, is that private universal jurisdiction cases implicate potential abuses (because individuals are more likely to file abusive lawsuits) while accepted principles of universal criminal jurisdiction do not; the latter involve governmental action (rather than private lawsuits) to commence the case.[87] Criminal cases are less likely to trigger problems of overlapping jurisdiction because government officials must decide whether the case will proceed.[88] Government officials deciding whether to file a criminal case will carefully consider the ramifications of filing the case, including the potential damage to international diplomacy. Private individuals filing a civil lawsuit on their own behalf will remain unmoved by such global concerns and will not factor them into their decision to file a civil complaint.

Unfortunately, the argument represents a failed understanding of comparative criminal law. In the United States and other common law countries, it is indeed true that criminal cases are initiated only if a public prosecutor decides to bring charges. However, plenty of civil law jurisdictions do not have such a clear dividing line between civil and criminal cases. Indeed, in these jurisdictions, a private party (*partie civile*) can commence a *criminal* case against an individual purely by bringing a private action in court, thus triggering the criminal law machinery that, in the United States, is triggered only by the public prosecutor.[89]

The rest of Goldsmith's amicus brief was couched in terms of *fidelity* to international law. Alien Tort Statute cases authorize impermissible judicial intrusion into matters that are properly the exclusive sovereign prerogative of other state governments. By authorizing suits for human rights abuses in other countries, the Alien Tort Statute was violating international principles of jurisdiction that ensure that states do not use expansive legal jurisdiction as a way of meddling in the affairs of other states. "Outside the United States, however, ATS litigation is not seen as a vindication of international law," Goldsmith wrote. "Rather, it is seen as an instance of American international law exceptionalism."[90] With this argument, international law *required* that the Supreme Court restrict the remedies that aliens could seek in U.S. courts for violations of international law. *Clever again.*

When oral arguments commenced for *Kiobel* (Round 2), it was clear that Goldsmith's argument had won the day already. None of the Justices seemed interested in entertaining the idea that federal courts could hear suits in foreign-cubed cases. Chief Justice Roberts authored the Court's opinion, which stated that the presumption against extraterritorial application of congressional statutes applied in this case because the allegations did not "touch and concern the territory of the United States . . . with sufficient force to displace the presumption."[91] In other words, absent express indication to the contrary, the Court always assumes that congressional statutes do *not* apply to extraterritorial conduct.[92] Because the Judiciary Act of 1789 (of which the ATS was a part) contained no explicit statement, the presumption was not rebutted. Justice Kennedy, writing a concurrence that was signed by him only, took pains to note that some conduct might be sufficient to rebut the presumption against extraterritorial application of congressional statutes, although he declined to say what that conduct might be.[93] Justice Breyer's four-vote concurrence, signed by the other members of the liberal wing, expressly articulated what those cases might be:

> [T]he defendant's conduct substantially and adversely affects an important American national interest, and that includes a distinct interest in preventing the United States from becoming a safe harbor (free of civil as well as criminal liability) for a torturer or other common enemy of mankind.[94]

Since Breyer's concurrence only represented a four-vote plurality, it is unclear if a majority of the Justices would embrace this standard.

Despite Roberts's statement that the presumption against territoriality barred application of the ATS to foreign cases, the argument is far from self-evident. In fact, if there is *any* type of litigation where the presumption is naturally rebutted, it is precisely in the ATS context, which, by its very terms, applies *international* law in U.S. courts. To apply a presumption *against* extraterritoriality to a law that gives a cause of action for violating *international* law—a universal law that applies around the globe, not just in the United States—is to demonstrate a fundamental insensitivity to the very idea of international law as a unifying body of law that brings together each country under a common set of norms.

Furthermore, as Anthony Colangelo has demonstrated, the *Kiobel* decision rests on a conceptual mistake, because the presumption against extraterritoriality applies to conduct rules, but the ATS does not impose any conduct rules at all—it simply confers a cause of action for violating international law (since the law is jurisdictional).[95] Causes of action are neither territorial nor extraterritorial because they do not directly regulate conduct (instead, they simply allow a court to exercise jurisdiction over particular types of cases). The conduct-regulating rule in ATS cases comes from international law, which is neither conceptually nor legally confined to the territory of the United States.[96] Properly understood, the burden imposed by the presumption against extraterritoriality was easily met by the text of the Alien Tort Statute and should not have been the legal foundation for Roberts's opinion.

Kiobel left much unanswered; lower courts will inevitably fill in the gaps as they apply the *Kiobel* standard to ATS cases before them. But this much is clear: the ATS can no longer be used to sue corporations for complicity in foreign human rights abuses where the corporation's sole contact with the United States is the mere corporate presence of a U.S. subsidiary. Justice Roberts was clear that corporations are "often present in many countries, and it would reach too far to say that mere corporate presence suffices," a point that even Breyer endorsed in his concurring opinion.[97] However, the Roberts opinion avoided the controversy between the modern and revisionist positions regarding the status of international law as federal common law post-*Erie*. *Erie* was conspicuously absent from the opinion.

1.4 The New Realists Go to Washington

The *Kiobel* case was not the only situation where the New Realists had a direct impact on international law's reception in the U.S. federal courts. Bradley and Goldsmith's views on customary international law had a far more direct impact on the policies of the executive branch during the Bush administration.

While employed at the Justice Department's Office of Legal Counsel, John Yoo and Jay Bybee wrote a series of memoranda arguing that torturing suspected terrorists did not violate federal law.[98] They argued that torture did not violate international law or, in the alternative, that if it was found to violate international law, the president was not bound by it, and federal courts should not enforce it.[99] One argument for this conclusion was Bradley and Goldsmith's revisionist position on customary international law. For example, in his January 9, 2002, memorandum to Robert J. Delahunty, John Yoo stated that "[i]t is also clear that the original understanding of the Framers was that 'Laws of the United States' did *not* include the Law of Nations, as international law was called in the late eighteenth century."[100] Furthermore, Yoo explicitly relied on the Bradley and Goldsmith argument, in a footnote, to help support his argument that international law is not a part of federal law.[101] Although he conceded that the issue was in dispute, Yoo nonetheless concluded that "the legitimacy of incorporating customary international law as federal law has been subjected in these exchanges to crippling doubts."[102]

In fact, Yoo's argument perhaps swept far broader and deeper than Bradley and Goldsmith's argument. Yoo's argument was not confined to the status of customary international law in the post-*Erie* period. Rather, he argued that international law itself was not a part of the U.S. national legal culture and concluded that the political branches could violate customary international law at will: "it is well accepted that the political branches have ample authority to override customary international law within their respective spheres of authority."[103] He made the same arguments about legal positivism that Bradley and Goldsmith had made: that *Erie* represented a firm entrenchment of legal positivism and that any direct incorporation of international law into federal common law would violate this directive. Customary international law was spurious because it took place outside of the Constitution, laws, treaties, or executive proclamations.[104]

As an overlay to the Bradley and Goldsmith argument, Yoo was particularly concerned with keeping presidential authority immune from judicial meddling. The real problem with allowing customary international law to be imported directly into U.S. federal law was that it gave an additional source of authority for federal courts to limit the president's conduct—an intolerable result from Yoo's perspective. According to Yoo, "the President under the Constitution is given plenary authority over the conduct of the Nation's foreign relations and over the use of the military."[105] Incorporating customary international law into federal law risks upsetting that delicate constitutional balance, in particular the war-making discretion that the framers gave the president.

The upshot of this argument was that customary international law does not bind the president and cannot be enforced in federal courts; the Bush administration's pursuit of the armed conflict with al-Qaeda could continue without restriction from treaty-based or customary law. Prohibitions on torture that stemmed from customary international law could not prevent the president from ordering the CIA to torture detainees to acquire actionable intelligence about future terrorist attacks.[106] In this regard, the metaphysical debates about the status of international law within the federal system generated practical implications for ground troops. These debates not only provided a legal argument for the Bush administration's rejection of international law, but they also provided the legal foundation for torturing detainees. If international law prohibits torture but is not part of U.S. law, federal courts cannot enforce it, and the president is free to ignore it. In that sense, there is a direct line from the obscure, legal arguments about the applicability of *Erie v. Thompson* to the OLC memos justifying the use of torture by CIA interrogators. To pretend that the *Erie* question is a "pure" academic debate is to radically underestimate the influence that this intellectual argument had on executive branch officials during key moments of the Bush presidency. Devaluing international law was a necessary first step before giving CIA employees the legal authorization to ignore it. Doing so laid the legal foundation for the suggestion that international law could be ignored. If international law had retained its full intellectual force and vigor, it could never have been so cavalierly ignored.

As further evidence that abstract legal arguments influence the highest levels of government, one need look no further than an article by David Barron and Martin Lederman. They offered the single largest rebuke to the Bush administration's view of unfettered executive power in wartime, in the form of a two-part *Harvard Law Review* article entitled "The Commander in Chief at the Lowest Ebb."[107] The title of the article was a reference to Justice Jackson's famous turn of phrase in his concurring opinion in *Youngstown Sheet & Tube Co. v. Sawyer*, where he divided presidential power into three categories: (1) when the president acts with congressional approval, (2) when the president acts in the wake of congressional silence or inaction, and (3) when the president acts in the face of congressional constraints.[108] In the latter instance, presidential power is at its "lowest ebb" as the powers expressed in Article I and Article II of the Constitution conflict when both the president and Congress assert their authority in a given sphere.

Lederman and Barron's work dispelled the widely accepted narrative that Congress, since the mid-1960s, has largely abdicated its responsibility to regulate wartime affairs. In the standard story, Congress has—by inaction—written a series of blank checks for presidents to wage a succession of armed conflicts without congressional interference.[109] Lederman and Barron directly challenged this assumption in both the historical and contemporary contexts. Previous armed conflicts were governed by both the White House and Capitol Hill, and, more important, President Bush waged the armed conflict with al-Qaeda in the face of substantial congressional regulation. In particular, Congress had placed constraints—often over the loud objection of President Bush—on the detention of suspected terrorists, their treatment while in detainment and under interrogation, and their prosecution before military commissions.[110] Furthermore, after Lederman and Barron completed their study, President Obama faced extreme congressional limitations in his attempt to reverse some of these policies, especially his attempt to close Guantanamo, transfer detainees to mainland prison facilities, and prosecute senior al-Qaeda figures (most notably, Khalid Sheikh Mohammed) in the Southern District of New York.[111] Congressional inaction this was surely not.

The point here is not whether Barron and Lederman have the better argument. Rather, the point is simply that Barron and Lederman's alternative vision of presidential power was deeply influential in the early days of the Obama administration, in no small part because Barron and Lederman were subsequently selected as top attorney advisers in the Justice Department's Office of Legal Counsel, the very department where John Yoo had produced the original torture memos. Barron and Lederman's appointment to the OLC gave them the opportunity to implement their academic vision of presidential power.

Their highest profile assignment came when the Justice Department tasked them with reviewing the legality of targeted killings during the armed conflict with al-Qaeda. According to the *New York Times* and other published reports, Barron and Lederman produced a memorandum that laid out the legal groundwork for these strikes, with special attention to the thorny legal issues raised by the targeting of American citizens.[112] The Obama administration had conducted dozens of targeted killings in Pakistan, Afghanistan, Yemen, and Somalia, but for the first time, the administration was considering targeting an American citizen, Anwar al-Awlaki, who was raised in New Mexico before moving overseas and settling in Yemen and was the chief spokesperson for al-Qaeda in the Arabian Peninsula. Barron and Lederman constructed a meticulously argued memorandum that concluded that targeting al-Awlaki was lawful under certain circumstances.[113] However, after reading a post on a legal blog, the two decided to focus more squarely on the issue of whether the strike would violate a federal law prohibiting the murder of U.S. citizens abroad.[114] In a lengthy ninety-page classified memo, Barron and Lederman concluded that a drone strike would not violate the federal statute.

After the legal analysis was completed, a drone strike killed al-Awlaki and raised a firestorm among civil libertarians who accused the president of waging war against his own citizens. It also rankled congressional leaders who complained that the president had exceeded his powers under Article II and under the 2001 law known as the Authorization for the Use of Military Force (AUMF) passed by Congress after 9/11.[115] Eventually, an insider leaked to NBC news a white paper summarizing the legal conclusions of the original Justice Department memo. The white paper was only a brief summary prepared for congressional leaders; the original memorandum applied abstract legal analysis to concrete facts about al-Awlaki and was officially classified.[116] A redacted version of the full memorandum was eventually released after it was declassified.

The leaked white paper makes clear that Barron and Lederman (and those working with them) never abandoned the theory of presidential power they had articulated in the *Harvard Law Review*. First, Congress passed very few explicit restrictions on the commander in chief's power to engage in targeting during armed conflict, so in ordering the strikes, President Obama was not acting with presidential power "at its lowest ebb." Second, according to the white paper, the president's actions were consistent with basic principles of the law of war, which permit deadly attacks against members of enemy forces.[117] These enemy forces include traditional military forces but also irregular fighting groups associated with non-state actors like al-Qaeda. Third, the killings were consistent with the federal law prohibiting the murder of U.S. civilians because lawful killings during armed conflict have traditionally fallen under a "public authority" justification that also exculpates police officers who kill during lawful police operations.[118]

Perhaps the greatest example of academic influence in the executive branch occurred in the detention context. When Congress passed the AUMF after 9/11, it granted authority to the president to use all necessary and appropriate force against al-Qaeda and organizations responsible for the 9/11 attacks.[119] However, many of those detained by the Bush administration and held at Guantanamo or elsewhere were not members of al-Qaeda proper, nor were they directly involved in the 9/11 attacks. In a lengthy *Harvard Law Review* article, Jack Goldsmith and Curtis Bradley concluded that detention authority extended to "associated forces" of al-Qaeda, even though the phrase "associated forces" was not mentioned in the AUMF even once.[120] They concluded that the AUMF conferred detention authority over associated forces because international law allows countries to construe third-party states as belligerents if they render assistance to one side of the armed conflict.[121] This is known as the doctrine of co-belligerency and it stems from the law of neutrality. Specifically, before declaring a third state as a co-belligerent with an enemy (and therefore subject to attack), the original state must give the putative co-belligerent the opportunity to declare its neutrality and stay out of the conflict.[122] If the original state refuses to make this declaration, it can be considered a co-belligerent and become a party to the conflict. Unfortunately, it is unclear how the doctrine applies to the armed conflict with a non-state actor such as al-Qaeda that has no formal diplomatic relations through which a statement of neutrality could be demanded or tendered.[123]

Regardless of the uncomfortable fit between the doctrine of co-belligerency and non-international armed conflicts with non-state actors, a deeper problem emerges. The concept of "associated forces" has no currency within the law of neutrality; it has no history and no precedent. It is basically made-up law. After the phrase first appeared in the Defense Department's order creating the Combatant Status Review Tribunals in 2004, Bradley and Goldsmith's *Harvard Law Review* 2005 article included a discussion of the concept, which greatly popularized the phrase and brought it into common currency among experts in the law of war. It then appeared the following year in the 2006 Military Commissions Act passed by Congress, which authorized the president to convene military commissions to prosecute (among others) any unlawful belligerent "who has engaged in hostilities or who has purposefully and materially supported hostilities against the United States or its co-belligerents who is not a lawful enemy combatant (including a person who is part of the Taliban, al-Qaeda, or associated forces)."[124] A subsequent version of the Military Commissions Act in 2009 changed the term unlawful belligerent to "unprivileged belligerent" and relied on the concept of material support instead of associated forces.[125]

When the Obama administration was confronted with explaining its detention authority to the federal court for the District of Columbia (and subsequently the U.S. Court of Appeals for the D.C. Circuit), it adopted the "associated forces" concept without bothering to ground it in positive law. In its submission to the federal court, the U.S. government proposed the following standard for the executive branch's detention authority:

> The President has the authority to detain persons that the President determines planned, authorized, committed, or aided the terrorist attacks that occurred on September 11, 2001, and persons who harbored those responsible for those attacks. The President also has the authority to detain persons who were part of, or substantially supported, Taliban or al-Qaida forces or associated forces that are engaged in hostilities against the United States or its coalition partners, including any person who has committed a belligerent act, or has directly supported hostilities, in aid of such enemy armed forces.[126]

The administration's lawyers conceded that the exact contours of the "associated forces" language was uncertain and imprecise, but they argued that further precision was unhelpful. "It is neither possible nor advisable," the brief continued, "to attempt to identify, in the abstract, the precise nature and degree of 'substantial support,' or the precise characteristics of 'associated forces,' that are or would be sufficient to bring persons and organizations within the foregoing framework."[127]

Despite the lack of positive law to serve as a grounding precedent for the concept of associated forces, the court of appeals adopted the language without further scrutiny. In its *Al-Bihani* decision, the D.C. Circuit Court of Appeals stated that the "associated forces" standard proposed by the government was appropriate, and the court did not seem bothered by the fact that the term never appeared in the AUMF passed by Congress. The court reasoned as follows:

> The provisions of the 2006 and 2009 MCAs are illuminating in this case because the government's detention authority logically covers a category of persons no narrower than is covered by its military commission authority. Detention authority in fact sweeps wider, also extending at least to traditional P.O.W.s, see id. § 948a(6), and arguably to other categories of persons. But for this case, it is enough to recognize that any person subject to a military commission trial is also subject to detention, and that category of persons includes those who are part of forces associated with Al Qaeda or the Taliban or those who purposefully and materially support such forces in hostilities against U.S. Coalition partners.[128]

In other words, only individuals who are already lawfully detained can be brought to trial before a military commission. So, *by definition*, all individuals who can be placed before a military commission must be subject to the administration's lawful detention authority.

The argument makes sense, although it ignores a crucial element: the provenance of the "associated forces" term. The idea was central for resolving a key problem in the armed conflict against al-Qaeda, but neither its content nor its exact expression has any direct grounding in positive international law. Although the term was used in the Military Commissions Act of 2006, it appeared there only after Bradley and Goldsmith suggested its use in their 2005 *Harvard Law Review* article.[129] And now that the term has come to dominate public discourse about the scope of detention authority in the armed conflict against al-Qaeda, legal scholars cite the *Al-Bihani* decision when using the term. But a mere citation to *Al-Bihani* fails to acknowledge the bootstrapping that accompanied the term's appearance. By moving from "co-belligerents" to "associated forces," the lawyers have effectively removed the concept from the body of law—international law—that once inspired it. If Henkin was guilty of bootstrapping the modern position on customary law into the Restatement on Foreign Relations, then surely the D.C. Circuit's acceptance of the Bradley and Goldsmith "associated forces" argument should be vulnerable to the same criticism.

In this respect, academic lawyers have a huge impact on the role of international law within the federal court system. Law professors launched the rear-guard action to eject international law from our domestic court system and reject the "modern position" regarding customary international law. In so doing, professors managed to squeeze shut the doors of the federal judiciary from hearing human rights litigation under the Alien Tort Statute. Never before has the federal judiciary been more hostile to hearing claims sounding in international law. And the same law professors continue to exercise profound influence in proposing legal standards and legal interpretations regarding everything from executive power to targeting and detention authority. The hostility toward international law within the American academy is not just an abstract and philosophical debate that is confined to the four corners of the *Harvard Law Review*. It has provided the intellectual and legal foundation for American presidents to ignore or marginalize international legal obligations at key moments in time. The result is a painful synergy between the American legal academy and the highest echelons of government lawyering. Although many lawyers have resisted and fought this trend, it is undeniable that the quintessentially American fascination with the questionable status of international law as "law" has been a corrupting influence on not just the academic study of international law but also, more broadly, on the practice of international law in Washington, D.C.

1.5 International Law as Interpretive Guidance

In August 2010, open war broke out in the D.C. Circuit over how to apply and understand the AUMF after Al-Bihani sought a rehearing of his habeas petition claiming that his continued detention violated both international law and the Detainee Treatment Act. The district court below had dismissed the habeas petition, and a three-judge panel of the D.C. Circuit Court of Appeals had upheld the district's court's dismissal. Al-Bihani then filed a petition for rehearing en banc before the entire D.C. Circuit of Appeals, one of the most conservative appellate courts in the country. The full court refused to rehear the case, issuing a terse three-sentence order dismissing the petition for rehearing.[130] Strangely, though, that three-sentence order triggered 113 pages of warring opinions from the judges on the proper scope of international law in federal courts.

Seven judges stayed out of the fray entirely, issuing a one-paragraph opinion asserting that the status of international law was an academic question with no bearing on the outcome of the case. Either way, Al-Bihani would lose his case, so the status of international law in the federal courts should be avoided, though the seven judges offered no reasoning whatsoever to explain this result. An eighth judge, Judge Brown, concurred in the result but took the seven judges to task for avoiding the key question, which was anything but academic: "Although we have avoided en banc review, we have done so through the costly expedient of making a rather common-place judicial proposition impenetrably obscure."[131] Brown was clearly hostile to the invocation of international law in federal courts, but he wanted the court to explicitly address the issue that lurked "below the surface of the briefs and opinions of this en banc petition process."[132]

Judge Brett Kavanaugh filed a blistering opinion concluding that international law principles could not be invoked in federal courts as a constraint on executive war-making authority. Kavanaugh relied heavily on Bradley and Goldsmith's post-*Erie* argument, concluding that direct application of international law in U.S. courts ended with the demise of the federal common law. In a telling omission, Kavanaugh discussed *Sosa* without quoting any of its language, relying instead on quotations from *Erie* as well as Bradley and Goldsmith's 1997 article pushing the revisionist position.[133] The omission obscured the fact that the Supreme Court in *Sosa* never adopted the revisionist position.

Judge Kavanaugh's opinion was so strident that it rejected the idea that the law of war could even be used as a tool to guide interpretation of the post-9/11 AUMF. If the AUMF was designed as congressional authorization for the president to pursue al-Qaeda and the Taliban, then it stands to reason that Congress intended that authorization to be consistent with international constraints on warfare. This would make international law relevant, not as directly applicable in federal court but simply as an interpretive tool to guide the statutory interpretation of the AUMF. Indeed, there is ample support for this modest argument. First, it is already a universally accepted canon of interpretation that Congress is acting consistent with international law unless it declares otherwise—a canon of interpretation known as the Charming Betsy presumption.[134] The basic idea is that if the Supreme Court is choosing between two different interpretations of a congressional statute, the Court should adopt the interpretation that accords with international law rather than violates it. In other words, one can presume that Congress is legislating consistently with international law unless it explicitly declares otherwise. Consequently, using international law as a framework for understanding the AUMF is simply a logical extension of the Charming Betsy presumption. Second, the Supreme Court in *Hamdi* used the international law of war as an interpretive gloss for understanding the scope of the president's detention authority emerging from the AUMF.[135]

Kavanaugh, in *Al-Bihani*, was swayed by neither of these arguments. First, he denied that the Supreme Court used international law to guide its interpretation of the AUMF, despite the following unambiguous language from *Hamdi*: "[W]e understand Congress' grant of authority for the use of 'necessary and appropriate force' to include the authority to detain for the duration of the relevant conflict, and our understanding is based on longstanding law-of-war principles."[136] Despite the clear reference to law-of-war principles, Kavanaugh claimed that the reference was ambiguous and that a narrower reading of *Hamdi* was appropriate: Congress authorized *at the very least* everything that international law requires and possibly *more*. In Judge Kavanaugh's view, international law is used as an interpretive gloss *augmenting* the scope of congressional authorization but never as an interpretive gloss *constricting* the scope of that authorization. International law would provide a one-way ratchet.[137] In this regard, Judge Kavanaugh departed company from Bradley and Goldsmith, who have long argued that international law provides relevant guideposts for understanding congressional authorization in the wake of 9/11.[138]

Second, Judge Kavanaugh essentially gutted the content of the Charming Betsy presumption by arguing that it survived neither *Erie*'s rejection of customary international law nor the rejection of judicial application of non-self-executing treaties in *Medellín v. Texas*.[139] A non-self-executing treaty requires domestic implementing legislation in order for the treaty to have legal effect in the domestic court system; in contrast, a self-executing treaty has immediate effect in U.S. courts, even in the absence of a congressional statute. In *Medellín*, the Supreme Court ruled that the U.N. Charter and the related Statute of the International Court of Justice were non-self-executing treaties, and therefore decisions of the World Court had no immediate effect in the U.S. court system because Congress never passed a domestic law implementing them.

In the end, the real animating impulse behind Judge Kavanaugh's hostility toward international law is the possibility that judges would use international law as a weapon in their fight to constrain the executive branch. It is almost as if he was channeling Eric Posner and Adrian Vermeule's complaint that judges are amateurs playing at security policy. According to Kavanaugh, "even if one disagrees with that broader proposition and concludes that use of the Charming Betsy canon is appropriate in some such cases, it should not be invoked against the executive branch, which has the authority to weigh international-law considerations when interpreting the scope of ambiguous statutes."[140] The real underlying principle is judicial deference to executive authority.[141]

Kavanaugh insists that any law-of-war constraints on presidential action, applied by the judiciary, stem from domestic sources, that is, the domestic law of war. But this is fallacy. The whole point of the law of war is to build a system of reciprocal constraints between nations in order to minimize the horrors of war. True, some of these constraints were then codified with self-executing treaties or statutes passed after non-self-executing treaties were drafted and signed. But remember that the issue here is not whether non-self-executing treaties can be directly enforced by the judiciary. Rather, the question is whether federal courts can use international law as an interpretive guide to understand congressional behavior. And since authorization for military force against international parties is an action primarily governed by international law, it is bizarre to suggest that background international norms cannot provide an interpretive guide to congressional behavior. Of course, Congress may, in its wisdom, provide the president with authorization to prosecute the war effort outside the bounds of international law, but in such cases, it ought to do so explicitly.

Judge Kavanaugh's argument places him in the strange position of saying that international law may constrain the United States but that the president is not constrained by it. While this may be a function of our divided system of government and the general preference for non-self-executing treaties that require further congressional action before being a valid source of law in domestic courts, none of this suggests that international law is irrelevant to statutory interpretation. *Erie*'s legal positivism (the idea that all law must flow from a sovereign source), even if it were to apply to the international law, cannot be used as a weapon to dispossess judges of the required tools to understand congressional action in the international realm. *Erie* may have rested on legal positivism and domestic sources of law, but it could not have transformed war from an irreducibly *international* event into a creature of purely domestic concern. To allow judges to interpret statutes with that international context in mind is simply to recognize that war, and war-making, is a concept deriving from international affairs and the international legal system that structures its basic concepts.

1.6 Conclusion

What emerges from this chapter is a portrait of a sustained, coordinated, and multipronged attack against international law. This is not
to suggest that it is conspiratorial, but coordinated effort should be
seen for what it is. Since international law is self-interested behavior, it cannot be a source of obligation. Since international law does
not emanate from a domestic sovereign source, it cannot form the
positive law that judges employ to decide cases. Furthermore, since
it is not real law, judges should not even *rely* on international legal
principles as an interpretive guide to understanding domestic laws
passed by Congress. Each of these arguments constructs an edifice
of parochialism from the raw materials of a naïve misreading of
Erie's legal positivism. The resulting diminution of international
law flows from many directions, but the tributaries can be traced
back to a common revisionist source.

2 :: Presidents and Leviathans

In a sense, the New Realist argument about international law is not really about international law at all. It is about the structure of self-interest and obligation—and the relationship these concepts have to the concept of law. According to the New Realists, you cannot find law in the midst of self-interested behavior. Since most agents engage in self-interested behavior, there is much less law out there than most international lawyers think. The New Realists are so enamored with this argument that they deploy it *twice*. The first time is in the domain of international law.[1] The second example of the argument is in the domain of constitutional law, where the New Realists argue that law plays no role in the resolution of horizontal disputes between the branches of the federal government.[2] These disputes are characterized by self-interested rational agents, like the president, who attempt to secure as much power as possible.[3] The only external check on how much power the president can grab is popular discontent when the president grabs too much. Politics, not constitutional law, constrains the modern presidency.

These two arguments are very similar. Indeed, the arguments are similar because at their heart, they have the *same* structure. The international law argument is *external* and concludes that state interactions are mostly governed by rational self-interest—not law. The bigger constraint is not law but power and diplomacy. The constitutional law argument is *internal* and concludes that disputes between Congress and the president are governed by rational self-interest; again, the bigger constraint is not law but power politics.

Given the similar structure of the arguments—indeed their essential repetition—it should be clear that the antidote for both is the same: self-interest and obligation are not mutually exclusive in international *or* constitutional law. Just as states are capable of following international law out of a dual sense of obligation and self-interest, so too can modern presidents act out of rational self-interest and yet feel constrained by constitutional law *at the very same time*. That is because rational agents accept the constraints of the legal system, whether international law or domestic constitutional law, because rational self-interest counsels in favor of working within a system of legal constraints. That is the very essence of living under the rule of law.

Given the essential similarity of the arguments, one might wonder why a whole chapter is necessary to respond to each version of the argument. One could simply note the similarity and move on. However, there are reasons to carefully linger over the constitutional version of the argument, in part because the stakes are so high. In THE EXECUTIVE UNBOUND, Posner and Vermeule do more than argue that law has little role to play in resolving constitutional disputes and interbranch rivalries. They also argue that the result of these disputes—the ever-increasing power of the president—is not only inevitable but salutary.[4] Posner and Vermeule's world is one of unbounded executive authority, undiminished by either law or congressional involvement. With other advocates of a powerful presidency, including John Yoo, the New Realists wish to remake the American political landscape in the image of the leviathan— that is, a single powerful leader with the authority and nimbleness to respond to emergency. Except in their eyes, we have entered a state of permanent exigency that never ends. What some see as a state of exception, the New Realists see as the permanent state of tomorrow. The power of this argument for the creation of an imperial presidency—based on the same New Realist argument they used to undermine the integrity of international law—threatens

to undermine the legality of the U.S. Constitution and the carefully calibrated system of checks and balances that the framers
bequeathed us. For that reason, a detailed examination of the argument is in order.

2.1 Public Opinion and Law

The heart of Posner and Vermeule's argument is that law rarely
limits the president. What really constrains the president is public opinion or, more specifically, the *possibility* of public outrage.[5]
When presidents calculate that the public will react negatively to
their policies, they pull back. This process changes their behavior,
not the allegedly "constraining" laws passed by Congress or the
Supreme Court decisions that apply the Constitution to limit the
powers of the executive branch.[6] The real process of constraint is
more about politics than law, they say. Once again, the argument
only makes sense if you buy into the underlying tension between
public opinion and politics on the one hand, and law on the other.
At issue is whether the reaction of the public, and its constraining
effect on the behavior of the president, must always be thought of as
"purely" political in nature, and never as a legal matter.

As New York University Professor Richard Pildes has demonstrated, the tension between politics and law is exaggerated in
Posner and Vermeule's account.[7] Constitutional law, and the rule
of law more broadly, provides the structure for the political process
and the public opinions that are generated within it. When citizens
feel that the president (or Congress for that matter) is acting illegally
or violating the Constitution, this fuels popular unrest.[8] It is not
as if popular opinion is wholly divorced from any consideration of
what behavior can be considered as legal or illegal. Rather, it is the
complete opposite: the legality or illegality of the president's behavior provides a meaningful structure for that discussion to happen.

Pildes poses an interesting hypothetical: a two-term president
who wants to run for a third term, despite the term limit imposed
by the Twenty-Second Amendment.[9] Most presidents would not
seriously consider this as an available option, correctly predicting
that open defiance of the Twenty-Second Amendment (absent a

formal repeal) would provoke both a constitutional crisis and popular outrage. Is this constraint legal or political in nature? Pildes correctly terms the dispute "semantic."[10] How do we know whether this type of self-constraint on behalf of a hypothetical (and greedy) third-term-seeking president is political or legal? Although the constraint stems from public opinion, the whole reason the public would react negatively to the possibility is because it openly defies the Twenty-Second Amendment.

Posner and Vermeule *might* respond that the public would only react negatively to the proposal if they disliked the president and were against the possibility of a third term. If the president enjoyed broad public support, the people might be willing to overlook the Twenty-Second Amendment. On the other hand, if the public disliked the president, the "legalistic" nature of invoking the Twenty-Second amendment would represent legal camouflage for pre-legal objections. The political objections to the president's seeking a third term would be cast in legal terms for purposes of *rhetorical* appeal. But that façade of legalism should not distract from the essentially *political* nature of the dispute and its resolution.

The argument involves the direction of causation. Is the public outrage pre-legal in nature and then simply expressed in legalistic terms? This would make politics the driving force of the causal story. Or, is the outrage essentially legal in nature, thus making the law the prime element of the causal story? The third alternative is that there is a dynamic relationship between the two forces, creating a reinforcing loop of political and legal objections that continually feed each other. It is not clear where the correct dividing line is between the political and legal, especially when the public disagreement surrounds a specific constitutional provision. At the very least, Posner and Vermeule offer no definitive account to explain where law ends and politics begins—a dividing line that Pildes calls enigmatic.[11]

In a sense, Posner and Vermeule's dichotomy between the labels "politics" and "law" is a distractor. The real question is the unstated rationale for decrying political constraints as extra-legal in nature. Again, the reason for this classification scheme stems from the same realist assumptions that underlie their theories of international law, which we will explore in great detail in chapter 3: acting out of self-interest is inconsistent with acting in compliance with the law. Posner and Goldsmith never explicitly defend that assumption in THE LIMITS OF INTERNATIONAL LAW, and Posner and Vermeule never explicitly defend the assumption in THE EXECUTIVE UNBOUND either.

Turning to the specifics of the constitutional argument, Posner and Vermeule argue that modern presidents accept constraints only out of self-interest. Having engaged in a rational calculation about expected outcomes, presidents usually refrain from self-aggrandizing institutional behavior because such behavior is likely to be counterproductive and lower their expected payoff.[12] In such situations, the self-interested calculation—not the law—is constraining the behavior of the executive. Specifically, Posner and Vermeule note that

> the system of elections, the party system, and American political culture constrain the executive far more than do legal rules created by Congress or the courts; and although politics hardly guarantees that the executive will always act in the public interest, politics at least limits the scope for executive abuses.[13]

Consequently, Posner and Vermeule refer to this system as one of *self*-constraint. Neither the Constitution nor Congress constrains the president; the president constrains himself (or herself) in order to achieve the best outcome, taking into consideration the reactions of other players. In this game theory dilemma, the president becomes one rational agent engaged in a two-person game with the American electorate. Another way of formulating the relevant game is to think of it as a two-person interaction between the president and Congress.

Posner and Vermeule believe that this view is warranted by the literature on rational choice theory. According to them, "[t]he question is a familiar one in the game theoretic literature on bargaining, and we adopt that literature's findings."[14] Specifically, "[g]ame theorists would treat the problem in the context of a standard bargaining game between two agents over a pool of resources or a 'pie' whose value declines over time as the agents haggle."[15] The problem is that Posner and Vermeule draw the wrong conclusions from the rational choice literature. Yes, rational choice theory provides a model for explaining how two self-interested agents will interact as they seek to achieve best outcomes, in many cases accepting restrictions on their behavior when doing so is the best avenue to optimizing their outcomes. However, there is nothing in rational choice theory that automatically dictates that such behavior is inconsistent with the concept of law.

In fact, this is precisely the heart of a legal system: a set of mutually applicable constraints that, when they achieve widespread acceptance, yield beneficial outcomes for the participants in the system. These participants become *constrained maximizers*. They recognize that mutually beneficial reciprocal constraints, formalized in a legal system (or, in this case, in a constitutional structure) provide meaningful benefits for all involved. Pildes puts the point nicely:

> *The Executive Unbound* offers a rich account of why self-interested presidents, motivated only by instrumental considerations, would choose to create or accept many forms of external constraint on their otherwise unlimited discretion; yet the book never explains why law would not be one of those constraints—indeed, why compliance with law would not be the most significant constraint even for presidents motivated only by instrumental considerations.[16]

Indeed, this is a prima facie plausible description of what it means to live in a society governed by the rule of law. But Posner and Vermeule refuse to recognize this philosophical truth, and they deny the status of law to all self-constrained behavior motivated by self-interest.

There is already a theory in constitutional law that bridges the gap between public opinion and legal change: popular constitutionalism dictates that constitutional change happens when the public itself alters its collective conception of the Constitution or "ratifies" interpretations offered by officials.[17] Although there are many different flavors of popular constitutionalism, one version holds that major

Supreme Court decisions are reactions to the changes in popular conceptions, rather than the other way around.[18] Bruce Ackerman argues that many of these critical changes in the Constitution are forged through important "constitutional moments"—identifiable points in time where a crisis or critical event spurs the public to change the popular conception and meaning of the Constitution.[19] All of this happens without a formal amendment to the Constitution.

Posner and Vermeule note that their argument is consistent with some versions of popular constitutionalism insofar as both theories place the electorate in the center of the theory and deemphasize the role played by the judiciary and other formal mechanisms of de jure lawmaking, whether congressional statutes, formal amendments to the Constitution, or Supreme Court opinions interpreting and applying constitutional provisions.[20] One small difference is that the Posner and Vermeule account includes a greater role for institutional and political elites—those individuals who are in charge of the federal branches during key moments of political showdowns.[21] The elites, rather than the public directly, play the game of brinkmanship that yields constitutional and political resolution of crises. The public is not wholly absent from the scene—the elites make their decisions based on the anticipated reaction of the public at large. According to Posner and Vermeule, "the process of constitutional change is roughly plebiscitary: the people do not propose, but they do dispose."[22] In that sense their account is consistent with popular constitutionalism.

There is, however, a significant difference between most versions of popular constitutionalism and Posner and Vermeule's theory of the self-constraining executive. Most versions of popular constitutionalism do not deny the label of "law" to the changes they describe.[23] Even the public's dynamic insertion into the lawmaking process (usually associated with legislators and judges) is not reason enough to label that process "extra-legal" or "merely political." In fact, some versions of popular constitutionalism explicitly rely on the concept of law insofar as they describe the public's participation in the process of "higher-lawmaking."[24] The real question, then, is why Posner and Vermeule are so adamant about denying the label to the process they describe.

The most likely rationale is the concept of law that Posner and Vermeule are working with. There are hidden assumptions here about the nature of law and how it differs from politics. One wonders if Posner and Vermeule subscribe to the view that "law" is limited to the commands of the sovereign backed up by the threat of sanctions. This "command" theory of law, famously associated with the philosopher J. L. Austin, associates law with a state's enforcement mechanism.[25] Since intrabranch disputes, for example, between the president and the judiciary, are not resolved by a police force capable of imposing sanctions, constitutional disputes between the branches are not real legal disputes. They are purely political. (And since there is no international police force capable of threatening sanctions for violations of international law, the "command" theory entails that much of international law is also not real law.)

One might object that the federal government has police forces at its disposal: the FBI, the U.S. Capitol Police, and the U.S. Park Police (to name just a few). But that isn't the real question. Consider the dispute in 1974 between President Nixon and Congress over whether he was required to turn over the Watergate tapes. The Supreme Court concluded that Nixon was required to fulfill the congressional subpoena for the tapes; the president was not above the law.[26] What would have happened if Nixon had openly defied the Supreme Court and ordered executive branch officials to ignore the Supreme Court decision?[27] The Supreme Court has no police force of its own that it could send to the White House to collect the tapes. The relevant police forces belong to the executive branch (with a limited number in the legislative branch). The result would have been a constitutional crisis, and the question is whether lower executive branch officials as well as the population at large would support Nixon's defiance or whether these individuals would consider the Supreme Court's decision determinative. But it is wrong to suggest that the absence of a police force to implement a sanction makes this hypothetical interbranch dispute a mere political dispute. It would be undoubtedly a legal dispute.

Austin's "command theory" lurks behind the scenes in Posner and Vermeule's account of interbranch disputes. However, it is not clear that the command theory is a correct description of the concept of law. Most philosophers of law reject it—at least since H. L. A. Hart's pathbreaking work, THE CONCEPT OF LAW, advanced an alternative account of lawmaking.[28] According to Hart, a legal system is characterized by primary rules governing conduct and secondary rules governing how government officials deal with the primary rules.[29] The most important secondary rule is a rule of recognition that allows the public to recognize when a putative law is valid. This rule must be widely shared and observed by public officials as a matter of *practice*.[30] Other important secondary rules include the rule of change, which dictates how laws might be amended or repealed, and the rule of adjudication, which governs how laws are applied and enforced when violations occur.[31]

Under a Hartian conception of law, it is clear that the commands of a sovereign are not an essential element of the concept of law. What matters is that there is some definitive rule (or set of rules) that identifies what counts as a law. Then there must be a shared attitude and practice with regard to that rule of recognition. As it happens, the decisions of the Supreme Court are binding, and there is an almost universally accepted attitude that its decisions are binding pronouncements of the law. As Chief Justice Marshall articulated in *Marbury v. Madison*, it is the province of the Court to "say what the law is"—and the public agrees with this fact.[32] Similar Hartian stories can be told about congressional and executive lawmaking, including statutes, executive agency administrative regulations, and even quasi-authoritative decisions of executive entities such as the Office of Legal Counsel. In other words, interbranch disputes are legal disputes, not just political disputes, so long as there is a widely shared rule of recognition about them.[33]

There is some dispute about whether Hart's version of the rule of recognition can accommodate the popular views of the citizenry.[34] One interpretation holds that the relevant social practice with regard to the rule of recognition is the practice of government officials, including legislators and executive officials.[35] A second interpretation holds that the relevant social practice is the practice of *judicial* officials—"a form of judicial customary rule existing only if it is accepted and practiced in the law-identifying and law-applying operations of the courts," according to Hart.[36] In order to accommodate popular constitutionalism, the theory might make room for the widely shared attitudes of the public as the relevant "recognitional community" for the rule of recognition.[37]

If Posner and Vermeule were to adopt a Hartian view of the law, they might be more willing to describe the interbranch political process as legal. It would allow them to shed their Austinian anxieties about the lack of orthodox enforcement in such disputes. And it would facilitate the conclusion that acting out of self-interest and legal obligation are not mutually exclusive. In fact, self-constraining rational agents will often seek *legal* structures that provide reciprocal constraints on behavior. The use of the legal system to provide structure for these constraints is not just possible or plausible; it is downright inevitable. The legal system provides the richest and most developed set of norms to codify such restrictions, so it is no surprise that rational, self-interested agents would harness the power of a legal system as a way of operationalizing a system of constraints.

Posner and Vermeule falsely denigrate this possibility as inconsistent with "Madisonian liberal legalism," or the idea that legislatures govern, executives carry out the law, and a *legal* system of separation of powers constrains the president from upsetting this delicate balance. According to Posner and Vermeule, the president is never constrained by this structure, and Madison's model is a relic of the past.[38] But the real problem is not with Madisonian liberal legalism, it is with Posner and Vermeule's Austinian understanding of constraint. Because the executive engages in a system of self-constraint instead of an external constraint backed up with sanctions, it cannot be law-like. But the law is built upon a reciprocal system of mutually beneficial constraints. So the executive *is* bound by law, so long as one correctly understands the concept of law and its relationship to rational self-constraint.

2.2 Presidential Power: The New Realist's Normative Argument

Legal scholars who favor broad presidential power in war-making usually circle back to a familiar criticism of Congress: a legislative body is too slow and too fragmented to offer quick, decisive action in times of great national peril. According to John Yoo, only a unitary executive branch vested in a single individual—the president himself—can lead our nation during national emergencies.[39] As such, the president should be entitled to fight the War on Terror without interference from Congress; he should be entitled to create military commissions, sign international agreements, and launch military forces—all without substantial congressional obstacles.[40] In THE EXECUTIVE UNBOUND, Eric Posner and Adrian Vermeule go so far as to suggest that we live in a world of permanent exigency and that we always need a strong and unencumbered president to engage in war and foreign relations, and to manage the modern administrative state.[41]

Yoo's argument for the primacy of executive action stems, in part, from constitutional text and history.[42] The framers reserved to Congress the power to *declare* war—a choice of words that Yoo believes is very significant.[43] A declaration is a verbal act, an ex post decision to classify an existing state of affairs into a particular logical or legal category. Under this view, the president has the authority to commence hostilities and to make war, and Congress retains the power to place the United States in a state of war with another sovereign nation. This is a reactive decision after the president has already committed troops to deal with a particular military situation. In Yoo's reading, if the framers had wanted this authority to reside exclusively with Congress, they would have granted them the authority to "engage" in war rather than simply the authority to declare war.[44] Yoo concedes that Congress retains the right to interfere with military action by applying the power of the purse.[45] If the president engages in military actions that Congress considers foolhardy, Congress can simply refuse to appropriate the necessary funds for the operations.[46] In recent history, however, Congress has "refused to exercise the ample powers under its disposal," according to Yoo,[47] resulting in further delegation of power to the executive branch.

Similarly, Posner and Vermeule argue for the primacy of executive branch action, although they do so for different reasons. The argument's inspiration comes from Carl Schmitt, the Nazi political philosopher. Although the Constitution's framers (not just in the United States but also in many other democracies) place their faith in legislative deliberation, the reality is that legislatures have a backward-looking focus on past problems.[48] For urgent problems that develop in real time, whether a modern fiscal crisis or a military intervention, the executive branch is at the front lines of developing a strategy to confront the threat. The legislature simply operates too slowly to be able to act quickly enough to solve urgent problems. Under the Schmittian view, the reality is that legislatures end up delegating more and more authority to executive branch officials to respond to these emergencies. That is the lesson that Posner and Vermeule take from both 9/11 and the 2008 economic crisis. In both cases, although there was some legislative pushback on particular presidential proposals (such as military commissions), the net result was more delegation of authority from the legislative branch to the president.[49]

Why does this happen? Under the Schmittian view, the process is inevitable because the *structure* of the legislature prevents meaningful action.[50] Deliberation is time-consuming and involves more bargaining (much of it along ideological lines) than meaningful reflection.[51] Floor debates are "carefully orchestrated posturing for public consumption" and a "transparent sham" rather than actual deliberation yielding improved ideas.[52] Party leaders make decisions "behind closed doors" while individual members usually fall in line or risk losing benefits conferred on them by their party.[53] In any event, the whole process comes much too late when a time-sensitive crisis emerges. Posner and Vermeule summarize the Schmittian idea this way: "The basic dilemma, for legislators, is that before a crisis, they lack the motivation and information to provide for it in advance, while after the crisis has begun, they lack the capacity to manage it themselves."[54] The end result is executive delegation.

Posner and Vermeule identify a final problem with legislative action. Far in advance of a crisis, legislators sit behind a "veil of uncertainty" about the future, which blunts the partisan gridlock since legislators have difficulty predicting who will emerge winners and losers under any new proposal.[55] This increases impartiality but also decreases motivation. When a crisis emerges, however, the situation is exactly the opposite. Legislators no longer act under a veil of uncertainty, since the situation's immediacy makes clear which actors will emerge with distributional benefits under any new proposal. But with the increase in motivation comes a decrease in impartiality. The result is more gridlock, less action.[56]

These criticisms rehash a tired point straight from Thomas Hobbes.[57] The British philosopher argued that life in the state of nature was nasty, brutish, and short, and that the only escape from it was a social contract that places ultimate authority in the hands of a sovereign power—someone who could protect everyone by enforcing the law.[58] For Hobbes, a corporate body like parliament was ill suited to this role because its internal divisions rendered it susceptible to conflict and confusion, like a multiheaded mythical creature pulling in too many directions.[59] In part II, book 19, Hobbes writes that "the resolutions of a monarch, are subject to no other inconstancy, than that of human nature; but in assemblies, besides that of nature, there ariseth an inconstancy from the number."[60] Hobbes then puts the point even more sharply: "a monarch cannot disagree with himself," but an assembly certainly can.[61] And when a legislature disagrees with itself, the end result is civil war. This is precisely what Hobbes witnessed in his own day.[62]

Only an all-powerful leviathan—a monarch—could avoid the irrationality and corruptibility of parliament.[63] For Hobbes, only absolute rule could save us from absolute anarchy. He also believed that the objections to monarchical rule were exaggerated. Although a monarch could use his power to enrich "a favourite or a flatterer," so too could a legislature.[64] Although a legislature is divided, it is just as corruptible as a monarch: "they are as subject to evil counsel, and to be seduced by orators, as a monarch by flatterers; and becoming one another's flatterers, serve one another's covetousness and ambition by turn."[65]

Hobbes has other, less convincing arguments for the primacy of executive authority. First, he argues that monarchs have a unity of interest with their states, so there is never a split between public and private interests—an infirmity that he finds endemic to legislatures.[66] Though the split between public and private interests is crucial (it represents the seeds of corruption), it is doubtful that monarchs are immune from it. Hobbes believes that monarchs are only as rich as their subjects since the monarch's riches come only from the "riches, strength, and reputation" of his subjects.[67] In a more practical sense, weak subjects are unable to fight and win wars on behalf of the monarch, so the monarch has a vested interest in strong subjects.[68] This argument is weak, however, because there is a big difference between an army and the public writ large; plenty of monarchs starve the masses but feed the army.[69] Furthermore, monarchs are famous for preferring some constituencies over others, raising distributional concerns among those who have fallen out of favor. No alleged unity of public and private interests will prevent that.

Second, Hobbes argues that a monarch receives better advice and counsel "when, and where he pleaseth," including from experts who can give technical knowledge with the comfort of secrecy.[70] This produces better decisions. By contrast, legislatures work in the bright light of day, where honest information and advice is never rewarded; instead, it is replaced with the "flame of the passions, never enlightened, but dazzled."[71] Their very size prevents legislatures from deliberating in secret, though the practice of the U.S. Senate Intelligence Committee would suggest otherwise. And although it is true that public debate in the legislature is often uninformed or driven by ideological posturing, it is unclear whether secrecy itself ensures that executive deliberations are free from ideological concerns.

The fact that the new plea for a strong executive branch is an old idea does not make it wrong. Isn't it true that the U.S. Congress is plagued by political logrolling at best and irrational policymaking at worst? These criticisms all trade on a particular asymmetry: the president is supposedly a rational agent because he is a single human being, unified in thought and action, while Congress is a motley crew of politicians, unified neither by thought nor policy and therefore incapable of exercising rational agency.

But the asymmetry is illusory, or, at the very least, exaggerated. Posner and Vermeule dismiss these objections quickly, though they only consider the familiar point that the executive branch has grown so large that it is now almost as unwieldy and divided as Congress.[72]

In fact, by raw number of employees, the executive branch is much larger than the legislative branch, which would suggest a greater capacity for internal division in the executive branch.[73] However, Posner and Vermeule correctly note that the executive and legislative branches have completely different *structures*; the executive branch is essentially hierarchical, with the president sitting at the top of the decision tree.[74] Although this is true, it isn't the real issue to be confronted. The *real* question is whether there is a deeper coherence to the activities of Congress, where Posner and Vermeule only see a corporate body that in key moments of crises "fretted, fumed, and delayed."[75] At the level of rational behavior, Posner and Vermeule refuse to take collective action seriously, which limits their ability to understand the essential unity of the behavior of Congress.[76]

Even a cursory look at the economic and philosophical literature on rational choice demonstrates that groups—whether corporations or Congress—are capable of exercising a very distinct type of rational agency.[77] Groups, especially deliberative bodies like Congress, are capable of deliberating in common, selecting ends that they wish to achieve and ranking preferences among them.[78] They can also collectively decide the necessary means to achieve those ends.

Some theorists suggest that the collective agency of Congress (or corporations for that matter) is illusory, a mere shorthand for a complex aggregation of individual agents.[79] The collective agency is essentially reducible to large numbers of individual agents who are morally and rationally significant. The collective only has rational significance indirectly or *derivatively* because it is composed of individual agents who are themselves significant.

This view is profoundly mistaken. In fact, attributing collective agency to a corporate body is often the only way to make sense of its behavior. This fact was demonstrated conclusively by Kornhauser and Sager in their discussion of the doctrinal paradox and again by Philip Pettit in his discussion of the discursive dilemma.[80] Both involve situations where we must *decide* whether to view a group of individuals as acting as individual agents or as part of a collective agent. Consider a three-person jury deciding a case with a special verdict form.[81] First they consider the issue of whether a legal duty applies; two individuals (*a* and *b*) vote yes. Then they consider whether there was damage to the victim in the case; two individuals (*b* and *c*) vote yes. Consequently, they award a recovery in the case. How can this result be explained? Only one individual (*b*) out of three thinks there was *both* a legal duty and damages in the case. However, the group as a whole decided by majority vote that there was a legal duty and then also decided in favor of damages; consequently, the group concluded that recovery was warranted. This is collective reason, and the behavior of the jury only makes sense if it is viewed as a collective agent, deliberating in common and issuing a collective decision.[82]

Now return to the present inquiry. If you look at the level of individual House or Senate members, the resulting decisions often look irrational. But if you zoom out and analyze the behavior of the group—*as a group*—you witness a rational agent that uses a specific decision procedure to resolve conflicts between its beliefs and desires. Although the decisions are often reached through messy negotiation (yes, even logrolling), the result is collective decision-making that is both rational and meaningful. The result is *legislation*.

It is true that the process of creating legislation may be just as unpalatable as making sausage, and many proponents of strong executive action have made a career of cataloging the foibles of congressional stupidity. One need not look far to find them; there is plenty to criticize in congressional behavior in recent history. However, as a comparative matter, one wonders how much of the division and stupidity found in the legislative branch is replicated in the executive branch. The difference, of course, is that most decisions of the executive branch are made in secret and are not subject to public evaluation; this produces an apple-to-oranges comparison between the two branches. If executive interagency deliberations (and accompanying turf squabbles) were as visible as public hearings in Congress, the executive branch would develop a reputation for disunity as well. The simple fact is that the executive branch has used secrecy as a shield to prevent exposure of its own sausage-making process.

One can take the argument one step further, moving from the disunity of the large executive branch to the disunity of the president himself. Hobbes falsely assumed that a monarch could not disagree with himself, but the internal process of deliberation, even *within* a single individual, is often fraught with incoherence and disunity.[83] Why then do so many political theorists, from Hobbes and Schmitt to their contemporary analogs, assume that individuals are relatively free from internal conflict? The answer stems from an extension of the secrecy point above. The internal deliberations of a single individual are even more secret—they are epistemically removed from observers who have little to no access to the competing thoughts and tensions within a person's mind. There is a natural assumption that *intrapersonal* rational tensions are somehow less significant than *interpersonal* rational tensions, although that assessment might be heavily influenced by the fact that interpersonal tensions are manifest for all to see, while intrapersonal tensions remain hidden from view unless articulated in language. But if we could somehow see inside the brain and witness belief- and desire-formation in an individual human being, it too would look messy and disjointed.

The alleged asymmetry exaggerates the degree of unity within the executive branch. To summarize, there are two separate points here. First, individual human beings are hardly a paragon of perfect rational unity—individuals have all sorts of competing beliefs and desires that are often downright contradictory, and the manner in which they resolve these competing beliefs is not always exemplary.[84] The only difference between the conflicted individual and the conflicted group is that the conflicted individual has an intrapersonal procedure to resolve the conflict, whereas the conflicted group has an interpersonal procedure to resolve the conflicts.[85] The important point is that both are capable of exercising rational agency.

The second point is more pedestrian. The executive branch is hardly reducible to a single individual human being, the president. Rather, the modern executive branch now contains thousands of employees, each of whom reports to a variety of cabinet and subcabinet authorities or executive agencies. Many of these actions produce tensions and contradictions that require resolution. True, the executive power is formally vested in the president of the United States, such that the president himself can resolve disagreements, but the disagreements within the executive branch are legendary—even in the context of foreign affairs and war-making.[86] So both branches are examples of corporate agency. The relevant difference between Congress and the executive branch is not the internal differences among its members—it is the decision procedure that governs the corporate agent.[87] Congress decides by majority and super-majority, depending on the question, while the executive branch decides based on deliberation and consultation, followed by a decision by the appropriate cabinet head, which is subject to reversal by the president himself. Both are corporate; it is the voting procedure that differs.

In the final analysis, the argument against legislative rule and in favor of executive primacy relies on unsupported assumptions about the coherence of executive action and the incoherence of legislative action. Posner and Vermeule, like Schmitt and Hobbes before them, assume that single individuals are immune from the failures of rationality and at the same time exaggerate the failures of rationality that plague collective agents like legislatures. The reason for this assumption is that political observers witness political dissension in the legislative branch, but executive disunity is shielded from view, either by secrecy or the simple fact that individual deliberation is inherently *personal*. But the very transparency of the legislative process, despite its messiness, is democracy's greatest virtue.

2.3 Democratic Decision-Making versus Schmittology

This then leads to an underlying inquiry about the nature of efficacious decision-making. In THE EXECUTIVE UNBOUND, Posner and Vermeule demonstrate little faith in the democratic decision-making procedure of Congress and an almost religious faith in the royal prerogatives of the modern presidency—a development that they fully endorse and encourage.[88] But what ought to be brought to the forefront is not the issue of rational disunity; it is the appropriate decision procedure that our political theory ought to support. Posner and Vermeule wholeheartedly reject Madisonian democracy while advancing Carl Schmitt's version of executive authority—a surprising figurehead to select for their arguments. James Madison was a Founding Father, an author of the *Federalist Papers*, and a revered patriot, so Posner and Vermeule's suggestion that our Madisonian Republic is now dead sounds, well, un-American. Combine that with their explicit avowal of Carl Schmitt—a Nazi political philosopher—as the intellectual father of unbounded executive authority. Moreover, Schmitt's Nazism was not tangential to his overall philosophy, like Heidegger, but in fact was essential to this political extremism.

Schmitt argued that faith in parliamentarianism was misplaced.[89] In fact, he diagnosed in liberal political theory an almost religious faith in the "rational deliberation" of seasoned legislators.[90] Schmitt found this faith to be misplaced, a not-so-quaint relic of the Enlightenment's obsession with dialectical reason.[91] As a practical matter, legislatures were dominated by political concerns and backroom dealing, neither of which justified the faith that liberal political theorists had placed in these institutions. In this sense, Schmitt's work represents a neo-Hobbesian attack on legislative primacy, while the work of Posner and Vermeule represents a neo-Hobbesian-Schmittian attack on the same target.

Schmitt combined these arguments with a second set of ideas that linked sovereignty with emergency. According to Schmitt, political rule could be separated into normal and exceptional states.[92] In exceptional states, the sovereign sets aside preexisting legal norms, what one might call the rule of law, which becomes a hindrance to effective handling of a crisis situation. The sovereign—by definition—is he who decides the state of exception, he who decides whether the state is in a state of crisis or not.[93] Law only applies when the sovereign decides that it *can* be applied. This effectively subrogates law to power, a rejection of Hans Kelsen's theories placing the *Grundnorm* at the center of the legal system.[94] For Schmitt, sovereign power was the base of the entire structure. Moreover, Schmitt felt that this ultimate sovereign power was itself not constrained by law, because making it constrained by law was internally self-contradictory. If the sovereign has the power to decide whether the law applies or not, then no law could review whether that decision is lawful or not.[95] Such a power of extrasovereign review would assume that there is a preexisting legal norm that could stand in a position of legal authority over the sovereign. And this is precisely what Schmitt denied.

Schmitt's ideas proved incredibly useful for legitimizing the Nazi state.[96] Hitler suspended the previous German constitution and declared a series of emergency states, heralding the very state of exception that animated Schmitt's writings. Hitler himself was in a position to decide when legal norms should give way to the demands of exigency; as such, Hitler himself stood above the law and could not be constrained by it. So there is a straight line to be drawn from Schmitt's ideas to the *Führerprinzip*—a far more explicit and tangible connection than anything found in Heidegger's philosophy of *Dasein*.[97] Furthermore, Schmitt's philosophy of law captured the rather distinct relationship between law and power in Nazi Germany. Schmitt argued that the vague and indeterminate standards that proliferated in German law (as they do in all liberal democracies) could be harnessed by sympathetic jurists who wished to make the legal system more conducive to the Nazi program.[98]

In this sense, Schmitt represents an odd standard-bearer for the New Realists; Hobbes would have been a far more efficacious rhetorical choice. True, Posner and Vermeule are not making their argument to the general public. So perhaps it is irrelevant that no politician could stand up today and be taken seriously by the electorate if they denigrated James Madison and suggested that we follow the teachings of a Third Reich Nazi philosopher. Academics are supposed to reject ad hominem attacks; they should attack the theory itself and not the man who speaks the theory. The theories of Madison and Schmitt should receive a fair hearing on the merits.

Thus what matters is whether there is room for Congress' collective decision-making in the context of the modern presidency's stewardship of crisis situations and the conduct of foreign relations and war. Here again, the social science literature is instructive. It turns out that crowds display a collective wisdom that single individuals do not, a fact that is abundantly demonstrated by the capacity of markets—which are, after all, just a large collection of individuals making decisions—to make accurate predictions.

Markets harness the wisdom of crowds to make accurate assessments of risk and even predict future events.[99] The idea is an old one and was scientifically evaluated by Francis Galton's famous study of a fat ox weight-judging competition in 1909.[100] The result was that the collective evaluation of a large number of individuals was more likely to be accurate than a single individual assessment. The philosopher John Stuart Mill also believed that freedom of speech—including dissent—was crucial for a well-ordered society, because only through deliberation and dissent could a collection of individuals, a society, reach the correct conclusions.[101] The theory of rational choice supports this understanding.[102]

It was precisely these insights that prompted John Poindexter, while working at the Pentagon, to suggest the creation of a futures market for predicting terrorist attacks—on the assumption that a self-interested crowd would do it better than the CIA.[103] Of course, the proposal was not just politically unsavory—it might have exaggerated the conclusions of the social science literature. But it is far less controversial to point out that the 535 members of Congress, voting individually, might actually produce better collective decisions in some contexts than single individuals.[104] As political philosopher Jon Elster has convincingly argued, the design of a democratic assembly should foster rational belief formation by optimizing deliberation and representation.[105] In practical terms, the best-designed assemblies minimize the role of interest and passion but maximize the diversity of opinions and ideas (which Elster refers to as "epistemic quality").[106] Indeed, the collective judgments of a corporate body like Congress are more than just an aggregation of individual whimsy—they may exhibit collective reason on the basis of common deliberation and a robust decision procedure that pushes Congress toward greater consistency over time.[107] Indeed, the philosophers Christian List and Philip Pettit have modeled how a legislature of individual politicians could reason collectively regarding financial policy and a new budget.[108] The wisdom of crowds need not come at the expense of coherency; a divided Congress can act intelligently.

What the New Realists and Hobbes denigrate as the greatest failing of the legislative branch might turn out to be its greatest strength. Legislative deliberation allows the corporate body to receive and digest a wealth of information, synthesize differing viewpoints, consider objections, and pursue a course of action based on majority voting. Although the process appears disjointed—so many different and conflicted viewpoints—the same could be said of a market.

2.4 Executive Action During Emergencies

In taking a page from Schmitt's playbook, the New Realists conclude that only executive action can successfully lead the country during times of emergency. Since 9/11, there has been plenty of discussion of states of emergency; the entire Bush administration unfolded with an aura (some say cloud) of emergency. Posner and Vermeule believe that slide into emergency was inevitable—and should not be feared.

Posner and Vermeule begin TERROR IN THE BALANCE with a pithy and succinct articulation of their thesis: "When national emergencies strike, the executive acts, Congress acquiesces, and courts defer."[109] Then the process reverses itself: "When emergencies decay, judges become bolder, and soul searching begins."[110] Then another emergency comes along, and the cycle begins again. This could be an accurate statement of the post-9/11 legal and political culture in America.

Their argument proceeds in three parts. They present three theories. The first two theories they accept; the last one they reject. The first, the Trade-Off Thesis, holds that security and liberty are inevitably in conflict. If policymakers opt for more individual liberty, they necessarily decrease collective security; if the government reduces individual liberty, they can improve security conditions for the public.[111] Although many scholars have tried to argue around this certain tension, Posner and Vermeule consider it unavoidable. It is a tough decision. And those who resist it are fooling themselves.

There is a close connection between the Trade-Off Thesis and the New Realist argument for executive supremacy. The trade-off between security and liberty requires a dynamic response to the conditions of the day. In situations of acute emergency, the government should decrease liberty in order to safeguard security; when the crisis evaporates, the government can revise the relative balance between the two principles. This process entails institutional deference to the executive branch because only the executive branch has the technical knowledge and administrative flexibility to make quick and difficult decisions about security-liberty trade-offs. This is a specific instantiation of the more general Hobbesian and Schmittian argument.

This suggests that judicial interference in executive branch decisions about security-liberty trade-offs is particularly dangerous. This is called the Deference Thesis.[112] Posner and Vermeule are blunt and barely hide their skepticism of judicial involvement: "When judges or academic commentators say that government has wrongly assessed the net benefits or costs of some security policy or other, they are *amateurs playing at security policy*, and there is no reason to expect that courts can improve upon government's emergency policies in any systematic way."[113] The executive branch is filled with technical expertise and subtle public policymaking that maximizes individual liberty without sacrificing collective security. Judges make ad hoc and amateurish decisions that upset this delicate balance.

On the other hand, Posner and Vermeule reject the Ratchet Theory, a familiar argument among social scientists that concludes that repeated cycles of emergency and security regulation have the cumulative effect of permanently reducing civil liberties.[114] The Ratchet Theory is often associated with liberal criticisms of government security initiatives.[115] In essence, the theory holds that the government responds to a security crisis by reducing civil liberties. This first part of the argument is broadly consistent with the Trade-Off Thesis. However, at this point, the Ratchet Theory goes beyond the Trade-Off Thesis and concludes that governments rarely roll back all of their security initiatives at the conclusion of the crisis. The result is a net gain for security regulation and a net loss for civil liberties as the changes become "cemented" into place.[116] Consequently, the Ratchet Theory predicts that over time, governments will use states of emergency as an excuse to change the status quo, not in temporary ways but in permanent ways that fundamentally alter the balance of power between the individual and the state.

The Ratchet Theory constitutes a substantial criticism of the Deference Thesis. If the Ratchet Theory is correct, broad deference to the executive branch in its handling of the Trade-Off Thesis is inappropriate, because the "flexibility" that the deference theory promotes would be a sham.[117] Judicial (and congressional) oversight of the process is the only way to ensure that civil liberties are not cumulatively reduced into oblivion by a succession of crises. Thus it makes sense that Posner and Vermeule categorically reject the Ratchet Theory: "there are just no systematic trends in the history of civil liberties, no important ratchet-like mechanisms that cause repeated wars or emergencies to push civil liberties in one direction or another in any sustained fashion."[118] They also reject versions of the Reverse-Ratchet Theory, or the idea that a backlash to government security regulations creates a cumulative effect *in favor* of civil liberties.[119] The fundamental unpredictability of the effects supports their reliance on the Deference Thesis, since only the executive branch has the flexibility and expertise needed to make the appropriate trade-off calculations.

At this point, it is unnecessary to engage with the specifics of the Trade-Off Thesis. For the sake of argument, let us assume that trade-offs are inevitable and inescapable. This itself is a debatable assumption since trade-offs appeal to both consequentialism and welfarism and seem to give little weight to deontological concerns (the idea that we have a duty to respect the inherent moral worth of each individual, which cannot be balanced away by the greater good).[120] As such, there is plenty of reason to resist trade-offs, since in many instances they require sacrificing the interests of some individuals in favor of a larger benefit to others. In any event, the real question is whether the Trade-Off Thesis constitutes a valid argument in favor of the Deference Thesis, not whether trade-offs in general are morally appropriate.

2.5 Why Schmittian Administrative Law Is Not Inevitable

If the argument for executive supremacy was limited to states of emergency, that would be one thing. But Posner and Vermeule have extended their arguments about executive deference during states of emergency to a generalized claim about executive power during non-emergency situations as well. In the first instantiation of the argument in TERROR IN THE BALANCE, they argued that judicial and legislative branches substantially defer to the executive during times of crisis with regard to trade-offs between security and liberty; in addition to this descriptive claim, they also made the normative argument that this deference was appropriate.[121] In THE EXECUTIVE UNBOUND, they extend this argument substantially, concluding that the supremacy of the executive is an inevitable consequence of the rise of the administrative state.[122] As such, the executive is—and should be—unbound by judicial and legislative interference.

The extension from the first version to the second version of the argument owes much to Schmitt and his famous theories of states of emergency. As explained above, Schmitt believed that by definition, only the sovereign has the power to decide if there is a state of exception or not. Furthermore, he also believed that the conditions for a state of exception were truly *exceptional* (by definition) and therefore could not be stated or controlled ex ante by legal constraints (such as a statute that defined the scope of emergency powers and when they could be exercised); ex post constraints were also pointless.[123] He also believed that existing legal standards were frequently vague and indeterminate—often deliberately so as to give executive officials an "escape hatch" when exigency demanded substantial departure from prior courses of action.[124]

Posner and Vermeule take the Schmittian argument as an allegory for the modern administrative state.[125] In doing so, they realize that they adopt a controversial figurehead, but they conclude that Schmitt's essential point (his "marrow") can be divorced from the worst excesses of the Nazi period and the downfall of the Weimar constitutional order (the discarded bones).[126] They conclude that panicky civil libertarians exaggerate the danger that unchecked executive power would lead to another Hitler—a point they end with the comforting reminder that "if it did, there would be nothing that civil libertarian judges could do about it."[127] The greater risk, they claim, is the "specter of authoritarianism" that will be trumped up by civil libertarian panic and prevent needed security reforms from being implemented.[128]

Posner and Vermeule conclude that the same "institutional features" exist in the modern administrative state.[129] The creation of numerous administrative agencies represents a nod to the Schmittian worldview. Only the agency has the technical expertise to regulate appropriately. Both Congress and the judiciary take a hands-off approach and give the executive administrative agencies broad discretion to regulate. First, Congress allows the agencies to issue their own regulations, and the courts use *Chevron* deference to give priority to an agency's interpretation of those regulations (as opposed to the court substituting its own interpretation of the regulations). Although courts retain the power to review and overturn agency decisions that are arbitrary and capricious, in reality, this only amounts to a "soft look" review, not the "hard look" review that courts claim they employ.[130] Consequently, legislative and judicial deference to executive expertise is not simply a function of the liberty-security trade-off—it is implicit in the structure of modern society, with a fast-moving economy and international legal order that demands rapid response and technical expertise.

For these reasons, Posner and Vermeule believe that Schmittian administrative law is inevitable.[131] Black and gray holes will always exist in legislative standards; black holes exempt entire areas of executive action from legal regulation (such as Guantanamo Bay), while gray holes involve vague standards that provide flexibility and "adjustable parameters."[132] However, Posner and Vermeule deny that the process starts with emergency deference, which then is extended (and perhaps ratcheted) during peacetime. This would be the simplistic Schmittian version of the argument. Rather, Posner and Vermeule claim that the causal chain runs in the opposite direction. The administrative state, with its grants of flexible parameters and deference to executive expertise, is the purest expression of the Schmittian system, which is then incorporated through a "reverse spillover" effect into the law applicable during states of emergency.[133] In other words, national security deference and the open-ended standards that make it possible was promoted and strengthened by the rise of the administrative state.

Pace Posner and Vermeule, the rise of the Schmittian administrative state—with virtually unreviewable executive action—is not inevitable. The problem with the argument is its implicit reliance on a Hobbesian narrative that disparages legislative action and lionizes executive competence. It represents presidential hagiography. In this neo-Hobbesian worldview, the legislature is ideological, plagued by technical impotence, and devolves into political compromise. In contrast, executive branch decision-making is technically sophisticated, immune from incoherent compromise, and quarantined from ideology. This represents a return to the Hobbesian idea that the legislature is rationally divided while the monarch is unified. But, as we explained before, that conclusion rests on an asymmetry because executive level decision-making is never subject to the same level of transparency and scrutiny and consequently *appears* far more unified than it actually is. In reality, congressional action through 535 members is just as much deserving of the label of rational agency as executive action that is filtered through a sprawling executive branch with final authority resting in a single individual. Of course, this point should not be exaggerated. In qualitative terms, Congress is more divided than the executive branch. But the point here is that the distinction is one of degree, not kind. Both branches of government feature disunity, and both are capable of exercising rational agency. Congress is always politically divided by multiparty representation, while the executive branch is dominated by one political party at a time. But even this point is capable of exaggeration: Congress is always, by definition, dominated by one *majority* party with the power of pushing through legislation. The plurality of voices and ideas from different constituencies may start with a torrent of deliberation, but they produce, through majority voting, coherent outcomes with discrete policy preferences.

Furthermore, Schmittian administrative law is subject to special interests and lobbying efforts that threaten the "technical expertise" that is supposedly the greatest asset of the executive branch. Although Congress is certainly not immune from lobbying efforts (especially because of the need for campaign donations), the greater transparency in the legislative process provides a built-in check on overaggressive lobbying efforts. In contrast, agency decision-making is particularly subject to special interest contamination because of the comparative lack of transparency in the administrative process. What passes for technical independence can often be an excuse for interest group politics.

2.6 Can Congress Constrain the President's Use of Military Force?

President Obama's tenure in office failed to meet the expectations of some voters. Although he campaigned on a platform of radical departure from Bush-era foreign policy, he failed to close Guantanamo Bay, continued the use of military commissions, and escalated the number and geographical scope of targeted killings. This not only angered his most ardent supporters, who felt betrayed that Obama the president looked so different from Obama the campaigner; it also provided fuel to Bush-era advisers who argued that Obama was simply continuing the core elements of Bush's legal and foreign policy. This narrative of continuation stands in some tension with the far-left view of the Bush administration as being exceptional, even by American standards of exceptionalism. But if the former Bush advisers are right, the Bush-era exceptionalism was hardly exceptional. It was par for the course and was supported, without interruption, by President Obama.

Jack Goldsmith has forcefully argued that Obama magnified Bush's foreign policy posture by substituting targeted killings for torture.[134] This claim prompted protests from Obama advisers who disagreed with the characterization. First, it is undeniable that Obama eliminated torture as an interrogation tool against suspected terrorists in detention—a marked break from Bush, who continues to unapologetically assert that the waterboarding of detainees was morally legitimate and strategically advisable.[135] Obama also halted the transfer of detainees to Guantanamo so that although he was unsuccessful at his attempt to close the detention center, he has not added a single detainee to its population. Any new detainees are either held by foreign governments directly (Iraq and Afghanistan) and not transferred to U.S. authority, or they are brought before federal district courts and charged with a domestic offense, such as providing material support for terrorism.

At the same time, though, Obama radically increased the number of targeted killings, leading to speculation that Obama is now simply killing people that Bush would have tortured. This is not what opponents of torture had in mind when they voted for Obama. The Obama administration also oversaw an expansion of surveillance powers for the National Security Agency (NSA); many of the details caused public and political consternation after they were disclosed by Edward Snowden, a former NSA contractor. Although Obama ordered the closing of CIA secret prisons known as black sites, the military continues to hold individuals for limited periods—though the administration does not apparently consider the individuals "detainees" in the legal sense of the term because of the transient nature of their incarceration. For Goldsmith, this is confirmation that criticisms of Bush were misplaced and that Bush-era exceptionalism was far from exceptional. He echoes the ACLU in their fear that Obama "will enshrine permanently within the law policies and practices that were widely considered extreme and unlawful during the Bush Administration."[136]

In POWER AND CONSTRAINT: THE ACCOUNTABLE PRESIDENCY AFTER 9/11, Goldsmith develops an account of why Obama continued so many of the Bush counterterrorism policies that the Democrats, and candidate Obama himself, initially opposed. It is a narrative that Goldsmith himself figures prominently in because "almost all of this program had been vetted, altered, and blessed— with restrictions and accountability strings attached—by the other branches of the US government," a process Goldsmith participated in.[137] As counsel to the Department of Defense and later assistant attorney general in charge of the Office of Legal Counsel, he helped ensure that Bush's policies were battle-tested and appropriately revised when opponents raised legal concerns about them. Goldsmith was in charge of withdrawing and revising the Yoo torture memos, and he also oversaw the OLC's legal advice on matters pertaining to detention and the use of force.

The narrative of continuation extends to the domain of unilateral president authority under the commander-in-chief power.

After Colonel Gaddafi began attacking his own citizens and Libya collapsed into civil war, President Obama decided to commit the United States to military action as part of a NATO-led coalition. The Security Council issued a resolution authorizing military action to protect civilians (and there were subsequent complaints that NATO's actions far exceeded that mandate). On the domestic front, it seemed that Congress would likely not authorize U.S. involvement in the military action; American voters were wary of contributing military personnel to a war that did not directly implicate U.S. strategic interests. Anticipating this result, Obama committed U.S. forces anyway, arguing that doing so was his prerogative as commander in chief of the armed forces.[138]

Under the War Powers Resolution, the president is only permitted to use military force in the absence of congressional authorization for up to sixty days. After that, congressional authorization is required, and the president has thirty more days under the Resolution to wind down U.S. involvement in a military action that Congress fails to approve. However, Obama exceeded this window and was forced to explain his seeming noncompliance with the ninety-day limit of the War Powers Resolution. He *could* have argued that the War Powers Resolution is unconstitutional as an impermissible infringement on his commander-in-chief powers, but such an explanation would have inflamed his left-leaning supporters, both in Congress and the electorate. Instead, he evaded the alleged contradiction and argued that the War Powers Resolution was simply inapplicable to the military campaign in Libya.

The task of making this argument fell principally to two sets of lawyers: Harold Koh, Legal Adviser to the State Department, and the Office of Legal Counsel in the Justice Department. The OLC issued a memorandum in April 2011, noting first that only war "in the constitutional sense"—that is, a lengthy and protracted armed conflict, usually between sovereigns—would trigger the Declare War Clause and require a formal declaration from Congress.[139] This determination required a fact-specific inquiry based on the "anticipated nature, scope, and duration" of the conflict.[140] Whatever Libya was, it was *not* war "in the constitutional sense." The OLC memorandum cited as support the

Haiti operation—the 2004 operation in which U.S. troops were deployed during a period of civil and political unrest during the end of Jean-Bertrand Aristide's presidency. At the time, an OLC memorandum written by Jack Goldsmith argued that the president had the authority to mobilize the U.S. military to protect U.S. personnel and assets, ensure regional stability, and maintain the credibility of U.N. Security Council resolutions.[141] The 1995 Bosnia operation, which involved 20,000 ground troops, was justified because the president was acting unilaterally to complete a "pattern of inter-allied cooperation and assistance" with NATO peacekeeping efforts, preserving regional peace, and maintaining the credibility of Security Council sanctions.[142] The new OLC memorandum concluded that since two of these factors were also present in the Libyan context (regional stability and the credibility of the U.N. Security Council), executive action to deploy troops on a limited basis was constitutional even in the absence of congressional authorization.[143]

The OLC memorandum was a lawyerly document not designed for public digestion (though it was unclassified). In contrast, Harold Koh's statements on the legality of the Libyan operation were pitched to lawyers and the general public alike. Koh is the former dean of Yale Law School, a leading scholar of international law, and a staunch supporter of international legal constraints on state behavior. He was as far from a New Realist as one could imagine. As State Department Legal Adviser, Koh argued that the Libyan mission was exempt from the constraints of the War Powers Resolution because the United States did not have troops in Libya, and no U.S. service members were likely to get killed during the operation.[144] U.S. involvement was limited to naval vessels off the coast of Libya, which were unlikely (though not impossible) targets for Libyan assets to strike. The United States was also deploying drones to help support the NATO operation. But there were no infantry troops or special operations personnel in Libya itself, thus supporting Koh's claim that the requirements of the War Powers Resolution were satisfied. In his testimony before the Senate Foreign Relations Committee, Koh concluded that Congress passed the War Powers Resolution to restrain the president from engaging in lengthy, protracted, and costly military campaigns such as Vietnam and Korea; it was a "No More Vietnams" resolution.[145]

Some international and constitutional law scholars, even former academic colleagues, reacted to Koh's argument with incredulity.[146] They questioned whether one could equate the legality of military action with the risk to ground troops—an argument that, if taken seriously, would enable future presidents to launch military actions (albeit limited ones) without congressional approval. With the advancement of drone technology, these military campaigns would become more and more likely. (Indeed, Koh had already taken criticism—though much of it unfair—from international law professors who questioned his legal defense of drone strikes against foreign nationals and even U.S. citizens.[147]) Furthermore, the rationale for congressional involvement in military decisions had little to do with risking American lives, or, at the very least, was only partially related to the risk posed to American citizens. Soldiers represent nations whose interests "advance and retrograde" with their troops.[148] The people share in the spoils and burdens of warfare. If the battalion is defeated, so too is the nation; if the army wins, the nation is victorious. Congressional involvement is essential for military actions taken in the name of the people, and the War Powers Resolution was Congress' attempt to insert the most deliberative branch of government into the process.

The hostility toward Koh's legal opinion was driven by a sense, possibly illegitimate or at the very least exaggerated, that Koh and Obama were indirectly undermining the War Powers Resolution without directly saying so. In the past, advocates of a strong executive with an expansive reading of the commander-in-chief power have argued that the War Powers Resolution is unconstitutional. Critics complained that Obama effectively subverted the War Powers Resolution with a legal argument that was too clever by half—ultimately unconvincing in its account of what counted as "hostilities." Since the Supreme Court has never passed judgment on the War Powers Resolution and will never do so because of the political question doctrine, so too there will never be any judicial review of the OLC's legal analysis regarding Libya.

Say what you will about the Bush administration's fidelity to international law; the fact of the matter is that President Bush sought and received congressional support for the armed conflict with al-Qaeda and the Taliban in Afghanistan (embodied in the 9/11 AUMF), and he also received congressional support for the invasion of Iraq. Critics will rightly complain that the Bush administration consistently interpreted the 9/11 AUMF in the broadest possible way, even to the point of applying it to "associated forces" of al-Qaeda and the Taliban even though no such language was ever included in the 9/11 AUMF. Consistently overbroad readings of the AUMF may have subverted the original congressional intent in passing the authorization, thus negating some of the credit that Bush should receive for involving Congress in the decision. As to Iraq, the Bush administration could be accused of securing congressional consent with negligent intelligence (WMDs that turned out to be illusory) or worse, a deliberately deceptive account of Hussein's military capabilities and his ties to al-Qaeda (which also turned out to be false). So the picture of Bush as a paragon of dual congressional-executive decision-making is somewhat complicated by the details of these authorizations. But even with these details, Bush's pattern of seeking congressional authorization, and Obama's concerted working around congressional authorization in the Libyan operation, complicates the narrative of the Bush years as exceptional exceptionalism. In some respects, the temptations of unilateral executive power have flowed uninterrupted into the Obama presidency.

Perhaps Congress acquiesced in these actions because it did nothing. It could have withdrawn the purse strings and refused to appropriate funds for any military action that it disapproved of. This applies as much to the AUMF as it does to Bosnia and Kosovo, all of which continued uninterrupted thanks to the cash that was doled out by Congress. Indeed, Posner and Vermeule specifically cite congressional acquiescence (by refusing to withdraw funding) in the Kosovo operation as emblematic of Congress' deferral to the ongoing ex executive authority.[149] The concept of acquiescence goes back to Frankfurter's concurrence in *Youngstown*, which concluded that the past practice of executive action to which Congress had acquiesced could provide a "historical gloss" on the scope of executive power.[150] In other words, if the president acts and Congress does nothing to stop him (or regulate him), this creates a constitutional precedent. For example, the OLC opinion on Libya specifically relied on congressional acquiescence regarding military engagements ordered by previous presidents. However, as Curtis Bradley and Trevor Morrison argue, it is dangerous to infer meaningful consent or waiver from institutional acquiescence—which might be the result of the mechanics of congressional inaction more than anything else.[151] Moreover, the acquiescence theory appears to be a one-way ratchet—each time the president acts and Congress fails to act, the constitutional balance of power is altered in favor of the executive branch. With each new military intervention, presidential power increases simply because Congress refuses to defund the action, and in the process, somehow the constitutional understanding evolves in the president's favor. This is bootstrapping.

The Syria crisis provided more fuel for the continuation narrative. However, like a Rorschach test, scholars have viewed the Syrian situation simultaneously as evidence for Obama's commitment to broad executive power *and* his commitment to congressional involvement, depending on who you ask. After Secretary of State John Kerry announced that the use of chemical weapons crossed a proverbial "red line," the Obama administration was stuck in an unenviable position. They could either ignore the red line and risk being viewed as weak and ineffectual, or they could pursue an intervention and risk being perceived as foolhardy. Further complicating the situation, neither China nor Russia was willing to support a Security Council resolution authorizing military action.

Jack Goldsmith was a forceful critic of the Obama administration's position, although his arguments revealed a strong departure from the views of his former coauthor Eric Posner, who has argued that international law imposes no meaningful constraints on state behavior and that constitutional law imposes no meaningful constraints on executive behavior. In contrast, Goldsmith wrote in the *New York Times*, under the headline, *What Happened to the Rule of Law?*, that the Syrian intervention would violate the U.N. Charter.[152] Even the British government, which favored intervention but failed to gain parliamentary approval for an operation, "did not attempt the impossible task of squaring this conclusion with the language of the Charter."[153] Although Goldsmith argued that "interventions are driven by military, ideological and humanitarian interests with relatively little regard for international law," his arguments relied on the premise that Obama's behavior should be guided by international law.[154]

Goldsmith also concluded separately that Obama did not have the constitutional authority to launch an intervention in Syria without congressional approval—a conclusion that deepened his intellectual divide from scholars like John Yoo, who believe in an unencumbered president with regard to military affairs, as well as Posner and Vermeule, who argue that constitutional law imposes no meaningful constraints on executive action. Writing on *Lawfare*, Goldsmith concluded that unilateral action in Syria "is a constitutional stretch that will push presidential war unilateralism beyond where it has gone before."[155] Under the Goldsmith view, unilateral executive action is permitted in cases where U.S. property or persons are implicated or when the strike is required by self-defense. Syria involved neither.

Furthermore, the constitutionality of the Kosovo operation was allegedly based on a national interest tied to our regional security treaty obligations (NATO)—a situation not implicated in Syria. (In fact, the self-defense rationale appeared to cut against intervention since the Syrian rebels contained al-Qaeda elements.) Nor is the credibility of the Security Council at issue since it declined to authorize intervention. The only available arguments are the U.S. interest in protecting the legal prohibition against chemical weapons and the U.S. interest in preserving stability in the Middle East—factors that Goldsmith found wanting.[156] Goldsmith's argument proved prescient because with the world watching, Obama suddenly announced that he would do precisely what he had refused to do with regard to Libya: ask Congress for explicit authorization to use military force against Syria.

The lobbying campaign in Congress did not go well. Members of the House were skeptical that the United States could intervene successfully and push President Assad from power. Others were unconvinced that there was a legal justification under international law for the intervention. The administration might have relied on the Responsibility to Protect doctrine (RTP), although the better view is that the doctrine is more aspirational than an existing statement of the law that authorizes unilateral intervention in the absence of Security Council authority.[157] However, for whatever reason, the administration did not push RTP as the legal foundation for intervention and instead concentrated on Assad's use of chemical weapons. It is undeniable that the use of chemical weapons violates international law, though interestingly, Syria never ratified the Chemical Weapons treaty, so any prohibition that applied to Syria would have to be customary in nature. Assuming *arguendo* that such a prohibition existed and that Assad had violated it, there is little law to suggest that the use of chemical weapons triggers a unilateral right of intervention as the appropriate sanction against the violation. Some other argument would be necessary to justify the intervention; the State Department did not provide one.

The final problem with the Syria intervention was that it required siding with the rebel forces, a disparate collection of brigades without any unified command structure. The fighters included, in addition to secular army officers who had defected from Syria, Islamic extremists who had allied themselves with al-Qaeda. An uncertain percentage of the fighters might even have been foreign jihadists who traveled to Syria with the hopes of establishing an al-Qaeda stronghold in Syria. American intervention in Syria would therefore place the United States in the awkward position of being co-belligerents with al-Qaeda, a non-state armed group with which the United States has been engaged in an armed conflict since 9/11— strange bedfellows to say the least. Assad's fall from power would surely have triggered a civil war among the rebels that would have displaced him, and there would be no guarantee that the secular rebels would be victorious in that campaign. The United States might succeed in ousting Assad only to witness an even worse al-Qaeda-inspired government consolidate control over large sections of the Syrian state. That would be a disastrous outcome, and the Obama administration was unable to placate congressional concerns about such an outcome. Ironically, there is a better legal argument under international law to support American intervention *in favor* of Assad, since the United States is already engaged in an armed conflict with al-Qaeda, which would make the United States and Assad co-belligerents against a common enemy.[158]

There are two ways of reading the Syrian case as a precedent regarding unilateral executive action. First, it might be a precedent in favor of congressional involvement, a precedent that supports and magnifies the relevance of the War Powers Resolution. In future military conflicts, when lawyers and politicians are debating the constitutionality of military action, the Syrian example will provide valuable support: lawyers can draw parallels between the new conflict in question and the prior Syrian situation and conclude that since Obama requested congressional authorization in one, it should also be requested in the other. In that way, Obama's action builds a body of jurisprudence—through executive action rather than judicial decisions—that helps provide a historical gloss on the scope and authority of executive action. The decision to approach Congress could be viewed as a rare example of executive *degrandizement* (as opposed to the more typical executive aggrandizement).

The second way of reading the Syrian case is the opposite. Obama asked for congressional authorization for military action, but he never conceded that he was *required* to do so. His silence on this question was notable. The decision appeared to reflect prudential concerns about politics rather than legal concerns about the proper scope of the commander-in-chief power. Furthermore, Obama refused to foreclose the possibility that he might order military action even if Congress refused to authorize military force. He spoke in vague terms, but clearly, he wanted to preserve his options in case Congress voted against his proposal; this possibility only makes sense if one also agrees that congressional support is nice but not necessary. The message appeared to be very subtle: *I have the power to act unilaterally*, but like Bartleby, I would prefer not to do so. Predictably, this inherent and sly assertion of unilateral executive authority hurt his efforts to obtain congressional approval.

Unlike Posner and Vermeule, Goldsmith views the executive as deeply constrained, not just by politics but by law as well. This directly contradicts Posner and Vermeule's thesis in THE EXECUTIVE UNBOUND that politics provides the only constraints on executive action or more simply that constitutional law (insofar as it purports to restrain the executive) is not *real* law. In contrast, Goldsmith takes seriously the legal status of separation-of-power constraints built into the Constitution. These constraints come from both Congress and the federal judiciary: "Judicial review of the Commander in Chief's actions often left him without legal authority to act, forcing him to work with Congress to fill the legal void."[159] Lawyers play a significant role in this narrative, in sharp contrast to Posner and Vermeule; Goldsmith describes a "giant distributed networks of lawyers, investigators, and auditors, both inside and outside the executive branch, that rendered U.S. fighting forces and intelligence services more transparent than ever, and that enforced legal and political constraints, small and large, against them."[160] Accountability is not reducible to criminal prosecutions. A vast array of agents and fora exist to provide accountability, and these legal and quasi-legal mechanisms constrain government officials either ex post or ex ante as government officials worry about the result of these investigations.[161]

Law represents a series of meaningful constraints on behavior. These constraints can come in many shapes and colors. Some are enforced by the judiciary and others by Congress, and still others are self-imposed constraints based on the understanding that normative constraints, both forming them and complying with them, make life go better for us. A constrained executive must govern in a complicated and fractured universe, with both constitutional and international constraints, and there is a natural temptation to wish for an uncomplicated playing field, free from all constraints that result in complex and messy decision-making. But only Hobbes's Fool could sincerely wish that this come to pass, because running such a country would require trading soul for expediency. In a sense, advocates for an unfettered executive want to change one thing and leave everything else constant: remove the constraints on the executive but inhabit a world where everything else remains undisturbed. This promise is illusory; pull on one thread and the whole tapestry unravels. An America with a fully unconstrained executive would be a different America, one whose imperial presidency had frayed the edges of our Madisonian system of checks and balances. And the same thing could be said of the world community. Though it would be easier to direct our external affairs without the nettlesome constraints of international law, it is unclear whether we would benefit from being an exceptional nation in a Hobbesian world without international law—a world where every state would, by definition, be *exceptional*.

2.7 Conclusion

Although there are many pieces that make up the New Realist argument, the indispensable foundation is the concept of law at work here. Since interbranch disputes are not subject to "legal" constraints, in the sense of commands of the sovereign backed up by sanctions, the executive branch remains fundamentally unconstrained. The only constraints that the executive adopts are self-constraints. This is the first step on the road toward the inevitable Schmittian administrative state, where the executive branch responds quickly to emerging situations without interference from Congress or the courts.

But this entire picture is assembled from false images of the law. The executive branch *is* constrained because the Constitution imposes a lengthy set of restrictions on executive behavior. The fact that the public itself is involved in policing compliance with these fundamental norms—through public outrage when things go wrong—does not mean that the restrictions aren't legal in nature. The separation of powers embodied in the U.S. Constitution represents a system of mutual constraints among different actors, each one abiding by the constraints as their counterparts do the same. Just like states under international law, the different actors in our constitutional system are constrained maximizers, working to achieve the best results within the framework of constraints that each accepts. These constraints are not *external* to the law—making them political. They are *internal* to the law, the very foundation of our social contract.

Ironically, that is a lesson best learned from Hobbes. In a sense, the New Realists have taken the worst of Hobbes's arguments (about executive primacy) and left the best parts of Hobbes (about rational self-interest as the foundation of a stable system of constraint) to rot. In short, they took the bones and threw out the marrow. If they had digested the real core of Hobbes's argument, they would understand that the social contract involves the acceptance of mutual constraints into a system of law. And the motivation for coming to the bargaining table—and complying with the demands of the social contract—is rational self-interest. Even branches of government are subject to this analysis.

This competing picture suggests an alternate inevitability: an executive branch constrained by law, subject to judicial review, and engaged in a meaningful partnership with Congress. Under this portrait, each branch of government accepts the evolving constraints of the constitutional order, recognizing that these constraints produce benefits for each actor. The opposite strategy—acting as a straightforward maximizer—risks abandoning the cooperative benefits of working with the other federal branches, in turn provoking constitutional crisis and sparking popular outrage. Although it is better to work *within* the system, doing so is more than just a *political* choice; it represents life under the rule of law.

As a normative matter, this story suggests that we should support a constrained and *bounded* executive. Whether the current level of judicial involvement in national security affairs is warranted depends on several factors. But the important point is that the New Realists make both descriptive and normative claims about executive primary. The descriptive argument comes first and concludes that the executive is not constrained by law, which then paves the way for the normative argument that the executive should receive as much deference, and as little interference, as possible. The fact that we have cast serious doubts on the veracity of the descriptive claim should give us pause before we accept the prescriptive argument too.

3 :: The Attack: Misunderstanding Rationality

The assault on international law is not an isolated, ad hoc, or random event. It is not the product of diffuse market forces. It is, rather, a coordinated attempt to undermine and undervalue American commitment to international law, through legal arguments both abstract and concrete. The concrete arguments ensure that the United States remains estranged from international institutions; they also outline reasons for the United States to either ignore or downplay international obligations. The abstract arguments provide an intellectual foundation on which the more specific arguments rest. They transform international law from a real legal system that demands compliance to a voluntary legal system, composed of self-interested actors, that can and should be ignored at will. Both types of argument are crucial to the devaluing of international law.

Many liberal commentators who support international law are unable to effectively counteract these positions because they are constructed with highly technical arguments such as rational choice theory, economic models, and paradoxes of decision theory that usually require a PhD in philosophy or economics to understand. The jargon keeps criticism at bay.

In this chapter, I contend that the argument against international law is both wrong and dangerous. Plenty of people have
noted that the argument is dangerous. One only has to look at
American diplomatic isolation between 2000 and 2008 to understand the danger. But liberal critics have made few inroads when
they claim that these arguments are mistaken. Either their coun-
terarguments get bogged down in technicalities, or they fail to
pick up on the correct problems inherent in the skeptical attack
on international law.

Simply put, I will argue that the attack on international law rests
on a flawed conception of rationality. The underlying theory of
rationality is just plain wrong, so the conclusions derived from it are
just as erroneous. No amount of tinkering with the theory will fix it
because its underlying foundation is built on quicksand. But before
I explain the correct theory of rationality, we need to understand
how international law was attacked and why these arguments had
so much influence, both within legal scholarship and in American
foreign policy between 2000 and 2008.

3.1 The Game Theory Game

For at least several decades, game theory has played a central role in
the academic literature on international relations. Only recently has
it emerged in the international law literature as well. Political scientists in the international relations field learned as long ago as the
1960s—with the work of Thomas Schelling—that game theory offers
a sophisticated matrix for modeling state relations.[1] The economet-
rics of game theory came with the promise of predicting behavior: social scientists could not only explain why some states had
acted the way they did, but they also might predict future behavior under certain conditions.[2] The prisoner's dilemma provided an
answer for problems regarding coordination and cooperation that
had concerned the international relations literature for years.[3] The
prisoner's dilemma is the most famous model in game theory, and
scholars have been dissecting it for years; it is a rich source for our
intuitions about self-interest, cooperation, and the consequences of
failing to cooperate.

In the prisoner's dilemma, two individuals are under interrogation by the authorities. Prisoner A is told that if he implicates his co-felon, Prisoner B, and Prisoner B does not implicate Prisoner A, then A will receive no sentence and B will receive a heavy sentence. However, both are told that if neither implicates the other, they will both receive light sentences. What is the rational course of action, their best response to the dilemma? It would seem at first glance that they should both stay quiet because then they will both receive short sentences. However, Prisoner A has no way of ensuring that Prisoner B will also stay quiet; maybe prisoner B will try to get his get-out-of-jail free card by implicating Prisoner A? So if Prisoner A is pursuing a strategy of remaining quiet, but Prisoner B decides to implicate Prisoner A, then Prisoner A is out of luck because his strategy of staying quiet has come back to haunt him. He will receive a lengthy punishment, while Prisoner B gets off scot-free. A poor outcome indeed for Prisoner A.

As it happens, Prisoner B is thinking the same thing. He could keep quiet, but he has no way of ensuring that Prisoner A will do the same. So to protect himself against a worst-case scenario, his only rational course of action is to implicate Prisoner A in a preemptive strike of sorts. In the end, although both would have had better outcomes if they had kept quiet, they both talk and they both experience relatively poor outcomes.[4]

Most scholars treat the prisoner's dilemma as a parable about cooperation, or the consequences of the failure to trust a partner in a two-person game. If the two individuals in the scenario above trusted each other, they might have stayed quiet and enjoyed the results of that rational move. But they have no rational reason to trust each other, and, moreover, they have no way to enforce a cooperative arrangement between them. They are stuck and ultimately fall victim to their own self-interested rationality. It turns out that lack of trust—and therefore lack of cooperation—is present in everyone. Consider a classic example from international relations. Two states in an arms race would save money and increase their security by disarming their arsenals, but the fear that the other side will cheat and covertly retain their weapons spurs both sides to pursue a costly and dangerous arms race.

The central puzzle of the prisoner's dilemma literature was the uncertain and uneasy relationship between a state's selfish behavior in international relations and a state's commitment to international legal norms when those norms proved inconvenient or downright inconsistent with a state's self-interest. One school of thought concluded that states generally act in their self-interest and seek to ignore the prescriptive power of international legal norms when the norms are sufficiently inconvenient.[5] A second school of thought concluded that states are generally more receptive to international norms for a variety of reasons. For many scholars, receptivity to international legal norms could be explained by future costs associated with non-compliance (i.e., loss of reputation that might frustrate a state's ability to negotiate future agreements), thus collapsing international law compliance into self-interested behavior.[6] Or, in the alternative, some scholars concluded that compliance with international legal norms was internalized as a value that formed one part of a nation's self-interest.[7] In other words, fidelity to national values included, among other things, compliance with international law, because some countries view participation in the global legal order (or fidelity to its underlying norms) as an essential part of their identity.[8] Therefore, compliance with international law was a national interest to be included with other more egoistic national values. This novel move was simultaneously edifying and de-edifying in the sense that it elevated fidelity to international law to a high national interest (a good thing), yet simultaneously deflated international law compliance by turning it into just another interest in a field of interests, as opposed to a universal *norm* that demands compliance in the face of contrary self-interest. What each school of thought rejected was what might be called a naïve account of international law: that states comply with international law simply because it is *law*.

While game theory offered theorists of international relations a model for explaining state relations, the methodology has had a far more explosive effect among international lawyers. Recent accounts have harnessed alleged lessons learned from game theory in service of a new brand of realism about international law.[9] These skeptical accounts conclude that international law loses its normative force because states that "follow" international law are simply participants in a prisoner's dilemma seeking to achieve self-interested outcomes.[10] In short, these arguments can be distilled to the following elements. Effective multilateral agreements are rarely achieved, either in treaty or customary form.[11] Most states consent to international legal norms through a process of bilateral agreements with specific partners who in turn have their own set of overlapping bilateral agreements.[12] Compliance with these agreements, whether by treaty or customary law, is usually based on considerations specific to a particular partner rather than considerations regarding the content of the legal norm.[13] In other words, states comply with international norms in specific interactions with a particular state when there are good reasons to believe that the other state will reciprocate such compliance.[14] This explains why a state might adhere to a particular legal norm with one partner but not with another. According to this way of thinking, the vast majority of the content of international law fits this paradigm as opposed to one that posits general legal obligations to the entire world community.[15] Reducing international law to a series of overlapping bilateral arrangements facilitates the use of the prisoner's dilemma as a convincing model, though of course it is not necessary to limit the analysis to bilateral interactions. It is possible, after all, to have a multiple-player prisoner's dilemma, though cooperation becomes more challenging as the number of players increases.[16] In any event, the rhetorical advantage to the bilateral claim is clear: it makes the prisoner's dilemma that much more intuitive as a model for international law.

The New Realists proceed to argue that compliance in a prisoner's dilemma is based on reciprocity that is hard to come by.[17] A state will prefer to violate the treaty or customary rule while their competitor adheres to it, though this state of affairs is difficult to achieve because all competitors share the same preference.[18] So, in order to avoid the opposite result (mutual defection), states cooperate by signing international agreements to produce the next-best preference: mutual adherence to the norm. Now comes the theoretical payoff, in the form of multiple claims: First, cooperation in the form of international agreements only shows up in the very limited situations when participants in the game have equal or near-equal

bargaining power.[19] In contrast, most cases of international relations involve unequal bargaining relationships, where a weak state
is forced to adhere to the wishes of the stronger state or face unfa-
vorable consequences. This reduces the scope of international law.
Second, even in cases of comparable bargaining power, the application of the norm is based entirely upon reciprocal compliance.[20]
States generally only follow the norm if their bilateral competitor
also follows the norm. Unfortunately, international law has a relative paucity of enforcement mechanisms compared with domestic
law, making assured reciprocal compliance through coercion rare
and difficult to achieve. This further reduces the scope of international law. Third, even when both states in a prisoner's dilemma follow the norm, they are doing so out of state self-interest.[21] In other
words, it is within a state's self-interest to follow an international
legal norm if and only if the other player is also following that same
norm. Consequently, international law is really just self-interested
behavior, not a robust system of law that *demands* compliance even
when it conflicts with a state's self-interest.

Now comes the normative payoff in the form of a fourth claim.
Because international law is reducible to self-interested behavior, states have no independent obligation to follow international
law when it conflicts with their self-interest.[22] International law is
based entirely on the prisoner's dilemma structure of self-interested
behavior, thus it has no independent normative force. If states wish
to comply with international law, they may do so when it suits them.
They may also structure international law obligations to their own
benefit, but they ought not to be concerned with how these norms
affect the global community or humanity as a whole.[23] Indeed, the
claim is not just that states are not required to follow international
law when it conflicts with their self-interest but, in fact, that *they
should not* do so. A government that follows international law when
it conflicts with self-interest is breaching its fiduciary duty to its citizens and placing the welfare of foreigners above the welfare of its
citizens.[24] Partiality is not just permitted, but required.[25] This book
takes aim at the validity of the third claim and its normative payoff.
Since the third claim is based on a conceptual error, the supposed
payoff is illusory.

Predictably, the new realism about international law sparked a serious counterattack from both the professoriate and the international bar,[26] though such realism already had its adherents in some corners of the U.S. Department of State (in previous administrations).[27] Most law school professors writing about international law are deeply invested in the claim that international law has normative force and that states ought to follow it.[28] Consequently, scholars have mounted numerous defenses of international law, cataloging the effectiveness of human rights treaties and identifying the complex compliance and enforcement mechanisms that currently exist under international law.[29] Although most of these arguments are undoubtedly correct, they miss something fundamental and foundational about the new realism: the use of game theory as a mechanism for making claims regarding international law's *normativity*—a claim that was largely absent from the international relations literature on game theory.[30] Using game theory to understand international law in this way triggers a real problem: can a descriptive theory about the nature of international law today yield normative conclusions about the way the world ought to be?

Specifically, I argue in this book that the new realism about international law suffers from a profound misunderstanding about the significance of game theory. In short, the new realism misuses the methodology by concluding that self-interested behavior and normativity are mutually exclusive.[31] Indeed, that is the conclusion that the new realists draw from the prisoner's dilemma. This conclusion is false.

In order to defend this claim, we must engage in some preliminaries. First, section 3.2 of this chapter offers a more nuanced understanding of the prisoner's dilemma in international law and explains how the international legal order promotes the creation of the Nash equilibria among its participants. In game theory, a Nash equilibrium exists when each player cannot reap better returns by changing his or her strategy while everyone else's strategies remain constant. International legal norms have this potential because states benefit from complying with the norms in a world in which other states are complying as well. Section 3.3 then explains the compatibility between rational self-interest and the normativity of international law by introducing the idea of *constrained maximization*—a concept that grounds the argument that unfolds in the rest of the book. The essential notion in this section is the "rationality of plans," or the idea that rational agents adopt long-term plans that help them forgo short-term temptations in favor of richer gains in the future. Constrained maximizers agree to live with the restrictive rules of the community in order to maximize the benefits from living in that community—a type of cooperative behavior as opposed to going-it-alone. In keeping with this idea, section 3.3 briefly offers reasons why it would be rational for a state to follow international law even when it could defect with impunity—a point that is explored in greater depth in chapter 3. Finally, section 3.4 considers a few introductory objections. The first objection involves the naturalistic fallacy, which concludes that statements about the way the world *ought* to never be derived from claims about the way the world *is* right now—this is sometimes referred to as the *is-ought* gap for short. The second objection appeals to the unequal bargaining power of states; China, the United States, and Russia can essentially dictate diplomatic terms, while countries such as Haiti and Mongolia are largely required to accept them. Does this undermine international law as a system of rational constraints? The third objection deals with the alleged inability of nation-states to bear moral obligations. It is uncontroversial to say that morality requires an individual human being to act in a certain way. But what does it mean to say that morality requires a state to do something? At a fundamental level, can morality speak to collective agents (like states), or is this just shorthand for describing the moral obligations of the collective's members?

3.2 The Prisoner's Dilemma and Nash Equilibrium

The prisoner's dilemma story told by the New Realists draws the wrong conclusions from the methodology. We shall first question the specific details of the model and then proceed to the second question of the false conclusions drawn from it. As for the model, Goldsmith and Posner view international cooperation as a bilateral repeated prisoner's dilemma.[32] While this view is true in the most general sense, the model can and should be more specific. Properly conceived, international law is a Nash equilibrium— a focal point that states gravitate toward as they make rational decisions regarding strategy in light of strategies selected by other states.[33] In game theory, a Nash equilibrium is defined as a solution in which each player evaluates the strategies of his competitors and decides that he gains no advantage by unilaterally changing strategy when all other players keep their own strategies unchanged.[34] In law, a Nash equilibrium allows participants to gravitate toward a particular legal norm and choose "compliance" as their strategy if and only if the other players in the game are also choosing compliance as their strategy.[35] When a bilateral international agreement works, one state realizes that unilaterally choosing breach as its strategy would confer no benefit because the costs associated with that shift in strategy are too high. So the player sticks with compliance. If one player decides that a shift in strategy (i.e., breach) is indeed in his or her best interest, then the players fall out of Nash equilibrium.[36]

In domains where international law has the greatest purchase, the resulting equilibrium generates reciprocal compliance with international norms.[37] Consider a bilateral treaty negotiation regarding extraditions between two countries: State A and State B sign a treaty promising mutual extradition between the countries and establishing a legal framework to govern those extraditions. Suppose that State A has custody of a suspect and must decide whether to comply with its obligations under the treaty regime. State A realizes that failure to comply with the regime will not only risk retaliation from State B in future extradition matters but will also have numerous collateral effects—including possible retaliation in other bilateral contexts with State B, as well as a loss of reputation in treaty negotiations with other states, who may now be less willing to sign agreements with State A.[38] Consequently, State A decides that compliance with the legal norm is in its self-interest and that it has no reason to unilaterally change its strategy; the cost of shifting strategies is just too high. The states in this bilateral treaty regime are in Nash equilibrium with each other because neither party has reason to unilaterally change its strategy. In this case, their compliance with an international treaty norm can be understood through game theory's lens of self-interested behavior.[39]

Of course, one might point out that it may be beneficial for a state to defy the treaty when it proves to be inconvenient, thus transforming the state into a free rider that receives the benefits of the legal regulation but ignores the costs when they prove to be inconvenient.[40] This is certainly true, but the whole point of the structure of international law is that this outcome (free ridership) is more difficult to achieve, all other things being equal. Because states are linked together through mutual ongoing interactions, a state cannot benefit by changing its strategy away from compliance. If it does so, it incurs costs associated with noncompliance that overwhelm any putative benefits from its defection against the norm. The whole point of international law is to create a structure whereby the cost of shifting strategy away from compliance becomes higher than it would be without legal regulation in that particular area. As a result, each state in the Nash equilibrium decides to comply with the legal norm in question.

It is important to remember that the equilibrium need not be the most optimal or efficient legal regulation possible.[41] It might be the case that a different legal regime creates cooperation that produces greater benefits for every state.[42] But this kind of Pareto optimality (a state of optimal efficiency where additional improvements to one person would make someone else worse off) may be difficult to achieve. For example, it might be more efficient for the states to set up a bilateral international court to decide all cases of extradition between the two countries, though each state gravitates toward a Nash equilibrium of a bilateral treaty that is far below the Pareto optimal outcome of a bilateral court for these two players. There is nothing in international law that promises that a stable set of legal regulations between competitors will be the most efficient regulation possible.[43] Indeed, over time, the hope is that the legal regime might evolve closer to Pareto optimality as initial cooperation yields greater cooperation. But in some cases, the particular toolbox of compliance mechanisms in international law might limit the amount of optimality that can be achieved in this context.[44] Although international law yields stable Nash equilibria, it will never yield the kind of Pareto optimality that is found in a domestic legal system. The only way to achieve that higher level of efficiency is with a system of robust third-party constraints imposed by a government. But just because international law does not rise to the level of efficiency found in domestic law does not mean that international law is not rational and that states should ignore it. The comparison between international and domestic law is a red herring. The more appropriate question is the relative efficiency between a world with international law and a world without international law.

The same analysis would apply in a multilateral context. Consider the most important area of international legal regulation: the use of force, an example that will be taken up in greater detail in chapter 6.[45] The New Realists often use this contentious area of international legal regulation as a poster child for their contention that legal norms will give way to self-interest when the cost of compliance becomes inconvenient.[46] However, the Nash equilibrium here is clear. The norm in question is the legal prohibition on the use of force, in both the U.N. Charter and customary law, unless such use of force is taken in self-defense or authorized by the Security Council—the central clearing house for decisions regarding international peace and security.[47] Some scholars trace the norm back to the Kellogg-Briand Pact, before which aggressive war was simply recognized as inevitable (and therefore not presumptively illegal).[48] This is too simplistic since it was, at the very least, implicit in the notion of Westphalian sovereignty that states were free not just from outside interference in the widest sense but also from outside attack in the narrowest sense.[49] In the current scheme, the prohibition against the use of force is now coupled with the Security Council's authority to authorize use of force to restore international peace and security.[50]

Unfortunately, Security Council authorizations for the use of force are rare, and, since the threat of a veto is always present, states cannot predict with any reasonable certainly when the Security Council will authorize such use of force.[51] Thus, State A complies with the norm and eschews the use of force. This strategy of compliance is made with the hope that the other players in the game will also favor compliance. However, no state can assume that competitors will adopt the same strategy; competitors might choose violation as their strategy and, in so doing, reserve the right to use force at their discretion. Why would the second state choose this strategy? Perhaps because the costs associated with noncompliance are relatively low. Although they might be sued before the International Court of Justice (ICJ) and lose international standing (e.g., reputation), these costs pale in comparison to forgoing the use of force when your competitors refuse to do the same. This is why the international legal community has not navigated toward a Nash equilibrium that grants the Security Council the exclusive authority to authorize military force. The stakes are too high and the legal prohibitions insufficient to incentivize reciprocal compliance. Simply put, each participant would have an incentive to change its strategy away from compliance regardless of the strategy chosen by its competitors.

So, at its earliest incarnation, international law gravitated toward a norm regarding the use of force that allowed unilateral exceptions to the prohibition against the use of force in cases of self-defense. In discussing the use of force, nineteenth-century treatises regarding public international law made it clear that military force was legal in cases of self-defense or self-preservation.[52] This exception to the norm prohibiting the use of force is as old as the prohibition itself. Although states were unwilling to adopt a strategy of compliance with a blanket prohibition on military force, states have been willing to adopt a strategy of compliance with a more nuanced legal norm that always allows military force in self-defense.[53] A state can comply with this norm because even if a competitor in the game changes strategy, defects from the norm, and engages in aggressive warfare, the first state can still use force in self-defense to protect itself, consistent with the legal norm. In other words, the cost of compliance with the norm does not require that a state risk its national security.[54]

Consequently, states have a reason to stick with the strategy of compliance even given the uncertainty regarding the strategy of their competitors in the game. That is why a Nash equilibrium has developed around a prohibition regarding the use of force unless authorized by the Security Council or in self-defense. Each state benefits from the legal norm—a stable world order without aggressive force and constant warfare—and therefore complies with the legal norm because compliance with the norm is also consistent with purely defensive force when competitors in the game change their strategy.[55] So, no state has reason to unilaterally change its strategy in the game.

3.3 Law and Self-Interest

It is clearly correct, then, that international fidelity to the legal prohibition regarding the use of force can be described, using game theory, as self-interested behavior on the part of states. However, this much was already clear in the previous wave of international relations scholarship twenty-five years ago.[56] Although advancements in the game theory models have only added sophistication to the analysis, they are hardly new. The New Realists take all of this as evidence for a much more explosive normative claim: since compliance with international law is based on self-interest, international law has no normative pull.[57] The status of international law as *law* is seriously called into doubt.

There are many different ways of making this claim. One might conclude that international law is not law at all, or one might simply claim that international law is far less important than international lawyers think.[58] Or, one might say that states only comply with international law when doing so furthers their self-interest and reject it whenever it does not, making international law different not in degree but in kind from domestic law.[59] All of these claims add up to an assault on international law's normativity.

Of course, I am not the first to object to the new realism and there is now a wide array of literature providing renewed justifications for international law in the face of the New Realist attack.[60] However, none of the defenses have, to my mind, adequately emphasized the specific methodological mistakes made by the New Realists. Although game theory allows us to model international law as a game of self-interest, this picture is entirely consistent, *pace* Goldsmith and Posner, with international law's normativity. Simply put, self-interest is the *source* of obligation in the international system, not its antithesis.

In 1986, the moral philosopher David Gauthier published MORALS BY AGREEMENT, a novel interpretation of social contract theory that harnessed the power of game theory to explain why rational actors would agree to a system that constrained their behavior.[61] MORALS BY AGREEMENT provided, for the first time, a fully realized model of rational self-interested individuals agreeing to a social contract of morality.[62] The relationship between reason and morality has a long pedigree, going back as far as Plato's *The Republic* and, more explicitly, Kant's work on the categorical imperative and the wave of contractarian theories following Rawls.[63] But for Gauthier, game theory provided the best tools to explain how individual rationality and moral constraints might be consistent with each other.[64] Indeed, for Gauthier, the claim was even stronger: the latter could be derived from the former in the sense that one could demonstrate that rational agents ought to accept moral constraints.[65] In pursuing this account, Gauthier did not even resort to a universalized rational account of morality, that is, he did not shift the focus from individual-level rationality to group-level rationality, arguing that a third-person point of view required the individual to recognize, on pain of contradiction, that accepting moral constraints was best for everyone.[66] Gauthier was unimpressed by such sleight of hand.[67] His vision of morality required that we face the hard question: is it rational for individuals, considering their self-interest, to accept the normative constraints of morality?[68]

The answer—almost a revelation for Gauthier—lay in the prisoner's dilemma.[69] Rational agents must make decisions based on the expected moves of their competitors. Although the best possible outcome for a given player is defection in the face of compliance by all other competitors in the game, this outcome is also the outcome preferred by one's competitors. If all competitors defect, the resulting payoff is extremely low, effectively throwing the game back into a state of nature where no one complies with any moral constraints, thus producing the worst possible outcome. The rational solution to the game therefore requires acceptance of the objectively second-best (but, rationally, only possible) outcome: acceptance of reciprocal moral constraints on behavior.[70] The purchase one gets from game theory is that this acceptance is itself demanded by self-interested behavior. Rational agents seeking to maximize their own outcomes will choose moral outcomes so long as morality is a group endeavor.

Of course, this still leaves unresolved the cleavage between the rational agent at the social bargaining table—who is rationally compelled to accept reciprocal moral constraints—and the rational agent who must decide whether or not to comply with the social contract. So far, I have only demonstrated that it is rational to form international law—not that it is rational to abide by it. It is one thing to demonstrate the rationality of bargaining for moral constraints and quite another to demonstrate the rationality of ex post *compliance* with the results of the social contract.[71] Maybe the most rational plan of action is to be a free rider: talk the cheap talk of international law but then ignore it when it becomes inconvenient. For Gauthier, the theory of rationality itself provides a simple answer to this quandary. A rational agent living in a cooperative community is a constrained maximizer, or an agent who "enjoy[s] opportunities for co-operation which others lack," as Gauthier puts it, as opposed to a straightforward maximizer.[72] The straightforward maximizer ignores everyone and maximizes his or her lot by going it alone. The question is whether the constrained maximizer receives cooperative benefits that outweigh the risks associated with the strategy of constrained maximization—that is, the risk that competitors in the game will defect and reject compliance as their strategy.[73]

How can this be demonstrated? For Hobbes, the answer was simple: the sovereign itself ensures compliance, a fact that provided its own rationale for Hobbes's specific rendering of the Leviathan.[74] Once one steps outside the scope of a total sovereign, though, the picture becomes more complicated. Various social institutions, both informal and formal, exist to promote cooperation among constrained maximizers: increased trust between cooperators, reputational gains, and community structures only open to cooperators, all of which have instrumental value for further cooperation.[75] Defectors, though they achieve some benefits from their straightforward maximization, lose all of the benefits of cooperation and

suffer the community penalties for defection.[76] Consequently, constrained maximization is rational just so long as the community
has the correct ratio of constrained maximizers to straightforward
maximizers.[77] In a world filled with straightforward maximizers,
the gains from (putative) cooperation would not outweigh the risks
associated with the compliance strategy. However, in a world with a
significant proportion of constrained maximizers, the strategy has
a clear salience. Presumably, there is an empirical tipping point at
which the strategy of constrained maximization becomes rational.[78]
The strategy becomes a Nash equilibrium.

One might argue that the concept of constrained maximization is nothing more complicated than the concept of a long-term
interest. Agents are typically concerned with maximizing their
gains in the present and thus ignore strategies that will produce
a maximum gain over a longer time period. Whether one should
maximize benefits now or later depends on what discount rate the
agent applies to future benefits. If the discount rate is low (or zero),
the agent will consider future benefits at full value when engaging
in decision-making. If the discount rate is high, the agent will discount the future benefits and treat them as less valuable in deciding on a course of action today. Constrained maximizers certainly
recognize that both the present and future benefits of cooperation
will far outweigh the negative consequences (the lost selfishness)
associated with following the rules. But the strategy of constrained
maximization is about much more than simply long-term interests.
The benefits of cooperation may be far in the future or immediate;
similarly, the demands of constraint may impose themselves today
or tomorrow. The real distinguishing factor of constrained maximization is a matter of pure strategy: go it alone and reap the benefits
and consequences of such breach, or accept reciprocal constraints
and receive the cooperative benefits that go along with them.

One can see how the strategy of constrained maximization is
directly applicable to international legal relations.[79] When one state
decides on a strategy for diplomatic relations, it can choose to be a
straightforward maximizer or a constrained maximizer. However,
deciding to be a straightforward maximizer—although initially
an attractive option—carries severe costs. A state that pursues this

strategy will be branded a rogue nation and deprive itself of the benefits associated with cooperative constraints. Operating outside of the community of nations carries enormous costs, as North Korea, Iran, and other isolationist states can no doubt confirm.[80] Those who adopt a strategy of reciprocal commitments to international law live in not only a world of relative security—fewer military interventions and aggressive acts—but also a world of bilateral treaty arrangements that would otherwise be unavailable to them. The rub of the argument is that the alleged dichotomy between fidelity to international law and self-interested behavior turns out to be illusory.[81] The fact that states are self-interested in no way undermines the normativity of international law.

In the end, states cooperate by complying with international legal norms, and this commitment is necessarily grounded by their self-interest. The New Realists claim that acting out of self-interest undermines the normativity of the subsequent constraints, especially customary norms grounded in *opinio juris*. But why? In searching for a different account of legal obligation, New Realists frequently resort to their old bailiwick: the lack of international enforcement mechanisms to punish defectors or straightforward maximizers.[82] In short, *real* legal obligations stem from sanctions (of the type found in domestic law). While it is no doubt true that international enforcement mechanisms are feeble when compared to their domestic analogs, the fact is often repeated to the point of exaggeration.[83] It is certainly not the case that there are no viable mechanisms of enforcement; this point has already been exhaustively detailed in the literature, and I shall not rehash the evidence here.[84]

Why do the New Realists resist these arguments? Although the concept of constrained maximization is nowhere considered in THE LIMITS OF INTERNATIONAL LAW, some clues are offered in Eric Posner's work on social norms.[85] In LAW AND SOCIAL NORMS, Posner concedes that rational agents will engage in "principled" behavior and will reap the reputational rewards associated with using the rhetoric of principle.[86] The language of principle has a signaling effect to potential associates: this agent can be trusted because he will never betray you.[87] But under Posner's view of rational choice, such a blind commitment to principle is either illusory or insincere.[88] At some point, the costs of adhering to the demands of principle will become too high, and any rational agent (according to Posner) will defect and violate the demands of principle.[89] But saying: "I will follow principle but only if the costs aren't too high" will not help to attract collaborators who are rightly scared away by such conditional language.[90] Thus, the result is that people cling to the rhetoric of absolute commitment to principle, and when self-interest demands defection from the principle, "they cheat and try to conceal their opportunism behind casuistry."[91] Unprincipled individuals seek to have their cake and eat it too by attempting to blend in among a crowd of principled agents.[92] This strategy works because it is very difficult for the public to distinguish between the principled and the unprincipled.[93]

The same view apparently underlies Posner's attitude about national compliance with international legal norms.[94] States will adopt the language of principled adherence to international law, but when self-interest demands defection, they can—and should—act out of self-interest.[95] Such a state may very well attempt to conceal its behavior and develop obfuscations in an attempt to explain away the defection.[96] The state will attempt to defect and still reap the rewards of constrained maximization.[97]

The question is whether a state can successfully adopt the insincere rhetoric of constrained maximization (i.e., fidelity to international law) while at the same time defecting and ignoring international legal norms. But, in this respect, there is a relevant asymmetry between individuals and nations. While the individual can hide his decision-making process from potential collaborators, most modern nation-states conduct their decision-making through various internal actors. These debates are often—though not always—public or semipublic. Disputes with domestic constituencies are laid bare for the entire world to see.[98] If a domestic constituency presses the government to ignore international law out of self-interest, this plea will be heard not just by its own government but also by the world. The ability to act insincerely is *comparatively* more difficult in the case of nation-states than it is with individuals. To the extent that some states, such as North Korea, conduct deliberations in secret, these states appear to be the least likely to insincerely claim adherence to international legal norms. Such rogue nations are often the least likely to publicly tout their adherence to and participation in international legal and regulatory regimes.

However, this still leaves a theoretical tension between the demands of rationality (occasional defection) and the demands of morality that counsels adherence to principle even in the face of rational opportunism. For Goldsmith and Posner, there is no moral basis to tell a state to follow international law when rational self-interest counsels in favor of defection.[99] And if indeed there arises a situation in which the gains of defection outweigh the loss of cooperative opportunities at any given moment, rational choice would appear to demand defection. Since our account of morality is closely linked with rational choice, there would appear to be no basis to tell a nation to forgo self-interest in favor of principle.

Gauthier's initial answer to this conundrum was to frame his account in terms of dispositions to cooperate—dispositions that were themselves rational (and moral) insofar as one found oneself in a community with a sufficient number of agents who were similarly disposed.[100] In his later work, Gauthier pushed beyond the concept of dispositions to cooperate in favor of an account of agency that linked intentions with plans and strategies that operate over time.[101] In other words, although rational choice theory—including Posner's version—evaluates an agent's all-things-considered judgment at each cardinal point in time, rational human agency operates in a far more subtle way. Were rational agents to recalculate rational choice at every cardinal time point, they would be exhausted and weighed down by the process of deliberation to the point of total collapse—literally, paralysis by analysis.[102]

Instead, rational agency should be understood in terms of strategies selected following moments of deliberation, after which the chosen strategies only come up for reevaluation at certain points in time.[103] What is missing from Posner's account, in other words, is the concept of *plans*—an idea that will be explained in greater depth in chapter 4.[104] And plans are sticky in the sense that rational agents form an intention to follow a plan and do not give up the plan at the drop of a hat.[105] Living life as a rational agent requires the use of plans; rational agency would be unimaginable without them.[106] Of course, it is important not to get hung up on the word "plan." We often employ plans without using the word. Agents often employ "rules of thumb," standard operating procedures, or cognitive shortcuts that all serve the same purpose: unifying present and future choices under a coherent and consistent framework (which also helps us avoid paralysis by analysis).

One might object that the stickiness of plans is irrational.[107] In other words, a truly rational agent should be constantly reevaluating the rational benefits associated with his plan and all alternate plans.[108] The rational agent should be playing chess like Deep Blue (reevaluating the benefits of every possible move at each move) and not like Garry Kasparov (pursuing and committing to a long-term strategy to win the game). To the extent that human agents are incapable of calculating like Deep Blue, perhaps one should count this limitation as a failure of rationality.

Gauthier, drawing partially on the work of Bratman and others, points out that the answer is not so simple.[109] Even if defection at any given moment is rationally beneficial, this is not the right comparison. Pursuing the strategy of rational choice at each cardinal time point may turn out to be less effective than choosing an *overall* strategy or plan that is rationally justified and then sticking to it.[110] Indeed, consistently pursuing rational choice at each time point may end up being self-defeating in the long run.[111] Plans provide stability for agents to pursue long-term interests and should only be abandoned in favor of new plans, not in favor of momentary and isolated desires.[112] An agent who is too easily lured from a stable plan by opportunistic defection is a *myopic* chooser.[113] Another way of stating the point is that the rationality of compliance with the reciprocal constraint—following the rules and resisting the temptation to defect—is *conditional* on the constraint's place within the larger, rationally justified plan.[114]

The structure of this argument is well known to moral theorists who debate the relative merits of act utilitarianism and rule utilitarianism.[115] Act utilitarians evaluate the consequences of each individual act and identify the moral thing to do based on this calculation.[116] By contrast, rule utilitarians evaluate general moral rules based on their guidelines and then identify certain rules as amoral regardless of their consequences at any individual decisional time point.[117] One reason for supporting rule utilitarianism is that, in the end, it may produce superior consequences globally, as compliance is better achieved in a world with sticky moral norms rather than constantly shifting moral evaluations. Ironically, constant reevaluation of the consequences at each moment in time may end up being self-defeating.

None of this is new in the moral or political theory literature. Within the recent debate in the international law literature, the basic assumptions regarding rational choice among the New Realists have gone relatively unchallenged. Some have questioned the wisdom of applying rational choice to international law; others have accepted the methodology but simply claimed that it yields different results.[118] But what is badly needed is critical reevaluation of the *version* of rational choice theory used by the New Realists.[119]

There is strong reason to believe that states are rationally justified in pursuing a strategy of constrained maximization and sticking to it even when faced with the temptation of opportunistic defection. Even if states could masquerade as principled—a doubtful proposition—constant defection from international legal norms may produce negative outcomes over time. It might be more rational for states to pick the strategy that is rationally justified and stay with it: either try one's best to engage with international institutions, or ignore them. Although it is unclear if this thesis could be empirically tested, it is highly suggestive that the most successful nations in the world participate in international legal institutions, whereas rogue nations on the periphery often are beset with hunger, famine, and war. Indeed, even the Bush administration, under the sway of Yoo and Goldsmith, did not *completely* reject international institutions or behave as opportunistically as their framework prescribes.

3.4 Objections to the Moral Obligation of States

At this point, several other objections to my account must be considered. The most worrisome objection is that Gauthier's theory of morality, and this chapter's extrapolation of that theory to the domain of international law, has fallen victim to the naturalistic fallacy—a reasoning error that occurs when one assumes that one can conclude how the world ought to be based on how the world is. A second objection outlined here concerns the unequal bargaining strength of states—one alleged reason for stronger states to refrain from a strategy of constrained maximization. The third objection is that states are collective entities that are unable to bear a moral obligation and that only individuals are directly subject to the demands of morality. If this view is correct, it would be nonsensical to say that a state has a moral duty to follow international law.

Let's start with the first objection. If the entire project is designed to derive morality from reason, then it would indeed appear as if we have attempted to jump over the "is–ought" gap. There is a long history of moral theories that combine insights regarding rationality with moral conclusions. One of the most famous is John Rawls, whose book A *Theory of Justice* revitalized social contract theories of morality by considering the principles of justice that a rational agent would negotiate, assuming the agent knows nothing about his present or future circumstances (the so-called "veil of ignorance"). In his later work, Rawls famously distanced himself from any attempt to *derive* morality from reason,[120] though in his earliest work, he described his social contract theory as one piece of a general theory of rational choice, similar to John Harsanyi.[121] Indeed, the whole project of deriving morality from reason long predates the era of social contract theory ushered in by Rawls and his contemporaries. In fact, the project comes from Kant and his obsession with practical reason, and ultimately reaches its apex in contemporary moral philosophers such as Rawls and Alan Gewirth.[122] In his later work, Rawls took great pains to emphasize the role of a "reflective equilibrium" in his methodology: not a top-down derivation from rationality to morality but rather a theoretical device for navigating toward a coherent vision of justice as fairness. In the Rawlsian approach, the task is to consider our intuitions about the original position where the social contract is negotiated, and then also consider our intuitions about the principles of justice that emerge from that negotiation process with the hope that a reflective equilibrium emerges with a fair negotiating process and a fair outcome. The rationale for this approach was that it would avoid the naturalistic fallacy inherent in any approach that derived the *ought* of morality from the *is* of rationality.[123]

Have *we* fallen victim to the naturalistic fallacy here? The answer requires an important clarification. In deriving morality from rationality, we are not deriving morality from the *fact* of rationality. Rather, we are deriving moral value from rationality as a *value*.[124] Simply put, constrained maximizers ought to pursue compliance as their strategy if they are committed to rationality as a value. If they aspire to be rational, then this is what rationality demands, though there is nothing that *requires* them to be rational. Moral value turns out to be somewhat parasitic on normative rationality—precisely the lesson that game theory has taught both moral philosophers and international lawyers.

Are individuals committed to rationality as a norm? They certainly are, and undeniably so, insofar as they hope to exercise rational agency.[125] Indeed, even the most elementary forms of agency require a commitment to rationality in the form of means–ends reasoning, the transitive ordering of preferences, and the law of noncontradiction.[126] It is very difficult—perhaps impossible—to imagine interhuman relations, including language, without this commitment to basic principles of rationality. And the fact that individuals may be imperfectly rational is entirely irrelevant to the point here. Normative commitments may fall well short of perfection, or even large-scale success, but that is not evidence that a person is not committed to the value in question. No one achieves perfect rationality, just as no one achieves perfect morality. But this is trivial; the point is that if individuals are committed to rationality, then they ought to be committed to a strategy of constrained maximizing in the form of accepting reciprocal moral constraints. And, as it happens, all individuals are committed to rationality as a norm because this value commitment is constitutive of rational agency itself. *Committing* to rationality is part of what it means to be a rational agent.[127]

Can the same thing be said about states? Are they committed to rationality as a value? The question is best pursued from the opposite direction: how could we deny that states are committed to rationality as a norm? States have interests and pursue collective projects on the international stage in order to maximize those interests.[128] Those projects involve rationality over time and necessarily require basic principles of rationality such as the transitive ordering of preferences and fidelity to the principle of noncontradiction.[129] The only relevant difference between states and individuals is the lack of phenomenological unity among the former.[130] While each individual typically enjoys a unified phenomenological point of view, states are composed of many individuals, each of whom represents its own unified phenomenological point of view.[131] But the lack of phenomenological unity of the state does not prevent it from exercising rational agency. Although the phenomenological unity of the individual certainly facilitates rational integration (viz., self-knowledge and direct epistemic access to one's own thoughts), none of this implies that there cannot exist external means of displaying a shared commitment to rationality. This is precisely what a state achieves through government—a system of representation and deliberation and diplomatic representation on the world stage.[132] To deny the rational agency of states would be to deny the foundations of international relations.

We must now redeem a promissory note and account for the fact that states bargaining for international legal norms do not stand in a position of equal bargaining strength.[133] Up until this point, we have assumed that participants in the prisoner's dilemma are bare self-interested agents, without further consideration of their particular strengths and weaknesses that might affect their ability or willingness to defect. Indeed, the New Realists make much of the unequal bargaining power of states and conclude that stronger states will ignore international law simply because they can.[134] Given that the unequal bargaining power of states is undeniable (even though it stands in tension with the formal equality of all states under international law), it would seem that our account is impoverished at best and irrelevant at worst.[135]

This anxiety is misplaced. The unequal bargaining power of states is relevant under our model because it affects the costs of noncompliance and the benefits associated with cooperation. As to the former, stronger states will face less retaliation for their non-compliance because weaker states might feel that they need to sign agreements with the stronger state even if previous defections alert the weaker state to the risk that the strong state will again defect. The unequal bargaining power might bring the weaker state to the table in spite of this prediction. Second, the benefits associated with cooperation are less significant for stronger states. Their stronger status might open up avenues of cooperation simply because they are stronger and because other states therefore need their cooperation—cooperation that is entirely independent of their strategy of constrained maximization.[136]

Three points are in order here. First, the difference in bargaining power will be most salient when strong and weak states bargain against each other, but the difference will be irrelevant when strong states bargain against each other and weak states do likewise. Second, the difference in bargaining power does not prevent strong and weak states from signing agreements; it simply increases the likelihood that the stronger state might be tempted to defect. In cases where the stronger state is strong enough to eschew constrained maximization entirely in favor of a strategy of straightforward maximization, the state may indeed defect. This is most likely in contexts where international law has weak enforcement mechanisms. In contexts where the enforcement mechanisms—however diffuse and informal—are working properly, constrained maximization will continue to be viable even for strong states.[137]

Third, and most important, the fact that some states will defect in favor of straightforward maximization in certain contexts is completely irrelevant for situations where constrained maximization continues to be most valuable. Indeed, this is the logical error made by the New Realists. They point out the situations where unequal bargaining power and lack of enforcement allow stronger states to ignore international law with impunity, that is, to act in their own self-interest.[138] In such cases, it is indeed correct to suggest that international law is ineffective. But the New Realists then use this fact as a pivot to say something about situations when international law is effective, that is, when states agree to follow international law because the value of constrained maximization is high. Since this latter situation is also governed by self-interest, the New Realists implicitly conclude that even these domains of international cooperation have little or no normative pull because there is no sense of legal obligation.[139] This is an error. One should see immediately that the underlying current of self-interest works differently in each case. In the latter, self-interest entails constrained maximization and fidelity to international norms; in the former, self-interest entails defection. The fact that some states will violate international law when reason counsels defection does not mean that they are not following international law when reason demands respect for it.

It should come as no surprise both that there are areas where international law remains ineffective due to insufficient enforcement mechanisms and that the absence of enforcement is less of a constraint for the most powerful nations. Though this is a pedestrian point, it does direct us toward one aspect of the New Realist critique that demands further study: the degree to which power imbalances change the tipping point at which a state has reason to shift from straightforward maximization to constrained maximization. This question is largely empirical and ought to be studied more systematically by scholars with training in empirical legal studies. However, the goal of such research would not be to undermine the normativity of international law, but rather to determine with empirical rigor those areas where international law is least effective and where systems of enforcement ought to be strengthened.[140]

This chapter now concludes by briefly rejecting another alleged reason why states need not follow international law: the supposed inability of collective entities to bear moral or legal responsibilities. According to the New Realists, corporate bodies (including states) are incapable of bearing such obligations.[141] Although corporations enjoy legal rights and bear legal responsibilities, they do so because their constituent parts—officers, directors, employees, and shareholders—all benefit from, and consent to, corporate obligations.[142] Shareholders accept the risk of paying for corporate obligations (including unforeseen liabilities) because they also accept the promise of future dividends based on their equity stake.[143] Although states do not demonstrate the same kind of internal organization, they nonetheless do organize themselves so that they can act on the world stage, form alliances and agreements with other states, and enjoy all of the cooperative benefits of constrained maximizers. The citizen does not receive dividends like a shareholder, however, the citizen certainly enjoys the cooperative benefits of living in a state that engages in international relations: everything from economic opportunities fueled by trade to the peace dividends that flow from the prohibition on the international use of force. Citizens do not consent in the same way as do shareholders who purchase stock, but their acceptance of the benefits of citizenship certainly functions as tacit consent.[144]

The New Realists also claim that states cannot be morally bound by international law because they are incapable of *consenting* to their obligations, a fundamental precondition of international treaties and customary law.[145] To understand their point, consider an analogy to another type of collective agent, the corporation. The members of the corporation (e.g., shareholders) have voluntarily joined the corporation by deciding to buy shares. So, under this view, corporations have the power to make binding commitments because doing so increases the autonomy of its individual members: thus, the corporate power to consent to obligations has instrumental value because it enhances the well-being of its members who voluntarily joined it.[146] When the corporate commitment is too burdensome to the individuals, the individuals demand that the corporation change the commitment.

In contrast, citizens of a state allegedly have no such authority. Once a state accepts a legal obligation, it remains operative for future generations even after the original citizens are dead.[147] The legal obligations of a state endure even if all individual citizens responsible for consenting to that obligation have since died.

Although international legal obligations are surely dynamic in nature as states abrogate, amend, supplement, and revoke treaties constantly, several important doctrines limit a state's opportunities for revising customary international law.[148] Under the persistent objector doctrine, states are only allowed to exempt themselves from an emerging customary law if they have persistently objected to the law, that is, if they have clearly and unambiguously communicated, at regular intervals, their desire to exempt themselves. This is a burdensome requirement. Also, the doctrine of jus cogens holds that some legal norms are so important that they are peremptory in nature and cannot be ignored through persistent objection.

Furthermore, the New Realists reject the possibility that the autonomy of states has intrinsic value.[149] The warrant for this conclusion is that states, unlike individuals, have no life plans and therefore are not valid subjects of the principles of autonomy that are required for an agent to realize a life plan.[150] This conclusion bears scrutiny.[151] If a state lacks the agency necessary to realize a life plan, it is unclear how a state has enough agency to exercise supposedly self-interested behavior on the world stage. Implicit in the notion of self-interested behavior, and consistent with the prisoner's dilemma, is the notion of a rational agent with enough foresight to have long-term interests (through subsequent iterations of the game). If the possibility of a state's life plan is rejected, then so is the entire applicability of the game theory methodology to international law and international relations; one would effectively have to throw out the baby with the bathwater. A state's normative agency inevitably entails the construction of long-term interests, which renders the state capable of consenting to (and bearing) legal obligations.

One might respond that there is a difference between a state's capacity for agency and whether this autonomy is intrinsically valuable. On this view, states are capable of exercising collective agency, though this agency only has instrumental value insofar as it facilitates or maximizes the autonomy of individual citizens whose life plans may require organization into collective units (states) that can operate on the world stage. Something along these lines is arguably implicit in the work of Will Kymlicka, a political philosopher who argues for communitarian principles because the "community" is an essential ingredient for an individual to flourish.[152] The irony and novelty of Kymlicka's theory is that he supports a communitarian political philosophy by appealing to the central tenet of political liberalism—the moral importance of the individual. If this view is correct, then the community has no independent moral value—its value is derived from the fact that living in a community is the best way of making individuals happy. Transplanted to the international realm, this view would suggest that states have no independent value. That is, the life plan of the state has no independent intrinsic value and is only important because of the benefits that flow to its individual members.

I reject this view of the collective entity as having no independent moral value, though I cannot defend fully the claim in this limited forum.[153] Nations, both in the cultural abstract and in their particular organization as nation-states, contribute to the rich tapestry of human existence.[154] However, merely assuming for the sake of argument that states have no independent autonomy does not by itself entail the conclusion that states are incapable of bearing moral obligations. There is a missing proposition in the argument, namely, that moral obligations at the collective level evaporate if they fail to maximize the autonomy of individuals. This need not be the case. Isn't it possible that states have no independent significance but that the state still has a moral obligation to keep its promises and fulfill its legal obligations?

One might coherently argue that once properly formed from the material of rational individuals, states become distinct entities whose interrelations are governed by an autonomous sphere of legal relations that are independent of the domestic laws governing their citizens internally. Just as one might call a corporation a legal or metaphysical fiction (though I do not subscribe to this view),[155] one might just as well dismiss a state with the same epithet. But the fiction might be sufficiently robust that its own collective agency generates corresponding moral duties even if its moral significance originally emerged from its constituent parts. A state without citizens would have no value; however, once a state is composed of individuals and begins to exercise collective rationality in its engagement with other states, it becomes capable of bearing moral obligations. Indeed, I have tried to demonstrate in this chapter that a state's collective rationality (in the form of constrained maximization) *requires* that it follow international legal obligation.

3.5 Conclusion

Although the New Realists offer an academic argument, it is important to remember that their game-theory-fueled skepticism codifies a view that extends far beyond the academy—it has pervaded American foreign policy for much of the last decade.[156] Although many commentators have exposed the flaws in such reasoning, few of the criticisms have—as we have done here—explicitly focused on the link between national self-interest and fidelity to legal norms as being a specific example of the more general relationship between rationality and morality. The New Realists focus on the relationship between a state's self-interest and the obligations that international law imposes on it. The insight developed in this chapter is that this argument can only be evaluated by first coming to terms with a larger idea: the relationship between rationality (what a state has reason to do) and morality (what a state ought to do).

As it happens, this is well-traveled terrain in the philosophical literature. My own view is that, in the international realm, there is a convergence between what a state has reason to do (based on self-interest) and what a state ought to do according to morality. Under certain very complicated conditions, the two actually coincide. That is the whole point of the strategy of constrained maximization. This is an ambitious claim; those who reject the view that morality and rationality coincide will naturally also reject its relevance for a theory of international law. For these thinkers, the notion that morality and rationality coincide may leave little room for our folk concept of altruism or for doing what is right when it requires significant sacrifice. Don't agents sometimes have to sacrifice their own interest when they do the moral thing? Isn't this the very definition of altruism?

But my account of the relationship between morality and rationality leaves open the possibility that in any one scenario, fidelity to norms may require significant sacrifice; the account simply insists that, as an overall and long-term strategy, constrained maximization is rationally justified. For the very same reason, states might still comply with international law with *opinio juris*—a sense of obligation—knowing that in any one context it might involve a sacrifice but with full knowledge that in the long term, constrained maximization is in the nation's self-interest. In a way, this is the lesson that was lost in our foreign policy over the last decade.

4 :: Solving the Prisoner's Dilemma of International Law

Now comes the time to offer the solution to the dilemma. Why should states accept the constraints of the international system? According to the New Realists, states are simply self-interested agents caught in a prisoner's dilemma. Their compliance with international law is really just rational, self-interested behavior. Consequently, when rational self-interest suggests defiance of international law, states can and should ignore the constraints of international law.[1]

In order to understand where this argument goes wrong, it is necessary to delve into the complexities of rational behavior. What makes a certain course of action rational? The New Realists are operating under a conception of rationality based on the idea that at each moment in time, rational agents should consider their best course of action; if their best course of action involves turning their back on promises or commitments they have made, then it is rational to do so.[2] However, this theory of rationality is dead wrong because it ignores the fact that rational agents—both human beings and nation-states—are *planning* agents.[3]

This chapter lays out this planning conception of rational agency and explains why it entails that compliance with international law is rational. The view was first introduced in chapter 1 to explain why the New Realist account is faulty, but I must now provide a full derivation of the argument. I will do this by starting from the beginning, building a theory of rational agency from first principles. This requires working through some famous thought experiments that philosophers of human agency have pondered for decades—including the toxin puzzle and the deterrence paradox.[4] My solution to these puzzles will help explain why individual human beings can—and should—evaluate the rationality of their actions by considering "large chunks" of strategic behavior rather than evaluating individual choices at each point in time. (And that is precisely what the New Realists are suggesting that states do.[5]) Strangely enough, doing the latter yields suboptimal results for rational agents—in other words, it makes their lives *worse* overall. That is hardly the rational thing to do.

4.1 The Toxin Puzzle and Taking the Long View

To start off the discussion, we should consider one of the famous paradoxes of rationality, although it is one that is basically ignored by the New Realists in their discussions of economics and game theory.[6] The paradox is called the toxin puzzle, and it was first described by George Kavka:

> You are feeling extremely lucky. You have just been approached by an eccentric billionaire who has offered you the following deal. He places before you a vial of toxin that, if you drink it, will make you painfully ill for a day, but will not threaten your life or have any lasting effects. (Your spouse, a crack biochemist, confirms the properties of the toxin.) The billionaire will pay you one million dollars tomorrow morning if, at midnight tonight, you intend to drink the toxin tomorrow afternoon.[7]

Sounds simple, right? The obvious answer *seems* to be that you should drink the toxin and take the money. One million dollars is a lot of money, and you could put it to good use. You only need to suffer through the sickness for one day, but then you recover, and at no point is your life in jeopardy.

Unfortunately, that answer is too quick. On deeper reflection, the rational response is more complicated. The billionaire promises to give you the money on Monday, *before* you have consumed the toxin. You only need to actually consume the toxin *after* you receive the money. But once you receive the *benefit* from the deal, what reason do you have to follow through and suffer the *burden*?[8] The original reason to suffer the burden was to get the money, but you have already received the money, so the reason to suffer the burden has evaporated at this point. So it seems that you should take the money and then not drink the toxin.

Things get worse. You cannot get the money so easily, because remember, the billionaire did not promise you the money for *drinking* the toxin, he promised you the money for *intending* to drink the toxin. But since it is rational for you to take the money and then refuse to drink the toxin, then you do not really *intend* to drink the toxin in the first place. And the eccentric billionaire knows this. So you do not—indeed *cannot*—get the money that the billionaire has offered.

This seems deeply paradoxical. The billionaire's toxin offer seems like a good proposition to me. I get a huge amount of money for just one day of discomfort, and this would improve my life overall. But I am held hostage, in a sense, by my hyperrational desire for an even better outcome: taking the money and then *refusing* to drink the toxin. Since that is an even better outcome, it ought to be my rational preference when it comes time to drink the toxin. Because the rationality of this ultimate defection is clear to everyone, including myself, then, as a rational agent, I cannot even *intend* to drink the toxin. My intent is to take the money and then not drink the toxin. So I logically cannot intend to drink the toxin; I cannot get the money. How is this possible?

One simple answer is to say that I have *promised* to drink the toxin, or that I have a contract with the billionaire to follow through and drink the toxin. But in this thought experiment, there is no promise and no contract involved. The billionaire does not ask you to promise anything or bind yourself with a morally or legally binding contract. His only condition is that you *intend* to drink the toxin. If your intention is sincere and rational, then you get the money. This is how the thought experiment is constructed, to write out promises and contracts from the equation.

But why are promises and contracts written out of the thought experiment? Isn't that how such situations are normally resolved in our daily lives, with promises or contracts that require us to hold up our end of the bargain? In a restaurant, one orders dinner and then consumes the food. After eating a big meal, you are stuffed and then the waitress brings the check. You look at the huge bill and ask yourself: *Why am I buying all of this food? I'm not hungry anymore. This doesn't make sense.*[9] The reason for following through on the intention to pay evaporated once your hunger was satiated with the consumption of the food. The answer, of course, is that you implicitly promised to pay the bill when you ordered the food, and failure to pay might constitute a breach of contract yielding civil and even criminal penalties. You better pay the bill or the restaurant might call the police. The dine and dash will get you into trouble.

The toxin thought experiment writes out these considerations of promises and contracts because it is exclusively focused on what *rationality* demands, not what morality or law demands.[10] The billionaire will give you the money if you intend to drink the toxin; since you cannot rationally intend to drink the toxin (your intention is to collect and defect), you cannot get the money, even though the money would make your life go better overall. That seems like a paradox of rationality before morality or law even enter the picture. Rationality should counsel a course of action that makes your life go better overall, not a course of action that leads to lost opportunities.

There are multiple responses to the toxin puzzle, and in this chapter, I shall concentrate on a couple of them. First, we should concentrate on the general relationship between *intending* a certain action and *executing* the action.[11] Indeed, that is what the toxin puzzle gets us to focus on, given that the billionaire ties the monetary bequest to one's *intending* the action rather than the action itself. Does an intention to perform an action give a rational agent a special reason to consummate that intention by performing the action to which the intention was directed?

Here is one possible solution, one that recognizes that human beings are planning agents. Paradoxes of rational agency often assume that rational agents will evaluate their best response and act accordingly at each moment in time. Think of a large supercomputer like IBM's Deep Blue deciding on what chess move is the best response, or your phone's GPS navigation system that you use in the car. Both will evaluate, at each chess move or at each street corner, which is the best alternative among all possible alternatives. So on move 100 of the chess game, Deep Blue will run through *every* permutation and decide the most strategic response in the chess game, and will reengage the same exercise on move 99 and move 101. If that counsels changing strategy, it will do so.

In contrast, human beings are *planning* agents. Instead of reevaluating our course of action at every moment in time, we select strategies that we think are rationally advisable. So a chess player might select a certain strategy for opening the game, or for defending his or her queen, or for developing his pawns. Now here is the important point about plans: they are *sticky*.[12] Human beings do not drop or switch plans at the drop of a hat. They stick to them, at least for some period of time, because *sticking* to the plan is inherent in the concept of a plan.[13] If you never stick with the plan and reevaluate your choices at each moment, then you do not really have a plan at all. A plan *liberates* the agent from obsessively reevaluating his course of action at each moment in time, a process that is both exhausting and potentially paralyzing.[14] We cannot reason like Deep Blue; we need plans that structure our course of action.

There is an important objection here. Just because human beings operate with plans does not make them rational, does it? Maybe our reliance on planning should be considered a rational defect, and that rational reconsideration at each moment in time, like Deep Blue, should be considered the rational norm to which we should all strive. Maybe our nature as planning agents is a reflection of human frailty, of our limited cognitive processing power; maybe it is a human condition that ought to be mourned rather than celebrated.

This is a good point, but it fails to understand the rational sophistication of plans.[15] Plans are more than just a second-best option when the first-choice option of constant reevaluation is deemed impossible or impracticable. Plans provide long-term structure to our daily lives, allowing us to achieve results that make our lives go better overall.[16] In other words, plans are rationally justified.

Consider the toxin puzzle again with reference to plans. When you intend to drink the toxin, you formulate a rational plan to get the money and drink the toxin. Then, when it comes time to drink the toxin, you follow through on the plan and drink the toxin. Knowing that this is your plan, your intention to drink the toxin is both sincere and rationally justified. You get the money. Your life goes better overall. The paradox disappears.

But wait a minute. This just sounds like we have substituted the word "intended" for the word "planned." Originally, we said that you cannot intend to drink the toxin, hence the paradox. Now, we are saying that you "plan" to drink the toxin, and that the paradox disappears. This sounds like a magician's sleight-of-hand move, not a sophisticated philosophical theory. Surely there is something more to the planning theory of human agency.

Indeed there is. The planning theory of human agency requires us to understand that we have been working with the *wrong* definition of rationality. The classical view, which the New Realists implicitly subscribe to, is that rationality is defined as taking the best course of action at each moment in time.[17] But the toxin puzzle teaches us that this definition of rationality yields inevitably to paradox.[18] So we need to recognize that the correct definition of rationality is slightly different.

Many theorists think that rationality demands that a rational agent should select his or her best response at each moment in time.[19] This is wrong, because in some situations, this leads to your life going worse, not better. The correct theory of rationality is to select the overall course of action that makes your life go better overall. Then, rationality demands that you fulfill the elements of your plan. Rationality demands that you *stick* with your plans, even in the face of opportunistic defection. It *maximizes* your total expected welfare.

How can this be? Shouldn't rational agents jump at an opportunistic defection? The key here is that rationality is evaluated in *larger chunks*, not isolated decision points. So the correct definition of rationality is that an action's rationality is evaluated with regard to its place within a larger, rationally justified plan.[20] An individual action is not rational because it constitutes your best response, like a computer in a chess game. An individual action is rational when it is part of a larger plan that makes your life go better overall.[21]

Some theorists, following Edward McClennen, refer to this as *resolute* choice.[22] In other words, a resolute choice is one that is not easily defeated by opportunistic defection. The fact that the choice is part of a rationally defensible plan gives the rational agent a *reason* to continue with that choice.[23]

An obvious problem develops here. Can this new account of rationality explain when one should stick with the original plan and when one should defect from the plan?[24] It would be difficult to offer a full account of plan revision here, but this much is clear. Nothing in the *stickiness* of plans prevents rational agents from reevaluating their commitment to a plan or revising its content. If new information is developed, then the plan can be revised or challenged.[25] What is certain, though, is that a plan should not be abandoned simply because the benefit has accrued but not the burden. In that situation, the rational agent has not acquired any new information at all; he is in precisely the situation he anticipated at the beginning of the scenario.

Let me explain how the concept of plans provides an answer to the toxin puzzle. The billionaire offers you $1 million if you intend on Monday to drink the toxin on Wednesday. On Monday, you develop a plan that includes both receiving the money and drinking the toxin. Come Wednesday, even though you have already received the money, you follow through with the plan and drink the toxin. Is this rational? Haven't you already received the money? What is to be gained from drinking the toxin at this point? The answer, of course, is that the rationality of that action is not to be determined by virtue of whether it is your best response at that moment in time. This definition yields paradoxical results. Rather, the rationality of drinking the toxin is based on the action's place within a rationally justified plan. If the overall plan makes the agent's life go better overall, then each *element* of the plan is rationally justified by virtue of its place within the whole.

Furthermore, the billionaire knows this to be the case. When you intend to drink the toxin, he understands this intention to be sincere and rational. So as a rational agent, it is possible to intend to drink the toxin. You receive the money and fulfill the plan by drinking the toxin. The putative paradox evaporates. The toxin puzzle is resolved.

There are many different ways of expressing this same point. Although there are important philosophical differences between them, their basic structure remains similar. For example, the philosopher David Gauthier once argued that rational agents could acquire *dispositions* to act in certain ways.[26] If a disposition makes an agent's life go better overall, then the disposition is rational, and the agent is justified in engaging in actions that are consistent with the disposition. To put the point slightly more colloquially, a rational agent can try to become the type of person who will engage in certain behaviors.[27] One can think of these dispositions as character traits, or elements of one's "second nature," as Aristotle thought of them.[28] So, for example, an agent might have a disposition to engage in cooperation, which might be rationally justified if it makes the agent's life go better overall (assuming that the agent lives in an environment with a sufficient number of agents with the same disposition).[29] Or, an agent might have a disposition to keep promises or a disposition to follow through (rather than abandon) on well-considered plans.

In MORALS BY AGREEMENT, Gauthier contrasts two different types of dispositions: to be a "straightforward maximizer" or to be a "constrained maximizer."[30] An agent disposed to be a straightforward maximizer will pursue his own interests without cooperating with other agents. On the other hand, a constrained maximizer will accept the constraints that come with living in a community in order to reap its cooperative benefits.[31] He will still try to maximize his position, but he will do so by accepting *reciprocal* rules that constrain his behavior in certain situations. Gauthier argued that any theory that defined constrained maximization as *irrational* was flat out wrong, because in many situations, having a disposition toward constrained maximization will improve the lot of the agent who has that disposition. It will make his life go better overall. So that disposition is rationally justified, and actions taken in accordance with that disposition are also justified.[32]

Dispositions are rationally justified if they improve the situation of the agent in question. Put in toxin puzzle terms, an agent with a disposition to fulfill his intentions by executing them would be in a better position than an agent who lacks this disposition. The former would receive the money while the latter would not. The latter would be unable to form the intention to drink the toxin and so would not receive the money.

The language of dispositions is a bit obscure, and it is not essential to solving the toxin puzzle. In *The Shadow of the Future*, Brian Skyrms argues that a rational agent needs to have a concern for the future—a fact that might encourage him to cooperate rather than defect in a prisoner's dilemma, so as not to lose the cooperative benefits from future partners in subsequent iterations of the game.[33] In simple terms, if you fail to cooperate in a prisoner's dilemma in the first round, your partner will have no reason to trust you in the second round, and neither will other partners in a universe with information-sharing about prior cooperation and noncooperation. The shadow of the future encourages you to cooperate now, even if cooperation does not immediately bring about the maximum payoff. But in the long run, it does.

This argument is not new.[34] Hobbes made much of this argument, putting the skeptical argument in the mouth of the Fool, who argues that keeping covenants was contrary to reason when there was no particular benefit to holding up one's end of the bargain.[35] Hobbes rejected this argument and concluded that the "shadow of the future" forces agents to consider these long-term consequences.[36] Unfortunately, Skyrms points out that Hobbes's Fool is not so easily defeated. In a prisoner's dilemma game with multiple rounds, there will come a time when there is *no* future at all, because the game is on its last round. In such situations, agents no longer have reason to cooperate, and so they defect.[37] Unfortunately, because agents in the game can predict this eventual outcome, the other agent will refuse to cooperate in the second-to-last round. By backward induction, the argument runs all the way to the beginning of the game, so neither agent will cooperate, even during the first round.[38] The structure of this argument applies to any prisoner's dilemma with a finite number of rounds. The only way around it is to assume an infinite number of rounds; even uncertainty about the number of rounds in a finite game will be insufficient to avoid the problem.

Of course, the toxin puzzle is a single-round incident. There is no "shadow of the future" to consider when drinking the toxin. The billionaire will not return tomorrow with a new offer to consider, nor is information sharing with other eccentric billionaires relevant. The puzzle forces us to confront the exact relationship between intentions and execution and between mental states and follow-through. The relationship between them, of course, is that both are unified in a larger whole. One can call the larger whole—what before I called the larger *chunk*—a plan, a strategy, or a disposition. There are deep philosophical differences between them, though they are unified by their long-term nature. Rational agents who operate at this deeper level understand that forming an intention and following through with the intention are unified in the overall plan. As Gauthier puts the point in *Rethinking the Toxin Puzzle*, "rational deliberation concerning future-directed intentions thus must consider both the formation and the execution of the intention."[39] He continues:

> At the time of formation, may one rationally expect to do better overall by performing the intention-requiring act than by performing any alternative? At the time of execution, may one rationally expect to do better by performing the intention-executing act than one would have done had one not performed the intention-requiring act? Deliberatively, the second question must be resolved prior to the first.[40]

Again, there is still room for regret and room for changing one's mind, although not just because one has accrued the benefit before the burden. Consider the following hypothetical, a variant of the toxin puzzle formulated by Gauthier. In addition to the gambit offered by the eccentric billionaire, there is now a slight possibility—a 10-million-to-one chance—that you have a rare genetic mutation that will render you permanently disabled by drinking the toxin.[41] You think the chance sufficiently rare that you intend to take the money and drink the toxin anyway. If, after forming the intention and receiving the money, you acquire *new* information that indicates that you actually *have* the genetic mutation, there might be reason to abandon your prior intention and refuse to follow through on the original plan. There is nothing irrational about *that*, because when forming the intention, you believed that the chance of holding the genetic mutation was 10-million-to-one. But after forming the intention, you acquired new information that changed your likelihood of being permanently disabled to 100 percent. The new information provides you with a reason to stay away from the toxin—a rational outcome despite the existence of the prior plan.

The devil is in the details, of course. How do we tell the difference between a stable plan whose original intention should be executed and an obsolete plan that can and should be abandoned as no longer being in the best interest of the agent?[42] Indeed, this is a crucial problem since, from the perspective of the agent in the original toxin puzzle, when it comes time drink the Toxin, certainly refusing to drink the toxin constitutes the best response at that moment in time. Why should we privilege the agent's best response on Monday rather than his best response on Wednesday? Especially considering the fact that Monday is now gone, and the only thing within the agent's control is his or her decisions on Wednesday. As Bratman puts the point:

> As time goes by we are located differently with respect to our plans. Along with a change in temporal location normally goes a change in the agent's causal powers. What is up to the agent is what to do from now on. So she will normally want to rank alternatives beginning from now on.[43]

Why privilege the prior ranking to the current ranking? One might refer to an agent who defects—and thereby selects a strategy of straightforward maximizing—as a *myopic* chooser, as opposed to a sophisticated chooser.[44] The myopic chooser only sees what is before him and fails to see the rational benefits of the larger chunk, whether we call it a larger plan or a disposition. The myopic chooser fails to take, in a sense, the long view of things.

McClennen argues that when faced with these temptations, rational agents should make a *resolute* choice.[45] By this, he means that when confronted with a conflict between an earlier set of preferences from which a plan was structured and a new set of preferences formed at a later point in time, a rational agent should privilege the earlier choice rather than be tempted by the immediacy of the new preferences.[46] The original choice should be *resolute*. In the toxin puzzle, that would mean that the intention to drink the toxin should prevail, even after the benefits have accrued and only the burdens remain. The original choice should function like a resolution to which the rational agent has committed himself.

Of course, it can be difficult to avoid temptation. Some theorists have argued that these two preference sets are incompatible, and so what the agent needs to do is bind himself so that the earlier set of preferences prevail instead of the temptation of operationalizing the later preferences (to refuse to drink the toxin once one already has the money). Consider the following hypothetical. The rational agent is given the original gambit offered by the eccentric billionaire. The agent intends to drink the toxin, and in an effort to defeat his anticipated later preference to refuse to drink toxin, the agent takes an irrationality pill.[47] The pill forces the agent to drink the toxin later by getting him to act irrationally, i.e. to ignore his new preferences and consequently privilege his original preferences.[48] Would it be rational to take such a pill? It sounds crazy to suggest that it would ever be rational to force oneself to act irrationally; it sounds like a paradox. But in fact, the paradox disappears once one realizes that the resolute choice—sticking to the original plan—is not an example of irrationality at all. The rationality stems from the larger chunk—from the original preference that gave rise to the plan—and there is no new information that provides a reason to change preferences. The only thing that has changed is the temptation and the fact that the agent is now, to use Bratman's phrase, "temporally and causally located" in a different manner with regard to the original intention.[49] But that is no reason to give privileged place to current preferences and declare them rational, such that the pill forces the agent to act irrationally. Rather, the pill forces the agent to stick to his resolute choice.

Thus the problem with the irrationality pill is not what it accomplishes but simply what it is called. It concedes too much by labeling later action as irrational. It really is a form of rationality, a form of resolute choice based on the legitimacy of the earlier intention. It should be called a rationality pill.

Does this answer all of the questions? Does the notion of *resolute* choice really provide a reason for an agent to stick to his original intention and follow through, even in the face of seemingly opportunistic abandonment? Bratman thinks not, because there is still a conflict between the past and present desires and little in principle to resolve a conflict between them. As Bratman says:

> [I]t is difficult to see why this shows that *at the time of action* one will not reasonably consult one's ranking of options that are at that time in one's control. If one is concerned with what is "maximally conducive to one's life going we well as possible," why wouldn't one be concerned with which action, of those presently in one's control, is "maximally conducive to one's life going as well as possible"? Faced with the toxin on Wednesday, however, the action presently in one's control that is maximally conducive to that benefit is, we may suppose, not drinking.[50]

The answer, for Bratman, lies in the fact that planning agents are not just concerned with their current preferences, but they are also concerned with their anticipated preferences when the plan comes to its natural end. If you envision this week that when your plan is complete next week you will come to regret your earlier preferences, this prediction is incredibly relevant to your calculus. As rational agents, we change our behavior all the time when our preferences are satisfied today but we know that we will come to regret those preferences at a later point in time. We balance today's preferences with tomorrow's preferences; we balance impulsive desires against future regret.

Bratman's story is built upon the "shadow of the future" as well, though in some sense, the temporal issue is reversed from how above we discussed McClennen's notion of a resolute choice. Resolute choice in the toxin puzzle involves privileging the earlier plan and sticking with it, unless new information arises. In contrast, the Bratman story of regret involves a recognition of how temporally extended agents will view their plan once it is all said and done. If you abandon or change your plan based on transitory desires, and if that choice fails to maximize your life outcome, you can envision today that you will come to regret that choice. The shadow of that "future regret" reinforces the stability of today's plan.

4.2 The Deterrence Paradox and the Limits of Follow-Through

So much for the toxin puzzle. We now need to consider another famous paradox, one that has troubling implications for both our theory of rationality and also our national security policy. It is called the deterrence paradox, and it was first formulated in the 1950s when game theorists were trying to understand the basic structure of deterrence that formed the foundation of our nuclear weapons policy.[51]

Famously, the United States developed a strategy known as MAD—mutually assured destruction. The idea behind the strategy was a commitment—a *public* commitment—to retaliate against any nation that launched nuclear weapons against the United States. Moreover, the commitment was not just to a partial nuclear strike. The promise was to completely destroy the adversary, such that any decision to destroy the United States would trigger a decision to destroy them. Everyone would be dead. Mutually assured destruction.

In one sense, this seems like an obvious policy. If the United States is attacked with nuclear weapons, of course it should respond in kind with a nuclear strike of its own. But stop for a second and consider the rationality of the policy. The goal of the policy is to issue a *threat*. The threat is designed to ensure that adversaries (principally the USSR) do not attack the United States. They would know that attacking the United States would be met with a deadly counterattack, thus ensuring mutual destruction. Nobody wins.

But consider the situation more carefully. The United States issues the threat of MAD. The USSR decides to launch its missiles anyway, which are about to land in the United States and kill its inhabitants in a few minutes. The United States is then faced with a decision about whether to retaliate or not. However, the rationality of the retaliation was based entirely on its efficacy in preventing the USSR from launching its missiles. In this case, though, the threat has failed. The USSR has already launched its missiles. What is to be gained from the United States killing Russian civilians halfway across the globe? It does not improve the situation of the Americans, and it only worsens the situation of the Russian civilians. There is no benefit. Consequently the United States has no rational reason to launch its weapons once the threat of a launch has failed to deter the USSR from launching its weapons.

Now here is the dilemma. The USSR knows that once the U.S. threat fails, and the USSR missiles are in the air, the United States will no longer have a reason to launch its own missiles. The United States cannot save itself, and launching its missiles will only serve to kill more Soviet civilians. Consequently, the deterrent threat does not work in the first place. The Soviets would never believe that the United States would follow through on a failed threat, so the threat is totally ineffective and fails to *deter* the Soviets (the whole point of the threat). MAD is an incoherent strategy so long as the actors are rational agents and each side believes that the other side is acting rationally. As a matter of game theory, nuclear deterrence is a fiction.[52]

What about the shadow of the future, you ask? Isn't there a reason to fulfill threats, even if they have failed to deter the original conduct they were meant to deter, so as to demonstrate resolve for future interactions? This sounds plausible, but the nuclear deterrence scenario is designed to be a single-round game. And that is not just an artifice of the game theory. In reality, nuclear deterrence is potentially a single-round situation since major world powers with large nuclear arsenals are capable of completely destroying their adversaries with a first strike or a retaliatory launch. There is no shadow of the future to consider in these cases.

This leads to a powerful dilemma. The United States wants to deter a potential Soviet nuclear strike, but once the threat fails, the reason to retaliate evaporates and a counterstrike will fail to improve the lot of the United States. Knowing this, the USSR is not deterred. (Incidentally, the situation works in reverse, too. The United States knows that the USSR will have no reason to respond after an American first strike, so the United States is not deterred by any threat from the USSR.) Is there a solution to this theoretical problem? Or was MAD simply a foolish and incoherent policy to begin with?

Based on our discussion of the toxin puzzle, there is a potential solution to the deterrence paradox. Just as the toxin puzzle involves a plan to which an agent has committed himself and to which the agent should follow through, so too the deterrence paradox involves a plan that requires rational follow-through, even when the original reason for formulating the plan appears to have run its course.[53] In the toxin puzzle, we learned that the rationality of an action is not to be determined by virtue of whether it constitutes an agent's best response at that moment in time. Rather, we learned that the rationality of an action is determined by its place within a rationally justified overall plan, a plan that makes the agent's life go better overall. Since drinking the toxin is one part of a rational plan, it is rational to drink the toxin. Similarly, since retaliating is one part of a rational plan of deterrence, it is rational to follow through and launch the counterstrike. Rationality is determined by the action's place in the overall plan.

This is a disturbing conclusion. In the toxin puzzle, the result of the *large-chunk* argument of rationality is a happy one—you receive $1 million. Only philosophers and game theorists will quibble with this result (on theoretical grounds). But in the deterrence paradox, the *large-chunk* argument suggests following through with the plan and killing innocent Soviet civilians, even when doing so could not possibly save the lives of American civilians. For some, this result represents a *reductio ad absurdum* of the entire line of argument.[54] If any of these *large-chunk* arguments suggest that retaliation is rational, something has gone wrong in the argument. This also suggests that our solution to the toxin puzzle might be wrong as well.

The entire theory of rationality needs to be reconsidered. Maybe the original view of rationality is better: agents *should* consider the rationality of their actions based on their preferences at each moment in time. At the time of retaliation, the United States has no preference for launching a retaliatory attack. Doing so does not benefit the United States and only harms the USSR. The present preference should take precedence over the earlier preference—resolute choice and plans be damned.

One potential solution is to recognize that the problem with the retaliatory strike is moral, not rational. For some, launching the retaliatory strike after the failed threat is morally impermissible because it sacrifices the lives of so many innocent civilians even when doing so has no causal benefit for saving the lives of other innocent civilians. So there is a moral objection to retaliation—not a rational choice objection to it. The two ought to be separate. For at least some theorists (although not Gauthier),[55] a theory of rationality does not exhaust what is morally permissible or required.[56] It might be rational to retaliate but morally objectionable to do so.

Perhaps there are other moral problems with the deterrence paradox. Consider the wrongful intentions principle.[57] There are different formulations of the principle,[58] but in broad brushstrokes, it states that if an action is wrong to execute, it is also wrong to *intend* to perform that action. So the intention inherits its wrongfulness from the action to which it is directed. If one is wrong, so is the other. The principle is intuitively plausible and makes sense of other moral intuitions (including why we punish attempts in the criminal law). In the case of the deterrence paradox, it is morally wrong to kill innocent Soviet civilians when doing so provides no utilitarian benefit to saving the lives of other innocent civilians. Since launching the strike is morally wrong, so is *intending* to kill the innocent civilians. Since intending to kill them is one part of a sincere *threat* to engage in a retaliatory strike, it is morally impermissible to even threaten to use nuclear weapons in retaliation.

Incidentally, I think this moral intuition lurks somewhere in the background when the International Court of Justice considered the lawfulness of the use of nuclear weapons.[59] In its famous decision, the World Court concluded (in a narrow majority) that both the use of nuclear weapons and even the *threat* of using a nuclear weapon was a violation of international law (though the court carefully carved out cases of so-called existential self-defense and concluded that its decision did not reach situations where the very existence of the state was at stake.)[60] The court's decision to equate nuclear strikes with nuclear threats drew special condemnation from Judge Schwebel, who, in a sharply word dissenting opinion, concluded that such threats, when effective in stopping a nuclear strike, ought to be encouraged rather than discouraged.[61] For example, Judge Schwebel noted that the United States threatened to use nuclear weapons against Saddam Hussein during the first Gulf War if Iraq used chemical or biological weapons. The gambit worked, and Hussein did not launch any WMDs. For Judge Schwebel, this was precisely the point of nuclear threats, and they ought to be salutary.[62] Of course, one difference between Iraq and the deterrence paradox is that the former was a bluff—the United States had already decided that it would not use nuclear weapons, though it did not communicate this decision to Saddam Hussein.[63] In contrast, the deterrence paradox assumes information sharing and publicity so that the threat to use nuclear weapons is not an insincere bluff.

Kavka was not so sure about applying the wrongful intentions principle to the special case of nuclear deterrence. The principle implies that intending to retaliate is morally wrong, even if the state never follows through on the intention by launching the retaliatory strike. This means that successful nuclear deterrence is not possible, unless the situation involves real deception, as with the Saddam Hussein case considered above. If you can deceive a partner, that is an obvious solution that avoids the issue entirely. But if you cannot successfully bluff, wouldn't it be morally better to *threaten* a nuclear retaliation if the threat prevents a nuclear holocaust? The threat seems like the right thing, despite the fact that the wrongful intentions principle counsels against it. According to Kavka, sometimes evil intentions "pave the road to heaven"— a surprising result but one that seems undeniable after sustained thinking about nuclear deterrence.[64] Avoiding disaster ought to be our prime concern.[65]

Do these moral considerations solve the problem? I think not. Even if we dispense with the moral considerations, there is still a seeming paradox of rationality here. Threatening retaliation seems to make sense. Also, it seems as if these threats are rational to make. However, it seems that once the threat fails, the reason for retaliation evaporates. Our prior theory from the toxin puzzle suggests that rational agents should follow through on prior plans rather than abandon them. We still need a solution for *this* problem.

Some scholars have wondered whether it would be rational to commit oneself to following through with the intention to retaliate so as to ensure that the earlier resolute choice wins the day. How could this commitment be ensured, especially when, at the time of action, the agent will reevaluate his preferences and find no reason to retaliate? One possibility is to construct a doomsday machine— with no manual override—that will automate the process of deciding on a retaliatory strike. Daniel Farrell refers to this as an "automated retaliation device," though it has been considered by others under many different names.[66] The device would detect the launching of a preemptive nuclear strike; in response, the device would launch the retaliatory strike that ensures mutually assured destruction. It sounds foolish to ever create such a device. But why? Putting aside practical questions of technical mistakes about the detection of the first preemptive strike, the machine would prevent the state from defecting from its prior intention to launch the retaliatory strike, even in cases when the threat of retaliation had failed to deter the original strike. The other side, knowing of the machine's existence, could not rationally launch a preemptive nuclear strike because it knew that its enemy had bound itself to its own resolute choice by building the automated machine that prevents the abandonment of its intention. One way of describing the machine is that it is a rational way to commit oneself to what becomes an irrational act at the time of execution. This would mean that one can have a rational intention to act irrationally. In this sense, the automated device is similar to the automated device we considered in the toxin puzzle, where the rational agent takes a pill that forces him to act irrationally when it comes time to follow through on an intention.

I dislike such descriptions. I do not believe that following through on either the toxin puzzle or the deterrence paradox is a case of acting irrationally.[67] Rather, following Gauthier, it seems clear that such an agent is engaged in a much more serious and sophisticated form of rationality because he has recognized that both intentions and their associated actions are a *package deal*. Gauthier concludes:

> The person who, in forming her intention, considers her reasons for and against drinking the toxin assesses her course of action—intention and execution—as a whole. She asks herself whether she has good reason to drink the toxin as part of her course of action, and, in concluding that she does, she recognizes that her reasons for forming the intention to drink outweigh her reasons for not drinking.[68]

This seems exactly right. Both intention and action are part of a plan, or strategy if you prefer, and it is implicit in rationality that a sophisticated agent will consider the whole rather than the part. Rationality is a package deal because the rationality of the act comes from its inclusion within a rational plan. If the plan is rational, so is the act; if the plan is irrational, so too is the act.

This still leaves the objection from Bratman, that the package-deal argument in such cases refuses to recognize the temporal and causal location of our agency. When it comes time to act, the rational agent must still evaluate his or her *present* preferences, because the original preferences are now in the past, and they are causally inaccessible. They are gone. What is real is *now*. Should the agent follow through on the original plan or change to a new plan? Maybe the correct plan is to intend to drink the toxin and then refuse to drink it. Perhaps that is the agent's new plan, but if so, he will not get the money because he never rationally intended to drink the toxin in the first place. Bratman's mistake here is failing to adopt the right definition of maximization: the agent should choose the course of action that makes his or her life go better overall. Forming the intention to drink and following through on that intention represents the best course of action for the agent and makes his life go better overall. Anything less will result in a life without the $1 million. Once you understand that rationality demands selecting a course of action that makes the agent's life go better overall—as opposed to simply selecting the best response at each point in time—the rest of the argument falls into place almost automatically.

If this is the correct answer to the toxin puzzle, does it automatically mean that nuclear deterrence requires rational follow-through as well? If it does, there is a risk that some will see the *package-deal* argument as a *reductio ad absurdum*. If successfully drinking the toxin and getting $1 million also involves, in another game theory "game," killing millions of Soviet babies, then *I want no part of this theory of rationality*, you might say. This is a serious and legitimate concern and one that deserves a response, not just at the level of moral theory but also at the level of rationality.

One answer at the level of rationality is that there are relevant differences between the toxin puzzle and the deterrence paradox. In the toxin puzzle, the benefit accrues first, but then the burden comes later. In the deterrence paradox, the benefit never accrues, and the burden is imposed on someone *else*, namely the Soviet civilians. But that does not seem like a relevant consideration for the structure of the argument. Is there a way out of this mess? Or should we conclude that rationality requires follow-through even in the case of nuclear deterrence?

In his later works, Gauthier added an element to his theory of rationality that is highly relevant here. He suggested that a rational agent should stick with a plan and follow through on the original intention if doing so makes the agent's life go better than if the agent had never formulated or committed to the plan in the first place.[69] This criterion retains the package-deal requirement, in the sense that intention and follow-through are evaluated as a package to determine if they make life go better for the agent. They are not to be carved out and evaluated independently, with both intention and act considered separately. However, what this criterion does is help identify the relevant comparison. You don't consider "intention + follow through" and compare it against "intention + no follow through." Rather, you consider the plan (intention + follow through) against not having had the plan at all.

Now the difference between the puzzles shows up. In the toxin puzzle, the agent compares follow-through with a state of affairs where the agent had never committed to the plan in the first place. In the first state of affairs, the agent becomes sick and gets $1 million—a good result. In the second (hypothetical) state of affairs, the agent gets nothing—not a good result. So follow through is rationally justified.

Compare this with the deterrence paradox. In that case, determining whether follow-through is appropriate requires comparing follow-through (mutual destruction) with a situation where the plan was never committed to in the first place. It is clear that follow-through is not beneficial because it confers no improvement. You are dead anyway. It is not superior to the situation where you refused to formulate the threat, and your advisory launched a nuclear strike and killed you because they were undeterred. In both situations you perish, and the only difference is that more innocent civilians (in the USSR) are killed as well. This does not confer a detectable improvement, so follow-through is not rationally justified.

Does this exception swallow the rule? Arguably not, because follow-through is permissible in toxin puzzle-type cases where the plan confers a benefit, but not in failed-threat-type cases such as the deterrence paradox. In the toxin puzzle, follow-though is better than a situation where no plan had been adopted at all. Without the plan, the agent receives nothing; with follow-through, the agent receives both the money and gets sick. The latter makes the agent's life go better overall.

4.3 Assurances and Cooperation

A final point remains. The lessons learned from the toxin puzzle and the deterrence paradox apply to a larger class of cases and provide a road map for understanding cooperative behavior. This will be crucial for understanding the rational behavior of states in the international system—which is the topic of this section. But first let us tackle assurance.

Consider this variant of a common thought experiment about cooperation.[70] Imagine you are a farmer considering whether to help a neighbor farm his property in exchange for his help in farming your property. While both farmers have fertile fields, neither is capable of maximizing his property's yield without assistance. Consequently, you propose to your neighbor that he help you with your property. Then, after the job is complete, you will assist him with farming his property.

But wait a minute, he says. After you receive the needed assistance, what reason do you have to assist him? The benefit has already accrued, and only the burden remains. What reason will you have to help farm his property when your field is already complete? The arrangement will no longer make sense for you. You will be in the same situation as the diner who has to pay the bill after already eating the food. So you will metaphorically dine and dash—a fact that makes your neighbor anxious about the arrangement.

Thus, you issue an assurance to your neighbor. You *assure* him that you will still help him after he has helped you. But he is skeptical of your assurance because he is unsure if you can rationally issue the assurance. What reason will you have to follow through on the assurance once you have received the assistance that you gained by issuing the assurance in the first place? With the assurance having performed its work (succeeding in getting you the assistance), the reason for following through on the assurance will evaporate. Consequently, as a rational agent, you will decline to follow through on the assurance.

Here is the real problem. Because the other farmer knows that it would be irrational for you to follow through on the assurance, he knows that the assurance is, in a sense, devoid of effectiveness. So he does not help you. As a result, the farmers fail to cooperate with each other, and their fields lay fallow.[71] This is just like the deterrence paradox. In the deterrence paradox, the threat fails to deter because there is no rational reason to follow through once it has failed. Consequently, the other side is not deterred and engages in the first strike. In the cooperation game, the assurance fails to assure the other side of cooperation because there is no rational reason to follow through once it is successful; because there is no reason to follow through on the assurance, it cannot be successful in the first instance. Rationality appears to demand no deterrence and no cooperation. This is not good.

Many of the solutions discussed above can be applied equally well to the simple cooperation game.[72] The shadow of the future certainly works well, so long as there is a future to cast a shadow over the present deliberations.[73] For example, you might follow through on your assurance to assist your neighbor because if you don't, he will fail to cooperate with you during the next growing season. This second stage of the game provides a reason for you to follow through on your assurance. Because he knows that you have reason to follow through on your assurance, he has reason to accept the assurance and provide the assistance. The shadow of the future provides reasons for cooperation today.[74]

However, as we saw before in our discussion of Hobbes (and Skyrms), the shadow of the future is open to counterattack. If the game is finite, there will come a last round when there is no more shadow of the future. In that iteration of the game, you will have no reason to follow through on your assurance. You will defect and spend your last amount of energy on yourself rather than working for your neighbor. This is not an infinite game. Your neighbor, knowing the game to be finite, will not cooperate on the second to last round. By backward induction, there is no reason to cooperate during the first round. With a finite number of rounds and information sharing, cooperation based on the shadow of the future appears to break down as a solution to the problem.

However, consider how assurances work if you adopt a plan- or strategy-based understanding of rationality. A rational agent should adopt the plan or strategy that makes his life go better overall. The plan should maximize his overall benefits over the course of his life, rather than simply maximize his benefits at any particular point in time. The latter would be a myopic strategy. As such, a rational agent should adopt a plan of cooperating with his neighbor by assisting him in exchange for assistance in return. In conformance with this plan, the rational agent should issue the assurance that he will perform the assistance once the time comes. The rationality of following through on the assistance should be evaluated not by virtue of whether it constitutes the agent's best response at the time of choice of follow-through. Rather, the rationality of following through depends on the action's place within a rationally justified plan. Since cooperation is far better for the agent than noncooperation, the plan is rationally justified. Consequently, it is rational for the agent to follow through on his assurance when it comes time to decide whether to provide assistance or not. The other farmer, knowing this to be the case, will find the assurance reassuring and will provide his assurance too. Cooperation is rational.[75]

This solution to the cooperation game broadens the previous discussion to a much larger class of cases, where its applicability will have profound consequences. In our prior discussion, the problem of rational follow-through was confined to obscure cases of intention follow-through (the Toxin Puzzle) and cases of failed threats (the deterrence paradox). However, now we see that the problem of intention follow-through infects almost every case of rational cooperation. And cooperation is at the heart of almost every moral and legal system we have. Moreover, we see that the *large-chunk* solution of evaluating rationality based on plans and strategies not only solves obscure thought experiments like toxin and deterrence but also provides a meaningful foundation for rational cooperation, too. It is rational to cooperate and not just in situations where the shadow of the future provides the rational agent with a reason to take the long view. It is rational to cooperate simply because following through on one's commitment is one part of a larger plan that makes the agent's life go better overall. This is a meaningful change to the classical view of rationality that assumes that the agent's rational point of view should be evaluated exclusively from the perspective of his best response at any single point in time.

4.4 Why the New Realists Fail to Understand Rationality

Before we apply what we have learned from the toxin puzzle and the deterrence paradox, we should summarize our theory of rationality before we apply it to the theory of international law advanced by the New Realists. Classical economic theory assumes that rationality requires an agent doing what constitutes his or her best response at each moment in time. This is incorrect because it leads to paradoxical situations where doing what is best at each moment in time fails to maximize payoff when viewed from the perspective of the agent's entire life. We have called this *making the agent's life go better overall*. One source of the paradox could be that a simplistic theory of rationality fails to take the *long view*. In other words, the shadow of the future should mandate that rational agents forgo their best response at each moment in time so as to maximize their payoffs over the long term.

Although the "shadow of the future" is one potential resolution of the paradox, I reject it as the sole and exclusive answer to the problem. Taking the long view is important, but adopting it does not entirely solve the problem. The issues with rationality run much deeper. Even in situations where there is no shadow of the future—no future iterations of the game—the paradox still emerges. In order to maximize the payoff in an agent's lifetime, the agent should forgo what constitutes his or her best response at some moments in time. That is the moral of the toxin puzzle. Sometimes, it makes more sense to formulate a plan and stick with it, where sticking with it means forgoing opportunistic situations that seem as if they deliver better payoffs at that moment in time. You can call these dispositions, intentions, strategies, or plans— for us, the difference is not terribly significant. What is significant is that rationality is a package deal—the rational agent needs to not just consider the atomic choice facing him at time x but should rather consider the expected payoffs of the entire plan to which that action belongs. I called the entire class of these arguments *large-chunk* arguments. As demonstrated in the previous section, they apply not just to thought experiments like toxin and deterrence but also to cases of cooperation.

Here is the payoff for this extended detour into the deepest mysteries of the concept of rationality. The New Realists have insisted that states that appear to "follow" customary international law are really just engaged in self-interested behavior.[76] When it suits them to follow international law, they do so, but this self-interested behavior does not meet the standard for *opinio juris* that is an essential requirement of customary international law.[77] And when self-interest counsels in favor of defection, states refuse to comply with international law. Therefore, much of what usually counts as customary international law is not law at all. It is politics, diplomacy, and self-interest, but not normatively generated behavior.[78]

Based on the preceding discussion, we can now offer a more nuanced response to the skeptical challenge posed by the New Realists. Their argument is based on an assumption—one that is never explicitly defended—that rational self-interest and *opinio juris* are mutually exclusive.[79] Either a state acts out of obligation or it acts out of rational self-interest.[80] If the latter, it necessarily cancels out the former. That is the assumption here. Observers confuse international law with rational self-interest and see "law" where little or no law exists. One consequence of this alleged insight is that the content of international law is supposedly much smaller than previously thought. Many "rules" of customary international law are not legal rules at all, and consequently, states that wish to ignore them can and should do so.

The argument is deeply mistaken for the following reasons. Rational self-interest and the essential normativity of international law are not mutually exclusive. Indeed, the very normativity of international law is based, philosophically, on the rationality of the strategy of cooperation to which the participants commit themselves. Let me unpack this intuition into a general theory of international law.

States pursue long-term plans and strategies.[81] The plan involves committing to legal rules that enshrine cooperation with international partners. That cooperation takes the form of everything from rules regarding bilateral investment (codified in treaties) to rules regarding the use of force and rules regarding the conduct of warfare during battle (*jus in bello*). From the perspective of state A, the rules are beneficial because they constrain the behavior of other states. However, state A also complies with the constraints of the legal system because doing so is consistent with a long-term strategy that makes life go better overall for state A. Cooperating in the international legal system represents a strategy that produces cooperative benefits.

Part of the compliance could be justified by the shadow of the future, though the behavior is not exclusively determined by taking the long view. A state may comply with international law because it realizes that its future partners will only trust it so long as it continues to comply with international law. If it starts rejecting international law, the international community might ostracize it. Scott Shapiro and Oona Hathaway have helpfully described this general phenomenon as outcasting—a central component of the international legal system.[82]

However, compliance is not limited to situations governed by the shadow of the future. There may be interactions that are sui generis and not subject to future considerations. Furthermore, there are deeper reasons for states to comply with international legal constraints. The argument is an obvious extension of the theory provided in the previous sections. States follow through and comply with the dictates of international law (even if the benefits have already accrued à la toxin puzzle) because doing so is one part of a rational plan that makes the state's life go better overall. Classical rationality is wrong if it assumes that states should evaluate the rationality of their actions solely on the basis of their best response at the exact time of follow-through. Large-chunk rationality counsels in favor of follow-through.

4.5 Rationality and Obligation

Gauthier takes the argument in the preceding section one step further: he argues that it is rational for an agent to behave morally.[83] In other words, acting morally is rationally justified. One can see right away the connection with the previous section. Say an agent has a disposition to act morally. If that disposition makes his life go better overall, then it is rational to do whatever he can to gain that disposition. It is also rational to act in ways that are consistent with that disposition.

Consider the idea of *constraint*. Morality imposes all sorts of constraints on our behavior. It tells us what we can do and when we can do it, and it forbids many things that we selfishly wish we could do. Normally, we think of constraints as unproductive— something that we are forced to do but would rather avoid if we could. But not necessarily. If living with the constraints of a cooperative community makes life go better overall for an agent, then acting in a *constrained* way might be both morally and rationally justified. Refusing to follow moral constraints could have disastrous consequences for an agent: isolation, inability to form cooperative partnerships, reaping only individual gains rather than the bounty harvested from collective action.

For Gauthier, acting rationally isn't just consistent with morality—it *is* morality.[84] If an agent living in a cooperative community were to perfectly understand the demands of rationality, he would be acting morally as well. He would form relationships, engage in cooperative activities that require reciprocation, and follow the rules of morality that stem from living as a constrained maximizer. Morality and rationality, rather than being at loggerheads, actually dovetail so long as the community is composed of enough individuals who are willing to cooperate with each other.

But here's the rub. The New Realists believe that states acting out of self-interest are not acting out of a sense of obligation. But this is false. States are doing both at the same time. They are following the dictates of rationality, which demand forming partnerships with other states and then living up to those agreements rather than defecting from them. Those partnerships often take the form of legal agreements, rules of customary international law, and participation in international institutions. States comply with international law because states are committed to acting out of rational self-interest and *also* because they are legally obligated to do so. Obligation and self-interest are not mutually exclusive. In fact, they both stem from the same root: the tree of rationality.

One might object here that not every philosopher accepts that rationality and morality converge. Parfit famously denied the connection.[85] Indeed, there are some reasons to be skeptical, although the previous arguments in this chapter suggest that the skepticism is misplaced. However, it remains perfectly consistent to deny the connection for regular human beings but still accept the connection for states acting in the international system. In other words, even if rational choice theorists like Gauthier are wrong about individual morality, they might be right about the international system.

Why would the structure be different at the individual level than it is at the global level? Shouldn't the structure be exactly the same?

Aren't rational agents all the same, regardless of whether they are individual human beings or collective entities such as nation-states? In one sense, this is a plausible intuition, but in another sense, the levels are different, and one shouldn't expect the same theory to fit both situations. For example, at the individual level, we are discussing the connection between rationality and morality, while at the international level, we are discussing the relationship between rational self-interest and the demands of international law. It might be the case that individual morality presents complexities that do not arise in the admittedly limited system of international law that currently exists.

There is a second objection that should be considered, which rests on the opposite intuition. If indeed human beings and nation-states are different, perhaps long-term planning (and large-chunk rationality) works differently for human beings than it does for nation-states. Consider the following asymmetry. When deciding whether to follow through on a commitment at a later moment in time, the individual must assess whether his later self should follow through on the burden even though his prior self already accrued the benefits. In such situations, nobody denies that your later self and your prior self are the same person. Your identity stretches across time, so this is not a situation where one person bears the burden and another accrues the benefit. It is one person who deals with both, just at two different points in time.

When dealing with nation-states, the situation is slightly more complicated. If the state is engaged in a particular long-term plan, the state may accrue the benefit in one year and bear the burden in a later year. During that time, the members of the state may overlap, but there might be significant changes in membership and composition. Some people move away; others die; new citizens are born. Unlike with individuals, it is no longer the case that the exact same people bear the benefits and burdens. Is it still rational to stick to a long-term project when the individuals who might bear the later burden might not be the same individuals who accrued the earlier benefit? Or does this provide a relevant reason to reject the large-chunk rationality argument for international law? Perhaps for this reason, rationality works differently for nations than it does for individuals.

Some philosophers deny that the two situations are all that different because individuals are far less unified over time than one might think. Derek Parfit is one obvious example. Parfit argues that personal identity over time is not very important at all.[86] What matters is how closely related your prior and later selves are.[87] In most cases, the connections between the two are close and significant, and that should affect our decisions. In some cases, however, the connections between our past and future selves have degraded. In Parfit's view, this might change our decisions about how we react to long-term situations. If this view is correct, then the continuity of states over time is not much different than individual continuity over time. Both vary over time. In a sense, Parfit takes our intuitions about states and applies it to individuals.

Parfit's view, while interesting, is highly extreme. As a matter of fact, most individuals see themselves as identical over time, not just closely related. (Parfit dismisses the relevant of these common-sense intuitions and argues that if some individuals are deluded about their identity over time, they can and should change their attitudes after engaging in considered reflection of the matter. In other words, he thinks that our belief in our own identity over time is a myth that could be unraveled by philosophy.[88]) More important, rational agency can persevere across time for individuals, and this fact persists even though individuals have biological and mental changes over time. Although people age, gain new experiences, lose memories, and change beliefs, their agency usually remains unified over time by virtue of the fact that people engage in long-term planning.[89] Whether this constitutes personal identity over time or not is unimportant.[90] It constitutes agency-over-time. And this is an important feature of our existence.

Consequently, the asymmetry remains. Individuals have agency over time. But what about nation-states? Does it matter that their composition changes? And unlike individuals whose composition changes at the level of cells and individual memories, the composition changes of nation-states take place at the level of individual citizens who are legitimate objects of moral concern. This raises a real problem of *distribution* that our theory of rationality must confront. If one set of individuals bears the burden while another set of individuals reaps the rewards, our account of rationality and morality needs to explain how this is justified.

Thankfully, there are solutions to this theoretical problem. Although nation-states are collections of individuals, they are more than just a *mere* aggregation of individuals.[91] The individuals are organized together in meaningful ways, cooperating and sharing the benefits and burdens of their membership in a collective. Indeed, the nation-state constitutes a very special kind of collective agent, different from a corporation or club. Rather, it represents a collective agent that acts with a unified purpose in particular areas of life. Some of those areas of life are internal—governmental organization, supported by the payment of taxes, and a system of support services funded by those taxes. National and subnational legal rules dictate and constrain the behavior of individual members. More important, however, are the ways the collective agent is organized for purposes of *external* affairs. The government engages in military defense against external enemies. A Department of State or foreign affairs ministry engages in diplomatic relations with foreign states. The executive branch negotiates directly with foreign leaders on matters of international concern. Even lower-level executive agencies might have direct contact with executive counterparts in other nations on matters of mutual technical expertise.[92] The point is that all of these relations are performed by individuals on behalf of the collective. The secretary of state does not engage in *personal* negotiations with foreign counterparts. Rather, the secretary of state makes commitments that bind the nation as a whole because the secretary of state speaks for and on behalf of the collective that she represents.

This unity of purpose on the international realm is essential for the conduct of international affairs. And it is more than just a convenient shorthand for a complex aggregation of individual activity. If individuals were simply acting as individuals qua individuals, they would engage in far different behavior. But because they act as individuals qua representatives of a collective, their actions must be understood relative to the rational commitments of the nation as a whole.[93]

We need to put the pieces of this argument together into a coherent whole. The nation is a collective agent that acts with a unity of purpose for matters of internal and external concern. As such, the nation retains a unified existence over time, even though its composition might undergo certain changes. The fact that some members come and go does not change the fact that the United States exists, and continues to exist, over many decades. In fact, international relations would be impossible if this continuity were denied.

This fact necessitates *two* levels of analysis. At the level of rationality, we need to evaluate whether the nation is acting rationally when it follows through on certain commitments when it has already accrued the benefits. From this perspective, we evaluate the ideas that we previously explored in this chapter. What is the nation's long-term plan? Will the plan make the nation's life go better overall? If yes, then the follow-through action is rationally justified, based on the large-chunk theory of rationality discussed in this chapter. However, at the internal level, the nation must be morally sensitive to questions of distribution. If a nation's plan makes the life of the nation go better overall, this does not end the analysis. A nation that is committed to internal fairness must account for situations where one set of citizens bears the burdens and another set of citizens accrues the benefits. In such situations, internal movements of goods may be necessary to compensate one group for their sacrifices. An obvious example is military service. Although the military conducts actions in the name of the state, its burdens are often disproportionately borne by one group (its service members). But this problem of distribution does not change the fact that the national action is collective in nature and ought to be rationally justified at the collective level.

Now for the final push of the argument. When a nation acts in accordance with a rational plan, it makes promises with other nations in order to induce their cooperation. Once that cooperation is received, the nation must decide whether it should follow through on its promises that it originally gave in order to induce its partners to cooperate. Some of these arrangements might be formalized either in treaty law or in rules of customary international law. The large-chunk theory of rationality suggests that the decision about following through on these promises must be made in conjunction with the overall plan: the action is rationally justified if, and only if, it is part of a *plan* that makes the life of the nation go better overall. These plans might require following through on promises even if the nation has already received the benefits.

The New Realists make the mistake of thinking that following through on these promises is merely a question of rational action. First, they think that states often fail to follow through on these promises because it is not in their interest to do so. Second, they think that even if states *do* follow through on these promises, they are doing so out of rational self-interest, not a sense of legal obligation. Consequently, their actions cannot give rise to international law. But they are wrong on both fronts. They are wrong on the first point because states acting out of rational self-interest should follow through on their commitments. They should do so when the follow-through is one part of a plan that makes the state's life go better overall. More important, though, they are also wrong on the second point. When states follow through and fulfill their promises, they are doing more than just acting out of self-interest. They are also acting out of a sense of obligation, because obligation and rational self-interest coincide.

Some might deny that obligation and self-interest coincide at the level of individual morality, but I think it is foolhardy to deny it at the level of international relations. The obligations created by international law are not antithetical to rational self-interest. Rather, the obligations of international law are what emerges from self-interest. How can this be so?

Go back to the various devices that a rational agent might use to ensure that he follows through on his commitments. He might take a pill, or he might build some sort of machine. These were all fanciful thought experiments designed to imagine scenarios where an individual tries to constrain himself in order to avoid myopic defection and stick with an overall rational plan that has tangible benefits.

Law is precisely one such mechanism. It is not a machine or a pill, but it is a complex organism that in many ways is far more effective than a machine.[94] We often assume that law constrains our partners. So if I sign a contract with you, the law provides me with security that you will perform your side of the contract. If you do not, I can sue you for breach of contract. That gives me confidence to enter into the bargain. However, it is often less understood that law works in reverse as well. The law constrains *me*, so that if I sign a contract, the law will ensure that I refrain from myopic defection. The law helps ensure that I take the long view of rationality. Moreover, the law communicates this to my partners. It provides assurance not just to me but to my partners that I will avoid myopic defection. That is what gives my cooperative partners confidence that I will follow through on my commitments. In that sense, every one is better off.

International law works in a similar way. It provides a state with assurance that its cooperative partners will follow through on their commitments, and it also provides the reverse: a self-binding tool to help states avoid myopic defection that is then communicated to potential partners. Without this system, much of international relations would be impossible. The key thing to understand is that the system is built from equal parts of self-interest and obligation, coinciding beautifully in a system of legal constraints designed to maximize outcomes. Without the law, none of this would be possible. A world without international law would represent a return to the state of nature, a world where only the limited rules of natural law were in force.[95] If this happened, every state would be worse off. To avoid this disastrous possibility, states both formulate and comply with international legal norms, pursuing self-interest by reciprocally imposing obligations on themselves. This is the deep structure of international law. And this deep structure is continually ignored by the New Realists.

5 :: War as Cooperation

Critics of international law often claim that blind compliance with international law will endanger the security of the United States. Like the trade-off between civil liberties and security, there is also an implicit trade-off between compliance with international legal standards and successfully fighting terrorism or defeating our military enemies abroad. Viewed in this way, compliance with international law might be a luxury we cannot afford. If we want to truly protect our nation, we need to preserve the flexibility to ignore and violate international law. To these critics, compliance with international law is a function of naïve and dovish liberalism.

This impulse lingers in the background of much of the New Realist attack on international law. The assumption is that international law—and the impingement of sovereignty that it represents—will hamper the ability of the United States to fight its enemies. This "fear" of international law pervaded both the White House and the Justice Department in the year following the 9/11 attacks, as officials sought to keep international law at bay so as not to interfere with U.S. military and intelligence activities. In the early Bush administration, the Geneva Conventions were "quaint" but dangerous obstacles to fighting terrorists and the Taliban, who did not deserve their protection; the international law on the use of force placed undue constraints on the ability of the president to respond to emerging threats; and the prohibition against torture had to be ignored in order to stop the next ticking time bomb. This portrait suggested that international law stood in stark contrast to U.S. national security interests. That is why international law itself needed to be attacked—in the court of public opinion, in legal filings in the federal courts, and in the pages of leading law reviews.

This portrait of international law is misleading. In truth, international law is created by states and is therefore highly biased *in favor* of state interests. This is most true in the laws of war, which are incredibly weighted toward state protection and are insensitive to the interests of terrorists, insurgents, and other violent non-state actors. In the war on terror, international law is our best friend, not our worst enemy. Consequently, this chapter is an exercise in applied theory, an attempt to correct the misperceptions. Importantly, it is also an account of the law of war based on the theory of rationality outlined in prior chapters, including large-chunk rationality, the package-deal argument, and constrained maximization. Only by understanding these theoretical underpinnings can it be clear that self-interest (national security) and obligation (international law) coincide even in the laws of war. The New Realists are wrong to assume that the two are at loggerheads.

The pervasive skepticism of international law is based on a fundamental misunderstanding of the laws of war—the branch of international law most directly relevant to our conduct in the armed conflict with al-Qaeda. The simple fact is that the laws of war are already incredibly permissive—much more so than the public understands—and give the United States wide latitude in how it fights al-Qaeda and other non-state terrorist organizations. Even some legal scholars misread the laws of war, believing they are far more constraining than they actually are. In reality, the laws of war provide the United States with all the tools it needs to aggressively fight al-Qaeda and prevent that organization (and other jihadist organizations) from launching attacks that could kill innocent civilians. As such, compliance with international legal norms, whether treaty-based or customary norms, is actually to our collective benefit when it comes to the War on Terror.

Why is the law of war so biased in favor of state conduct and state interests? The key point to understand here is how international law is formed. States are the main actors responsible for the creation of international legal norms. States participate in the process of law formation by negotiating and signing treaties with other states. States also participate in the formation of customary international law by engaging in customary practices that eventually ripen into laws that are explicitly recognized by the world community, even if they are not codified in treaty instruments.[1] Finally, states also participate in the formation of binding and nonbinding resolutions from the Security Council and other U.N. bodies since only states can be recognized members of the United Nations. Consequently, the process of law formation is entirely controlled (or monopolized) by states. Non-state actors like al-Qaeda have no leverage to change the law in their favor.

In recent years, scholars have often claimed that the state monopoly over international law is weakening. It is of course true that other entities are now legitimate subjects of international law. Individuals are subjects of international law insofar as perpetrators are directly responsible for violating core prohibitions of international criminal law; they can be prosecuted and punished before international tribunals, a rare or even unheard of event generations ago.[2] Similarly, individuals are directly protected by international law insofar as individuals are the beneficiaries of human rights that obligate states to treat citizens and noncitizens alike in humane ways.[3] Finally, international organizations, such as the United Nations itself, are recognized to have international legal personality and are capable of negotiating and signing international agreements.[4] A growing movement of scholars and activists have argued that international organizations should be legally responsible under international law when their interventions go awry or when personnel (such as peacekeepers) commit war crimes or atrocities (such as rape) under the color of law.[5] However, it would be an exaggeration to conclude on this basis that states have released their monopoly on the formation of international legal norms.

In this chapter, I offer a comprehensive analysis of the law of war, explaining both its basic structure and specific content that privileges state action. Specifically, section 5.2 will analyze who can be targeted during an attack, with special attention to terrorists who fall into the conceptual cracks between combatants and civilians.

Section 5.3 will then consider whether there are geographical boundaries to armed conflict and whether the laws of war apply outside of so-called "hot" battlefield zones. Section 5.4 will then analyze the relationship between the laws of war and human rights law, ultimately expressing skepticism about recent attempts to import human rights norms into the law of armed conflict. Finally, section 5.5 will conclude with a case study regarding the concept of military necessity—the legal principles governing when it is permissible to use lethal force and when a lesser method—say capture—is legally required. The upshot of this analysis is that the laws of war allow lethal force, rather than capture, so long as the victim in question is a lawful target. In other words, the U.S. program of targeted killings is entirely consistent with the basic principles of the laws of war. Put together, this portrait shows that compliance with international law is fully consistent with the demands of state security—an outcome that is quite surprising given that international law is the ultimate outgrowth of a system of constrained maximization.

5.1 War as Cooperation

Before continuing with these tasks, however, it is important to situate this discussion within the context of the previous chapters. In particular, the last two chapters sketched out an argument that equated self-interest with legal obligations. Rational agents, when faced with pursuing their own rational self-interest, will initiate and comply with a set of reciprocal constraints that bind members of a community. A legal rule is the most formal way of codifying these constraints. Furthermore, rational agents should follow through and *comply* with these regulations, even when it appears that ignoring them might yield better payoffs. Rational agents should reject this form of myopic selection as being inconsistent with a deeper theory of rationality.

It might seem that the law of war is a particularly inapt area in which to explore this phenomenon. If ignoring the law were ever rational, one would think it would be rational in the middle of war. Why is compliance with international law a good idea when matters of life and death are at stake? Furthermore, it would seem that war leaves no room for the type of cooperation that I have described as the basis for a system of reciprocal constraints. Indeed, it would seem that war is the opposite of cooperation. To suggest otherwise would seem counterintuitive.

If we have these intuitions, they should be revised. Despite how it appears, war involves plenty of cooperation. War is a legal institution—it is a legal concept that structures the violence between belligerents and imposes norms about winners, losers, and the spoils of war. As James Whitman explains in THE VERDICT OF BATTLE, the core elements of the concept of warfare emerged at particular points in history: the idea that war takes place on a battlefield; that the belligerents represent collectives who share the benefits and burdens of victory and defeat; and that victory on the battlefield represents a decisive verdict to which the participants then adhere.[6] As Whitman explains, these elements of warfare show that the concepts of "battle" and "trial" have clear similarities: they are both contests with consequences.[7] Just as a criminal or civil trial involves a culturally and legally defined contest with rules that pick winners and losers, so too does a battle constitute a culturally and legally defined contest with specific consequences for the winners and losers. War is much more than random killing.

War also imposes constraints and rules about acceptable methods of killing. The basic contours of the normative constraints are rather simple, though the details can get complicated. Uniformed soldiers may only kill other uniformed soldiers and should spare innocent civilians.[8] Innocent civilians should never be targeted, though they might be killed as collateral damage in attacks against legitimate targets so long as the collateral damage is not disproportionate to the value of the military target.[9] Soldiers may deliberately target civilians who are voluntarily acting like soldiers by taking up arms against the enemy.[10] When killing soldiers, unnecessary suffering should be avoided; killing the adversary is permitted, but imposing suffering for the sole purpose of sadism is strictly prohibited.[11] Surrendering soldiers must be taken as prisoners and treated humanely during their captivity until the end of hostilities.[12] Although this is just a skeletal description of the *jus in bello* landscape, it fairly describes its outer contours, leaving only the details to be filled in.

So where is the cooperation? Belligerents cooperate by following the rules of the game, by agreeing to conduct warfare within a system of moral or legal constraints. Following our previous discussion of constrained maximizers, rational agents are motivated by self-interest to accept a system of normative constraints on their behavior because a system of constrained behavior benefits everyone. This is especially true when it comes to warfare. Long ago, states recognized that so-called *unlimited* war was dangerous and to no one's benefit.[13] Consequently, the participants developed a system of ethical constraints on warfare (based on principles of chivalry) that limited how and when warfare could be conducted.[14] Most important, this system of constraint was supported by rational self-interest. Obeying the rules of warfare, even if doing so constrained one's conduct, was rationally beneficial because the alternative—total killing without limitation—was worse for all sides. As demonstrated in chapter four, rational self-interest supports both the implementation of the norm and the inevitable follow-through in the form of compliance with the rule.

It still might be strange to think of belligerents in a battle as "cooperating" with each other. But this result is inevitable once you recognize that a game is nothing more than following a set of rules in a contest—which is precisely the definition of a battle (although it is a deadly game).[15] An analogy might be helpful to cash out the intuition. Consider *People v. Russell*, a New York case that went all the way to the state's highest court.[16] On December 17, 1992, a group of individuals engaged in a gun battle in a housing project in the Red Hook neighborhood in Brooklyn.[17] During the battle, an innocent bystander—a public school principal—was hit by one of the bullets and died. Because the forensic evidence could not conclusively determine which defendant fired the fatal shot, they were all charged with second-degree murder (requiring that they acted with depraved indifference to human life).

The defendants were convicted based on the theory that they could all be considered accomplices. Although it was unclear who fired the fatal shot and deserved to be labeled the main perpetrator, such a determination was unnecessary.[18] Since each defendant met the mental element required for complicity (recklessness), they could be convicted as accomplices. However, there was one potential obstacle to this legal theory: accomplices must share a "community of purpose" when they work together to bring a criminal transaction to fruition.[19] How could the court link the defendants (who were firing bullets at *each other*) together through a community of purpose? In fact, it appeared that the defendants demonstrated the exact opposite of a community of purpose—they were trying to kill each other and by definition working at cross-purposes.[20]

The New York state court of appeals reasoned otherwise. They concluded that the defendants had tacitly agreed with each other to engage in the gun battle: "Indeed, unlike an unanticipated ambush or spontaneous attack that might have taken defendants by surprise, the gunfight in this case only began after defendants acknowledged and accepted each other's challenge to engage in a deadly battle on a public concourse."[21] In short, the defendants agreed to face each other in a gun battle, and without the other individuals' participation in the battle, there would be no "game" at all. Reasoning by analogy from prior cases that allowed the same legal theory in drag races that resulted in deadly crashes that killed innocent bystanders, the court concluded that there was a "community of interest" between the defendants in the Red Hook gun battle.[22] Their common interest was in the playing of the game (which requires cooperation), even though each person was trying to win the game (which defies cooperation).

To understand the point, you need to separate out two levels of potential cooperation. The first level involves cooperation in the decision to play the game—an understanding that requires at least some basic agreement, whether implicit or explicit, about the rules applicable to the game at hand. Without this cooperation, no contest can get underway. In this sense, there is always a thin "community of interest" between players of a game, even if they are working to defeat each other. Then there is cooperation that is internal to the game itself. Such cooperation only emerges if players are working in tandem on the same side in the game. This only happens if the two participants have the same, or consistent, objectives with regard to the game, as might be the case if two players in a game join together to fight a common enemy. In such cases, there is a thick community of interest between the co-participants who are fighting on the same side—they are working together to collectively win the game.

It does not matter whether you accept the "community of purpose" argument in *People v. Russell*. The court's use of the argument might have stretched to the breaking point the concept of "community of interest" as applied to accomplice liability. Nonetheless, the idea retains its salience in cases that have nothing to do with the criminal law, such as the concept of war. In that situation, the participants cooperate to engage in a contest with a set of normative constraints regarding acceptable behavior, and also agree to abide by the "verdict of battle." At a deeper level, of course, the participants work at cross purposes with each other, hoping to win the war by killing as many of the enemy as possible. But this should not obscure the fact that belligerents are cooperating with each other by agreeing to the normative constraints of modern warfare (as opposed to unrestricted killing).

One might object that some belligerents refuse to follow the rules of warfare, either because they do not care about the underlying principles of chivalry or because they are simply desperate to win. In these situations, one wonders if there is a sufficient community of interest between the belligerents since one of them refuses to follow the norms of restricted warfare. If cooperating in playing the game requires the following of rules, then it would appear that they are playing different games.

The key point here is that some rules in the law of war are reciprocal while others are not. The reciprocal rules apply only when both sides of the conflict are obeying them; if one side stops following the rules, the other side is released from its obligation to adhere to the norm.[23] In contrast, nonreciprocal rules are universal and apply regardless of whether the opponent is complying or not. The classic example of a universal, nonreciprocal rule is the entire category of rules that protect innocent civilians.[24] Just because your enemy is executing civilians—which constitutes a war crime—doesn't mean that you can start killing civilians too.

How then should belligerents handle situations where the enemy refuses to follow the rules? The traditional response has been to use reprisals to sanction an enemy who violated the rules, with the hope that the sanction would induce compliance in the future.[25] Consider an enemy who refuses to recognize that captured soldiers are entitled to humane treatment and status as prisoners of war, and instead simply executes them. This is a clear violation of the law of war. In order to pressure them into compliance, the other side might take the same number of captured soldiers and execute them, thereby sending the message: if you continue executing your prisoners, we will continue executing ours. So think twice before you violate the law of war. There will be consequences.

Traditionally, there were limits to what states could do under the rubric of reprisals.[26] Killing enemy soldiers, even captured ones, was considered acceptable under the law of reprisals (in order to save one's own soldiers at risk from future violations), but disproportionate reprisals were considered illegitimate. Today, however, the general assumption is that reprisals are no longer acceptable at all, though the law is generally unclear on the matter.[27] The recent rise of international criminal tribunals, and the possibility of ex post enforcement of law of war violations, has sparked many human rights lawyers to suggest that the need for self-help enforcement (taking matters into your own hands in the absence of an authority figure) in the form of reprisals is no longer necessary.[28] And the case law of the ad hoc tribunals certainly supports the view that reprisals against civilians are no longer acceptable under international law.[29] However, the evidence of actual law on this point is controversial.[30] Although the Additional Protocol I (API) to the Geneva Convention includes a prohibition on making civilians the object of reprisals, the United States is not a party to the Additional Protocol and has publicly stated that it does not adhere to a total ban on civilian reprisals.[31] Similarly, although Britain is a party to API, it included a reservation at the time of signing indicating that it would not be bound by a total ban on reprisals.[32] Furthermore, some countries (including Iran and Iraq) have resorted to civilian reprisals in recent conflicts, thus casting some doubt on whether the rule has ripened into customary law.[33]

The important point is that the law already has, built in at the ground level, a consideration for how to deal with noncompliant partners. Just because some participants do not follow *all of the rules* of the game does not mean that the participants are not playing the same game. Indeed, violations of some rules only count as violations if they are viewed against a general background of rule following—so the violations are understood as exceptions that demonstrate the existence of the general rule.

Now consider the armed conflict with al-Qaeda, the current example where the adversary does not follow the rules of armed conflict. The major failure of al-Qaeda is their refusal to recognize that civilians are not appropriate objects of attack. One might argue that this means that al-Qaeda is not cooperating in playing the game in the same way that the participants in the Red Hook gun battle were "cooperating" with each other.

The key point to understand is that the laws of war are multilateral in nature. It is not as if the United States constructs particular rules of warfare for its allies and then uses different rules of warfare for its enemies. Rather, the rules of warfare are, in part, constitutive of war itself—a concept that entails the distinction between belligerents and civilians, methods of warfare, and the notion that the population advances and retrogrades with their army on the field (and to the victor go the spoils).[34] This concept of warfare is widely shared in contemporary society, and most states accept almost all of the specific legal prohibitions that go along with the concept of war.

In instances where a state faces an enemy—either another state or a non-state terrorist organization—that refuses to follow the conventions of warfare, the state indeed faces a quandary about how to induce compliance. It can resort to reprisals, nonmilitary sanctions, or public opprobrium in the court of world opinion (in decreasing order of severity). However, none of this changes the fact that the conventions of warfare emerged from a widely shared intuition among the military powers that they should cooperate to reduce the worst horrors of war by redefining what it meant to engage in modern warfare.[35] This "cooperation" required that states forgo certain strategies, even as they were attempting to kill each other, based on the self-interested calculation that a world with legally regulated warfare was better than a world with unrestricted warfare. War, just like any other activity, benefits from constrained behavior.

5.2 Who Can Be Targeted? Combatants, Civilians, and CCFers

We now turn to the specific prohibitions embodied by the law of war in an effort to understand how even the constrained concept of warfare is nonetheless incredibly permissive and far less progressive than many assume. In this respect, the cornerstone of the law of war is the principle of distinction, or the idea that attacking forces can only aim at legitimate targets—combatants—while civilians are protected from intentional attack. However, there are two major exceptions that substantially weaken the force of the principle of distinction.

The first is the principle of proportionality. Under this doctrine, collateral damage against civilians is acceptable, just so long as the number of civilian deaths is not disproportionate to the value of the military target.[36] The principle is simple in theory but notoriously difficult to apply to particular fact patterns. Say an attacking force launches an attack against an apartment building used by armed militants to launch attacks. Unfortunately there are also civilians located in the building; it is, after all, an apartment complex. The attacking force decides to launch a missile at the building, killing ten armed militants but also killing twenty innocent civilians. At first glance, this might appear disproportionate because twenty innocent civilians were killed in order to neutralize ten legitimate targets—a smaller number by half. But this is the wrong calculation. The question is whether the killing of the twenty innocent civilians is disproportionate to the *value* of the military target. Although it is difficult to quantify military value and there are competing formulations of what "military value" means, it seems relatively clear that the relevant question is how much damage the ten armed militants will inflict on the attacking force. If the ten armed militants are holding an advantageous position, launching attacks that might kill twenty or thirty or even fifty soldiers, then the twenty collateral deaths no longer seem so disproportionate.

Much of this involves counterfactual thinking, which is one reason that collateral damage arguments are so controversial.[37] How much damage would the militants have inflicted had they survived? Of course, the answer is in many ways pure speculation since the militants *were* killed. The analysis seems to require the positing of an alternate universe, one where the militants are left alone and we calculate the damage they are able to accomplish with their military position. But this possible-world thought experiment is difficult to refute with empirical evidence.

Determinations of military value become even more difficult when the attacking force directs its fire at an installation rather than at specific combatants. Consider a munitions factory or a military telecommunications relay station. Destroying these installations might result in collateral damage to civilians, but the principle of proportionality requires that we ask how the war would have unfolded without these installations. How much would the enemy's fighting capacity be degraded by destroying the telecommunications station? Answering that question depends on knowing how second-best strategies are deployed when installations are destroyed and how successful those second-best strategies are likely to be.

Unfortunately, there is little case law on the concept of proportionality because the international tribunals never convict anyone of launching disproportionate attacks against civilian targets.[38] The reason is relatively simple. The rule of proportionality only applies if the attacking force is targeting combatants but also happens to kill innocent civilians. If the attacking force intentionally targets the civilians, then the rule of proportionality is irrelevant. The attacking force has violated the principle of distinction and has perpetrated a war crime. The analysis stops there.

International tribunals have been content to prosecute defendants for intentionally targeting civilians because the prosecutors (and the judges) take a very liberal approach to the concept of "intent."[39] Consider the same hypothetical from before: a military operation against an apartment complex that contains armed fighters and some innocent civilians. Even though the attacking force is aware that innocent civilians are in the building, their purpose in launching the attack is to kill the armed militants inside. The fact that innocent civilians are also killed is a regrettable consequence, though certainly a foreseeable one. At first glance, this seems like precisely the type of case that ought to be handled under the principle of proportionality because the attack is not intentionally directed against the civilians.

However, lawyers trained in civil law jurisdictions operate with a different definition of "intent." For them, intent certainly includes cases where an individual acts with purpose to achieve a particular result, for example, when a soldier shoots a particular individual with the desire to kill him.[40] Second, intent also includes cases of acting with knowledge, say, where a soldier is aware of the consequences of his action, though that consequence is not the motivating factor behind his action and not the reason why he did it.[41] Third, intent even includes cases of acting with recklessness, where the defendant is aware of the possibility of a particular result but decides to forge ahead with the plan anyway.[42] This third theory, often called *dolus eventualis* in many legal systems, involves liability for risk-taking behavior.[43] American lawyers would describe this as a case of recklessness and would never classify it as a type of intent.[44] In contrast, many European lawyers classify *dolus eventualis* as the lowest form of "intent," even though that liberal classification makes no sense from a common law perspective.[45] Common law trained lawyers view *dolus eventualis* and recklessness (liability for risky behavior that might produce injury) as the opposite of intentional conduct (such as deliberately murdering someone).

In the context of collateral damage, some international courts have concluded that soldiers are guilty of intentionally targeting civilians if they launch an attack against a building knowing of the possibility that civilians are inside.[46] For this reason, they do not need to consider whether the collateral damage is disproportionate or not. The principle of disproportionality only applies to lawful attacks; the cases prosecuted at the tribunal involve "violations" of the principle of distinction. That is the major reason international courts have not issued many opinions on what counts as disproportionate collateral damage. With a sufficiently expansive reading of the concept of intent and, by extension, of the principle of distinction, international prosecutors do not need to rely on the principle of proportionality, even though it is a cornerstone of the law of war.

These cases are probably wrongly decided because they turn the law of targeting on its head. The law of war gives attacking forces a huge advantage, allowing them to kill combatants and even civilians as collateral damage. The legal rules are weighted heavily in favor of permitting military attacks rather than restricting them. Even knowingly killing civilians is OK so long as they are collateral damage to a lawful military strike. Military ethicists refer to this as the doctrine of double effect—a moral principle that was first elucidated by Thomas Aquinas.[47] In short, it permits an agent to engage in beneficial conduct that has negative consequences—so long as those consequences are not intended by the agent and are not disproportionate to the intended benefit.[48] It has many applications to normal life (including all cases of self-defense), but the principles of distinction and proportionality in the law of war are among the most famous applications of the doctrine of double effect.[49]

The second major exception to the principle of distinction— though it may not be fair to classify it as an exception per se—is the rule that allows attacking forces to target civilians who take up arms and participate in hostilities.[50] This exception seems logical, because otherwise, enemy forces would have no incentive to organize themselves into a fighting force wearing uniforms. Instead they could simply engage in combat as civilians and retain the protection of civilian status. This result would undermine the very structure of the law of war. Civilians would fire at soldiers, who would be prohibited from firing back. Consequently, the law of war permits attacking forces to target regular combatants as well as civilians "directly participating in hostilities" (DPH).[51]

The rule allowing the targeting of DPHers is now of immense importance in the armed conflict with al-Qaeda. There has always been uncertainty about how to place terrorists within the basic categories of the law of war: civilians and combatants. In a sense, terrorists fall between the cracks of these two concepts, neither pure innocent civilians nor regular combatants. And the fate of al-Qaeda terrorists is no different; as they prepare and execute attacks, they operate as combatants. But in between these attacks, they lay fallow, blending into regular society as would-be civilians.

Many states, not just the United States, are concerned with the threat of terrorism. Consequently, when the major world powers came together to negotiate Additional Protocol I to the Geneva Conventions, the status of terrorists and irregular guerrilla fighters was a widespread concern among the negotiators. The final result was a provision (article 51) that allowed attacking forces to target civilians for such time as they are directly participating in hostilities. Although the United States is not a party to the Additional Protocol, this provision is largely considered emblematic of the customary norm.[52]

Unfortunately, the codification of the norm in API raises as many questions as it answers. First, how long does the "for such time" standard last? It clearly represents a temporal standard, that is, a civilian is only targetable when he is participating in hostilities—not before or after.[53] But if a terrorist fires a weapon and then stops firing, does that mean he is no longer participating in hostilities?[54] How quickly does the DPH status evaporate?

Even more troubling, how does one define *direct* participation in hostilities, as opposed to indirect participation in hostilities?[55] The use of the qualification suggests that there are at least two categories of participation and that only the direct variety opens up the participant to legitimate targeting. Experts are in a constant state of disagreement about this.[56] Everyone agrees that when a terrorist is firing a weapon, he is directly participating in hostilities, but after that the agreement ends. A broad view would include preparations for a terrorist attack, such as designing and building a bomb, in addition to actually carrying out the attack.[57] The broadest view possible might also include support services such as laundering money—acts that are essential for the success of the terrorist attack, although of questionable directness.[58] The narrowest view would limit participation in hostilities to the actual execution of the attack, such as the firing of the weapon or the triggering of the suicide vest. Not surprising, most states have official policies in their military manuals that reject the narrow view.[59]

Since the Additional Protocol was drafted, states have expressed concern that the provision does not give traditional armies enough leeway to fight terrorists and other civilian participants in war. In 2003, the International Committee of the Red Cross (ICRC) convened an expert working group to offer scholarly guidance on what constitutes direct participation in hostilities.[60] The meetings were contentious and controversial, and ultimately, the ICRC issued the report on its own without the signatures of the experts.[61]

One proposal that emerged from the ICRC process was a new standard to address the targetability of civilians in warfare. In particular, some states were concerned that non-state actors with armed organizations (like al-Qaeda) were getting preferential treatment under the law. Regular soldiers fighting for state armies were subject to being killed at any time, while fighters in non-state armed organizations could only be killed while they were engaged in hostilities. The asymmetry gave non-state actors a crucial (and arguably unfair) advantage in warfare.[62]

In order to rectify this unfairness, some participants suggested that non-state actors with military organizations should be treated in the same manner as regular armies, in the sense that they could be targeted at any time.[63] Gone would be the temporal requirement embodied in the "for such time" language of the Additional Protocol. The language used to express this standard was that civilians who exercise a "continuous combat function" (CCF) in a non-state military organization are targetable at any time, not just when they are participating in hostilities.[64] (Some military lawyers refer to these targets as CCFers.) This arguably puts al-Qaeda fighters and traditional army soldiers on equal footing.[65]

Of course, the CCF standard came after the Additional Protocol was drafted, and therefore the new standard is not embodied in any treaty or multilateral convention. However, it is widely considered to be emblematic of an emerging norm of customary international law, though it remains controversial.[66] Either way, it has substantial support among a wide cross section of states. It does not, however, solve every problem since it requires a definition of what counts as engaging in a "continuous" combat function. Clearly, an infantry soldier for al-Qaeda is engaged in a continuous combat function because that individual is the functional equivalent of a rifleman in a traditional army. But what about a cook who also happens to have received training in how to fire a rifle?[67] In one sense, a cook does not intuitively sound like the type of occupation that should be considered as a continuous combat function. However, if the underlying principle is one of symmetry, it should be noted that uniformed cooks in the U.S. Army are subject to lawful attack at any moment in time.[68] The rationale for their lawful targeting stems from the fact that even cooks graduate through basic training and receive introductory instruction in the firing of a weapon—a skill they rarely use but are capable of deploying in crisis situations. Perhaps the same could be said of an al-Qaeda cook?[69]

In trying to sort out these difficulties, U.S. courts have invoked the concept of "functional membership"—a variant of formal membership criteria that are traditionally based on wearing a uniform and being an official employee of the armed services.[70] Instead, functional membership criteria look to whether the individual is part of a chain of command and participates in the giving or taking of orders, thus establishing that he is a functional member of a non-state organization's military wing.[71] Formal membership criteria are inapplicable to non-state military groups because their members often wear civilian clothing and do not wear fixed emblems identifying their membership in the organization.[72] In application, the functional membership standard allows a court to determine whether someone is a continuous combat fighter in a non-state military organization by determining whether the individual is part of that military organization's chain of command.

In theory, the CCF exception constitutes wide support for the U.S. program of targeted killings against al-Qaeda militants. If the militants are continuous combat fighters, giving and taking orders in the chain of command of a military organization, then they are subject to attack at any moment in time, just like a uniformed member of a regular army.[73] (If the targets are not continuous combat fighters, then the attacks are probably illegal). These attacks could include a missile fired from a drone flying in Yemen or the tribal regions of Afghanistan and Pakistan. Despite the intensity of criticism from human rights lawyers and other activists, the

U.S. program of targeted killings is justified by basic principles of the law of war. Furthermore, it should come as no surprise that the law of war allows for such actions, because the law of war is substantially weighted toward state interests since it states themselves that create the law of war through the negotiation of treaty provisions and the development of customary norms through state practice.[74]

5.3 Geographical Constraints on Armed Conflict

The first thing to understand about the law of war is that it has two functions: a licensing function and a regulating function.[75] The licensing function transforms what would otherwise be an unlawful killing (under peacetime law) to a perfectly lawful killing (under the law of war) so long as the target is a legitimate target. This alchemic transformation is one of the most important but least understood aspects of the law of war—how it radically reorients the basic principles of killing from a broad prohibition under normal circumstances to a broad permission under the exigent circumstances of war. During war, soldiers may kill other soldiers with absolute impunity, provided they follow the more specific rules about means and methods of attacks. The regulating function of the law of war involves the elucidation, either in custom or treaty codification, of these specific prohibitions, including the prohibition against perfidy, the principles of distinction and proportionality, and the ban on weapons that cause needless suffering.

Legal scholars often focus exclusively on the regulating function, debating the specific meaning of the prohibitions, applying them to new weapons systems, debating whether particular customs have crystallized into norms of customary international law, and deciding whether violations of those norms constitute breaches of the law or constitute changes in the relevant customary norms. However, all of this ignores the licensing function and the fact that the law of war serves a radically permissive function: to legally sanction the killing of other human beings. Consequently, lawyers often have deeply conflicted feelings about the law of war. Some view it as the greatest achievement of international law, providing regulation and constraint to conduct that was previously lawless (the regulating function), while others view it with suspicion as the legal code that sanctions the worst murderous impulses of human beings.[76]

One can see this dichotomy playing out in the competing approaches to the geography of armed conflict. Traditionally, the international criminal tribunals have taken an expansive reading of the geography of armed conflict. They have consistently rejected arguments based on the so-called "hot" battlefield, or the idea that the laws of war are only applicable on a narrowly construed battlefield. In particular, the ICTY crafted a standard that defined an armed conflict based on the scope and intensity of fighting, though it rejected attempts by defense attorneys to cast these terms in a narrow light.[77] Rather, the judges at the ICTY concluded that the law of war was to be understood as broadly as possible.[78]

One can readily understand the motivation of the ICTY judges in construing the geography of armed conflict as broadly as possible. If the law of war does not apply during a particular interaction, then the defendants cannot be convicted for violating the laws of war. In other words, if there is no war, there is no war *crime*.[79] Although genocide and crimes against humanity do not require a nexus with an armed conflict, war crimes still require this nexus, and necessarily so. For this reason, international tribunals have generally promoted the expansion of the geography of armed conflict, and with it the expansion of war crimes law. In so doing, they are mostly concerned with the regulatory function of the law of war—a salutary development that in their view ought to be expanded.[80]

On the other hand, human rights activists and lawyers have the opposite motivation. They seek to constrain the geography of armed conflict because they view the law of war that comes along with it as morally disastrous.[81] It changes the legal baseline regarding killing. Human rights law (and domestic criminal law), which reigns supreme during times of peace, prohibits the killing of human beings (absent exigent circumstances such as self-defense). The law of armed conflict changes the basic presumption against killing, defining most killings in armed conflict as essentially lawful. For this reason alone, according to them, the law of war should be tightly policed, limited to discrete areas of time and space so as not to radically increase the licensing function that comes along with the law of war. Essentially, every expansion of the law of war comes with a price: the contraction of human rights law.[82]

This leads them to specific arguments in favor of a confined definition of armed conflict. The most notable variant is the "hot" battlefield argument.[83] Activists have deployed it with renewed vigor to argue that the United States violated the laws of war when it launched predator drones against al-Qaeda militants.[84] In short, the argument suggests that the attacks take place far away from any identified hot battlefield with intense fighting, thus displacing the law of war and its licensing function and bringing these attacks under the regulation of the much less permissive human rights law.[85]

In some cases, these arguments might have merit. But in most situations, they are vastly overstated. In Yemen, where the United States has launched strikes against al-Qaeda in the Arabian Peninsula (AQAP), the Yemeni government is fighting a protracted and intense civil war against Islamic extremists bent on toppling the government.[86] It is therefore most likely that the law of war applies to this conflict.[87] Also, it is undeniable that an armed conflict existed in Afghanistan, given the fighting by al-Qaeda and Taliban fighters against the central government there.[88] As such, drone strikes in Afghanistan took place during armed conflict and are governed by the law of war. Finally, even the tribal regions of Pakistan are arguably the site of armed conflict since the Pakistani Taliban and al-Qaeda militants continue to use that area as a launching pad against the Pakistan government.[89]

Human rights lawyers often resist this conclusion and argue that these territories are not subject to the law of armed conflict. As legal support for this argument, they often cite the International Criminal Tribunal for the Former Yugoslavia (ICTY) precedents that first defined the concept of armed conflict. Starting first with the famous *Tadić* case, these cases defined armed conflict based on the "scope and intensity" of armed violence in a particular area.[90] Critics of the drone strike then seek to apply this standard to Yemen or Pakistan and argue that the violence in these areas was of insufficient scope and intensity to qualify as an armed conflict.[91] However, these arguments completely misstate the holding—and spirit—in *Tadić*, which was based on the idea that the law of war should be construed as broadly as possible.[92] In fact, the ICTY in *Tadić* flatly rejected a defense attempt to foreclose war crimes jurisdiction because there was insufficient violence in the area where the alleged crimes occurred. In arguing that the law of war applied in a much broader area, the court concluded that "geographical and temporal frame of reference for internal armed conflicts is similarly broad . . . [because Common Article 3 applies] outside the narrow geographical context of the actual theatre of combat operations."[93] Consequently, the *Tadić* case actually stands for the opposite conclusion because it *rejected* the hot battlefield argument.

Critics of drone strikes sometimes make factual assertions that undermine the legal foundations of their arguments. For example, it is sometimes asserted that the United States is operating drones in areas where there is no armed conflict because the scope and intensity of fighting is too low. Then the critics decry the number of civilian casualties caused by the strikes, suggesting that thousands of innocent civilians are being killed on a regular basis by the aerial strikes.[94] This factual claim, while politically powerful, actually undermines the legal argument, because it belies the claim that the scope and intensity of the fighting is too low. The relevant scope of violence is not the fighting performed by the enemy; it is the total amount of fighting in the area.[95] Consequently, the U.S. deployment of drones in the area and the killings that result from them actually support the legal conclusion that the United States is engaged in an armed conflict in that area.

Critics of drone strikes also argue that a restricted geography of armed conflict is implicit in the notion of a non-international armed conflict. Under this view, the law of war operates differently, depending on whether we are considering an international armed conflict (between states) or a non-international armed conflict (either a civil war or an armed conflict with a non-state actor). For international armed conflicts, the law of war applies during engagements with the parties to the conflict, wherever they are found. But non-international armed conflicts are geographically bounded. As legal support for this argument, drone critics sometimes cite Common Article 3 of the Geneva Convention, which says that the

Convention applies to "armed conflicts not of an international character occurring in the territory of one of the High Contracting Parties."[96]

This represents a mistaken reading of Common Article 3 because it assumes that Common Article 3 was trying to define non-international armed conflicts. Under this view, since U.S. actions in Yemen or Pakistan take place outside the territory of the United States, it cannot be a non-international conflict. Consequently, the law of war does not apply to these drone strikes. However, this argument certainly fails because Common Article 3 is not an attempt to define non-international armed conflicts per se. Rather, it is an attempt to regulate certain non-international armed conflicts, that is, internal conflicts (civil wars) that take place solely on the territory of a contracting party and to which the Geneva protections then apply.[97] For other non-international armed conflicts, including the armed conflict against al-Qaeda, the customary norms of the law of war apply (which mirror the content of Common Article 3).

In fact, there are good reasons to reject the geographic conception of armed conflict entirely.[98] First, it should be noted that when the ICTY announced in *Tadić* the "scope and intensity" geographical standard for defining armed conflict, it did so without reliance on a particular source of law for this legal proposition.[99] It was, in short, an exercise in legal theory—a sui generis attempt to explain where and when the law of armed conflict applied. In that respect, it ushered in an interesting legal experiment, but it should not be exaggerated as indicative of a long-standing legal standard with deep roots in the history of warfare.

Second, the geographic conception of warfare is parasitic upon a deeper conceptual framework: the distinction between international armed conflicts (IACs) and non-international armed conflicts (NIACs). Traditionally, international armed conflicts were defined as armed conflicts between nation-states—placing the participants in a legally recognized state of war under international law that triggered a host of consequences, including the constraints of *jus in bello* between the states, as well as the international rules of neutrality with regard to third-party states.[100] But, non-international armed conflicts are more complicated to define. On one view, they are mere internal conflicts that do not cross international boundaries: rebellions, civil wars, and insurrections that pit government forces against rebels who have placed themselves in a state of belligerency against their own government.[101] Scholars who adopt this definition of NIACs are often led, conceptually, to accept the geographical conception of warfare since NIACs, under this definition, are geographically constrained to the territory of the government that is fighting the rebels. According to this view, the law of war only applies on the territory of the government fighting the rebels, not extraterritorially.

But this is not the only definition of NIACs, nor is it the correct one. As Justice Stevens recognized in *Hamdan v. Rumsfeld*, the Geneva Conventions refer to conflicts "not of an international character"—an expression that suggests that NIACs include all armed conflicts that do not fall into the category IACs, regardless of whether they are geographically limited to government territory.[102] Since Justice Stevens concluded that the U.S. armed conflict with al-Qaeda was an armed conflict "not of an international character"—because it was not an armed conflict between two nation-states—the Court in *Hamdan* then concluded that Common Article 3 of the Geneva Conventions applied to U.S. conduct in the War on Terror.[103]

At the time of the decision, the *Hamdan* holding was viewed as a great win for international lawyers and as a sharp rebuke to the Bush administration's legal position.[104] That was because the decision stated that the U.S. military was constrained by the laws of war in how it dealt with al-Qaeda fighters. United States soldiers were constrained by the ban on torture codified in Common Article 3, and the U.S. government was also constrained by Common Article 3 in the creation of its military commissions. Trials of enemy fighters needed to meet the international standards expressed in Common Article 3. The War on Terror was not lawless; it was, by contrast, bounded by the law of war. In this respect, the *Hamdan* decision was rightfully regarded as historic.

Although the *Hamdan* decision was treated at the time as a reprimand to the Bush administration, some human rights lawyers have come to view the decision with skepticism and regret.[105] While the *Hamdan* decision imposed the law's regulatory framework on government conduct in the armed conflict with al-Qaeda, it also, by definition, brought with it the licensing function of the law of war framework, too. Since the law of war paradigm applies to the armed conflict with al-Qaeda, U.S. military forces are permitted to kill, with impunity, enemy al-Qaeda operatives who are legitimate targets under the law of war. In other words, there is a straight line to be drawn from the *Hamdan* decision to the U.S. policy of targeted killings of al-Qaeda fighters. Since *Hamdan* declared that the law of war applied to the armed conflict with al-Qaeda, all of the permissive aspects of the law of war applied as well. This provides the conceptual foundation for drone strikes wherever al-Qaeda forces are operating, until al-Qaeda is so degraded that it is incapable of being a party to an armed conflict (launching attacks).

What did the human rights lawyers want instead? Some human rights lawyers would have preferred the opposite result: a holding that denied that the law of war applied to the war against al-Qaeda. Although this would have denied the regulatory aspects of the law of war to the conflict, it would also have denied the licensing function (the permission to kill). And in the absence of the law of war, human rights lawyers insist that U.S. conduct would be governed by international human rights law, which prohibits the killing of individuals without due process.[106] Targeted killings would be illegal. Ironically, *Hamdan*'s application of the law of war to the armed conflict with al-Qaeda has proven to be disastrous, according to some human rights lawyers.

This shows how much human rights lawyers have changed their thinking in the last ten years. Initially, critics of the Bush administration were happy with the result that the law of war constrained the government's conduct. At the very least, this ended the absurd assumption of the Bush administration that the executive's conduct in wartime was unconstrained by Congress, by the courts, and by international law. In this sense, the Supreme Court's decisions in *Hamdan*, *Hamdi*, and *Rasul* are to be celebrated.[107] However, over time, some critics of the United States have altered their opinion, now arguing that the law of war should not apply at all to the armed conflict against terrorists. That school of thought instead believes that the far more restrictive international human rights law paradigm should govern the conflict. This change in position was motivated by the recognition that the law of war is, despite first impressions, rather permissive in the type of killing it permits. While military lawyers have long understood this, it has taken human rights lawyers some time to reach this realization.

The insistence that human rights law should govern the armed conflict with al-Qaeda is ultimately unconvincing. The armed conflict is transnational in scope, and it constitutes an armed conflict because the parties to the conflict (the United States and al-Qaeda) meet the functional criteria required for engaging in combatancy: both parties are capable of launching wide-scale attacks; both parties are organized with a hierarchical command structure (though not necessarily with a linear hierarchy); and both are organizationally capable of complying with the laws of war if they choose to do so (though al-Qaeda refuses to recognize the principle of distinction).[108] As such, al-Qaeda and the United States meet each other as co-equal belligerents wherever they find each other, subject to the reciprocal risk of killing and entitled to the privilege of combatancy and immunity from prosecution if they comply with the requirements of belligerency under the law of war.[109] At some point in the future, if al-Qaeda's operations are sufficiently degraded so that it is unable to meet these functional standards, it will no longer be a party to an armed conflict with the United States, and the law of war (with both its regulatory and licensing functions) will no longer apply to U.S. operations against al-Qaeda.[110] Although this time has not yet come, Obama administration officials have already predicted this eventuality and have insisted that the government needs to plan, both legally and strategically, for how its operations will change once the war is over.[111]

5.4 Co-Applying the Laws of War with Human Rights

There is another avenue for human rights lawyers to inject the norms of human rights law into the armed conflict with al-Qaeda. But this avenue is no less modest than the previous attempt. Under this new argument, human rights law and the law of war can be co-applied at the same time.[112] Instead of viewing the two legal regimes as mutually exclusive paradigms—one applicable during armed conflict and the other applicable at all other times—the co-application view suggests that human rights law is universal and applies at all times. The law of war would then be an overlay that imposes additional constraints during times of armed conflict, though the ever-present constraints of human rights law continue unabated.

What is to be gained from the co-application thesis? For the human rights lawyer, the co-application thesis allows the importation of basic principles of human rights, such as due process and the prohibition against arbitrary deprivation of life. European human rights tribunals, tasked with elucidating and applying the European Court of Human Rights (ECHR), have recently rendered decisions that, on their face, apply in situations of armed conflict, thus giving fuel to the co-application thesis.[113] The practical upshot of this view is that the armed conflict with al-Qaeda might be governed by the restrictions of the law of war and international human rights law *at the very same time*. While drone strikes against legitimate targets are perfectly compatible with the law of war, they may violate the more restrictive norms of human rights law, which, in general, track the peacetime criminal justice process: detention, followed by trial under due process of law, ending in lawful punishment only in the case of conviction. Obviously, much is at stake in the co-application battle.

Although the co-application argument has some rhetorical appeal, there are important legal deficiencies. First, the United States has long insisted that the major human rights obligations imposed by the International Covenant on Civil and Political Rights (ICCPR) do not apply to government conduct outside of the country.[114] Such extraterritorial applications are not governed by the ICCPR since the United States has no jurisdiction or control outside of its territory.[115] Specifically, article 2 of the ICCPR states that "Each State Party to the present Covenant undertakes to respect and to ensure to all individuals within its territory and subject to its jurisdiction the rights recognized in the present Covenant, without distinction of any kind, such as race, colour, sex, language, religion, political or other opinion, national or social origin, property, birth or other status."[116] In the view of the State Department, the phrase "within its territory and subject to its jurisdiction" necessarily eliminates any extraterritorial application of the ICCPR. However, the issue was hotly debated within the State Department; former legal advisor Harold Koh argued forcefully in 2010 that the ICCPR applied extra-territorially. Consequently, the official U.S. position may evolve in the coming years.

This argument is consistent with the history and trajectory of human rights law. Originally, understandings about human rights were limited to states promising that they would not mistreat nation-als from foreign states. Over time, human rights grew into promises between states with regard to their treatment of their own citizens and residents.[117] However, the idea was to limit government conduct internally, that is, to transform what had historically been viewed as a matter of exclusive sovereign concern into a matter appropriate for international concern. By reciprocally promising never to mis-treat their own subjects, governments were establishing a system of mutual constraint regarding how they could engage with their own subjects. This was a major advance in international law. However, it provides no support for the idea that the ICCPR constrains the United States in its military operations overseas against individuals who are neither within its territory nor subject to its jurisdiction. There is no possible way that an al-Qaeda fighter in Yemen is subject to the jurisdiction of the United States government.

There are other problems with the co-application thesis. In importing norms from international human rights law into situ-ations of warfare, one runs into conceptual conflicts. Are the two bodies of law consistent with each other?[118] If they pull in oppo-site directions, how can their basic norms be co-applied at the same time? Consider the human right not to be deprived of life arbitrarily.[119] Under the ICCPR, "[e]very human being has the inher-ent right to life. This right shall be protected by law. No one shall be arbitrarily deprived of his life."[120] Indeed, this might be described as the most fundamental of all human rights. Although this is com-pletely uncontroversial as a matter of human rights law, it stands in stark tension with the basic norms of the law of war that permit the unrestrained killing of enemy combatants subject only to the specific prohibitions contained in the customary and codified laws of war. To put the point sharply, human rights law prohibits killing, while the law of war is designed to sanction it. If everyone has the right to life, why do soldiers have the right to kill as many enemy soldiers as they want? How can the two legal regimes be consistent with each other?

Advocates of the co-application thesis respond that the two legal regimes are consistent because the human rights prohibition against the deprivation of life is qualified in the following way: the deprivation cannot be *arbitrary*.[121] According to this view, the regular bread-and-butter killing during armed conflict—between soldiers—is not a violation of human rights law since the soldiers are not being killed arbitrarily. Co-application advocates need to make this argument in order to avoid a *reductio ad absurdum*: if human rights law outlaws all killing during armed conflict, then the law of war essentially disappears. That would not be co-application; it would be human rights law swallowing the law of war into a functional abyss.

The argument is ultimately not convincing. The killing of one soldier by another is indeed arbitrary, which shows that the human right to life cannot apply during armed conflict (it is a peacetime norm inapplicable to the law of war). The only way that co-application advocates can get around this conclusion is to say that such killings are not arbitrary because they are done pursuant to law. Which law is that? It would have to be the principle of distinction, the legal norm that permits killing of combatants but that protects innocent civilians. But that is a principle of the law of war, so the only way that human rights law can be made consistent with the law of war is by redefining the content of the human rights norm with principles from the law of war. That achieves the needed result only on pain of vicious circularity: the relevant human right is redefined with principles from the law of war (and then declared consistent with them) so the tension disappears.

The co-application advocate does have one advantage: the rhetorical appeal of concluding that human rights are universal and that they even apply in moments of armed conflict. Human rights are, after all, universal in scope and should apply to all human beings regardless of status or station.[122] It counts as a defect of the opposite view that it includes the idea that human rights are suspended in cases of armed conflict. The whole point of the theory of human rights is that the most basic of them are non-derogable, not subject to departure or utilitarian balancing when exigency demands.[123] No, human rights are rights that cannot be balanced away.

There is a solution to this problem. In its Advisory Opinion on the Legality of Nuclear Weapons, the International Court of Justice concluded that the law of war was *lex specialis* to human rights law.[124] The ICJ expressed a similar sentiment in its Advisory Opinion on the Legality of the Wall in the Palestinian Territories.[125] For some scholars, *lex specialis* means that the law of war is an exceptional legal regime with specific legal norms that knock out the general legal norms of human rights law. However, the ICJ was pointing to a more refined understanding of the law of war as *lex specialis* to human rights law. What it meant by the Latin expression was that human rights are universal, but the law of war provides the content of human rights law during times of armed conflict.[126] In other words, human rights law is universal in scope, but the situation of armed conflict has such specialized demands that the world powers decided to create a specific body of law to work out specific norms of human rights law that should apply during armed conflict. Instead of leaving it to the courts and other legal actors to work out how such norms would apply during armed conflict, the specialized body of law provides the answers. Instead of calling these rules the law of war, one might even call this body of law "human rights during armed conflict." The specific prohibition on torture, inhumane treatment, weapons that cause unnecessary suffering, trial before punishment for enemy fighters are all expressions of what human rights law demands in times of armed conflict. The only difference is that these norms are so well developed that they have morphed into their own legal regime. This is the proper meaning of the phrase *lex specialis*.[127]

5.5 The Concept of Necessity

One area where the dividing line between the law of war and human rights law really matters is the concept of necessity. In addition to the principles of distinction and proportionality already discussed, the law of war also requires that any military action adhere to the principle of necessity.[128] Only necessary killings are permitted under the law of war. In recent years, critics of the campaign of drone strikes have suggested that targeted killings are not truly necessary, since in many instances, the United States could capture (and prosecute) suspected terrorists with an infantry raid rather than killing them remotely with a Predator drone.[129] The upshot of this claim is that killing only meets the necessity requirement under the law of war if capture is unfeasible. In fact, the Department of Justice white paper on targeted killings, authored by lawyers at the Office of Legal Counsel, took for granted that the United States only launches drone strikes against terrorists when it deems capture unfeasible.[130] This suggests that maybe even the Obama Justice Department in 2011 believed that there is a duty to attempt capture if it is possible.

This view of necessity is wrong, but it becomes most plausible when principles from human rights law are incorporated into the law of war through the co-application thesis discussed in the previous section. The principle of necessity has a particular definition in human rights law, that is, the *least-restrictive means* to achieve a legitimate governmental objective.[131] Human rights tribunals have deployed this test in countless human rights cases where they must decide if a particular governmental regulation violates the human rights of individual citizens.[132] In these cases, the courts ask whether the government is pursuing a legitimate objective and then whether the government action is truly necessary, that is, the least restrictive means to get that result. If the government has an alternate, less obtrusive route by which to achieve the same objective, then the regulation is subject to nullification on human rights grounds.

Some human rights lawyers have imported this definition into armed conflict situations, suggesting that targeted killings are illegal because they are not the least-restrictive (or least harmful) means to disabling the enemy; capture would work just as well in

protecting the country from terrorism. This was part of the argument in the Israeli Supreme Court decision on *Targeted Killings*,
which included the following hypothetical: if a terrorist is sitting in
a café, the government should attempt to capture and detain him
rather than killing him outright.[133] Killing is only permitted as a
last resort.

What this argument ignores is that the concept of necessity has
a particular history and meaning in the law of war. This technical term of art was often referred to a military necessity. The concept was first codified in the Lieber Code of 1863, drafted by Francis
Lieber upon the request of President Lincoln for use by Union soldiers in the Civil War.[134] Article 14 of the Lieber Code states that
"[m]ilitary necessity, as understood by modern civilized nations,
consists in the necessity of those measures which are indispensable for securing the ends of the war, and which are lawful according to the modern law and usages of war."[135] Human rights lawyers
think that this supports the least-restrictive-means interpretation
of necessity or, at the very least, something very close it, because
killing is only justified if it is truly "indispensable" for winning the
war. If you can win the war some other way, then the action cannot
be indispensable.

But this conclusion is far too hasty because it selectively ignores
the next provision of the Lieber Code, article 15, which states in
part: "Military necessity admits of all direct destruction of life or
limb of armed enemies, and of other persons whose destruction
is incidentally unavoidable in the armed contests of the war."[136] In
other words, the Lieber Code stipulated by definition that killing
the enemy was always consistent with military definition. How can
this be? For Lieber, military necessity meant that the action in question was related to the war aim, in other words, that it was designed
to end the war as quickly as possible. Killing the greatest number of
enemy combatants is always related to the ends of war—because the
more enemy you kill, the quicker the war ends.[137] That is precisely
what the law of war allows.

Some lawyers are confused by Lieber's understanding of military necessity because it then becomes unclear what military necessity actually prohibits. If all actions designed to end the war quickly

by killing the enemy are deemed necessary, what conceptual work is performed by the concept of necessity? It is an excellent question, and one that Lieber answers in the Lieber Code, article 16:

> Military necessity does not admit of cruelty—that is, the infliction of suffering for the sake of suffering or for revenge, nor of maiming or wounding except in fight, nor of torture to extort confessions. It does not admit of the use of poison in any way, nor of the wanton devastation of a district. It admits of deception, but disclaims acts of perfidy; and, in general, military necessity does not include any act of hostility which makes the return to peace unnecessarily difficult.[138]

According to Lieber, then, killing is prohibited if it is unrelated to the war aim and it is motivated simply by sadism, vengeance, or a pure desire to inflict suffering on the enemy. It is precisely for this reason that the law of war bans weapons that cause unnecessary suffering—if the weapon does nothing to kill more soldiers but only increases their level of suffering when they are injured, then the weapon system will not advance the legitimate war aim of defeating the enemy. It could only be motivated by a desire to see the enemy suffer for its own sake.

A holistic reading of the entire Lieber Code demonstrates that the definition of military necessity is not confined to Article 14. This is the mistake made by scholars enamored with the least-harmful-means interpretation of necessity. Rather, the Lieber Code's definition of military necessity spans articles 14, 15, and 16, and only a comprehensive reading of all three provisions yields a complete understanding of this key concept of the law of war. Necessity demands that actions be indispensable for winning the war, and killing enemy soldiers is always an element of winning the war.

Put another way, these scholars confuse the licensing and regulatory functions of the law of war. These individuals are inclined to view necessity as part of the regulatory function of the law of war because that is the role necessity plays in human rights law. But in the law of war, necessity is more closely related to the licensing function of the law of war. Necessity is the conceptual ground for the privilege of combatancy: soldiers are permitted to kill other soldiers precisely because this type of killing is necessary for winning the war. Necessity does not, however, perform much regulatory work in constraining killing, except insofar as it prohibits killing for sadism or vengeance alone. This view does not take into consideration the fact that the law of war does not impose substantial constraints on methods of warfare; in fact it does. However, these constraints emerge from the other principles and specific rules in the law of war, not from the concept of necessity. The principles of distinction and proportionality constrain behavior, as do the specific prohibitions against perfidy or denying quarter to captured soldiers. But the concept of military necessity is in danger of being hijacked to provide a level of constraint that should rightly be performed by these other concepts in the law of war.

There have been attempts in the past to redefine the concept of military necessity to include a least-harmful-means interpretation of necessity. During the negotiations for the Additional Protocols to the Geneva Convention, delegate Jean Pictet, a noted expert on the law of war, pushed strenuously for a least-harmful-means interpretation of military necessity.[139] In particular, Pictet argued that "if a combatant can be put out of action by taking him prisoner, he should not be injured; if he can be put out of action by injury, he should not be killed; and if he can be put out of action by light injury, grave injury should be avoided."[140] This quote is now famous, and proponents of the least-harmful-means test use it to argue that the new definition has already been incorporated into the law of war, irrespective of human rights law and any co-application of its norms with law of war principles.

This argument, while intriguing, is ultimately unconvincing. Pictet did indeed hold a more restrictive interpretation of military necessity, and some scholars have described it as a "use of force continuum," meaning that attacking forces need to work their way through lower thresholds of force before passing to more extreme measures like killing.[141] Pictet did manage to convince other delegations, and he garnered support from other drafters, including Hans Blix of Sweden.[142] However, there is no evidence that Pictet's arguments won the day and that they were ever incorporated into a specific provision of the Additional Protocol.

The Additional Protocol did eventually include a prohibition on weapons that cause unnecessary suffering, but that did not represent a codification of the least-harmful-means interpretation of necessity.[143] The prohibition on unnecessary suffering limits the types of weapons that might cause suffering to soldiers without killing them: "It is prohibited to employ weapons, projectiles and material and methods of warfare of a nature to cause superfluous injury or unnecessary suffering."[144] If a weapon does not kill a greater number of troops, but only increases the suffering of those who are injured but survive, then it cannot be justified by the concept of military necessity. However, that has nothing to do with a least-harmful-means interpretation of necessity.[145] And the prohibition on unnecessary suffering is completely consistent with the definition of necessity in the Lieber Code, which stipulates that the killing of enemy soldiers ("all direct destruction of life or limb of armed enemies") is consistent with military necessity.

At stake here is whether the law of war permits killing legitimate targets even if there is some chance that they could be captured and detained instead. The least-harmful-means interpretation of necessity suggests that capture must be attempted first, or at least deemed unfeasible before recourse to killing. However, the least-harmful-means theory is a creature of human rights law, and it has won no place in the law of war, neither imported through the channels of human rights via co-application nor via Jean Pictet's efforts during the negotiations in Geneva.[146] Consequently, when the United States engages in targeted killings against legitimate targets (as identified by the law of war), U.S. forces are permitted to kill enemy targets without first resorting to capture. Although there may be policy reasons to prefer capture if possible, there is no legal requirement to do so under the law of war.

5.6 Conclusion

There is much talk about the law of war when war crimes are committed during conflicts where the participants are willing to ignore *jus in bello.* News reports have cataloged allegations of atrocities committed in Libya and in Syria, to name just two recent conflicts. There is, however, an important distinction to be made between atrocity, as that term is understood in war crimes law, and the killing of a large number of individuals. It might be perfectly consistent with the law of war to kill large numbers of individuals, provided the killings take place during an armed conflict, the individuals are legitimate targets, civilian casualties are not disproportionate, and the soldiers comply with the specific regulations of the Geneva Conventions. The law of war outlaws war crimes, but it does not outlaw war itself.

The general public often has a false impression of the law of war. They think it outlaws much more than it does. Officials in the Bush administration labored under a similar misperception. And the New Realists assume that the United States must ignore international law in order to protect its own national security and pursue its military objectives in an unconstrained manner. But in the long-term, compliance with the law of war is utterly consistent with national interest. First, the law of war is probably the least constraining area of international law; it is full of permissions and very few constraints. Second, the New Realists are wrong to think that self-interest and obligation are mutually exclusive. The United States complies with the law of war because it has good reason to do so: a world governed by the legal regulation of warfare is a far better world for the United States, which has organized its military forces around the basic legal principles discussed in this chapter: distinction, proportionality, and necessity. The law of war constrains its enemies and allows the United States to do what it does best: wage conventional wars in accordance with the basic principles of international law. The assault on international law loses much of its bite once it becomes clear that the tension between national security and international law is largely illusory.

6 :: Reengaging International Institutions

So far, our examination of the attack on international law has focused on its theoretical foundations. However, the attack has also manifested itself in particular diplomatic initiatives as the United States has migrated further away from international institutions and courts. This migration reached its apex during the Bush administration, often supported by New Realist arguments that provided the intellectual foundation for American exceptionalism. Intellectual skepticism regarding international law made this easier. The resulting foreign policy pushed the United States to reject the very international institutions that could have strengthened its security through a system of mutual constraints.

The core argument of this book is that a large-chunk theory of rationality entails that compliance with international law is consistent with national self-interest. Here is the most important point to be made. If this theory is correct, then the United States should embrace international institutions as part of a policy of constrained maximization. Rationality demands it, and the attack on international law has consistently obscured this basic fact. This final chapter lays out a roadmap for a policy of reengagement.

The estrangement of the United States from international institutions has proven to be an unmitigated disaster. Between 2001 and
2008 and beyond, the U.S. government pulled away from engagement with the United Nations and fought wars in Afghanistan and
Iraq with a "coalition of the willing" rather than an international
consensus. In May 2002, the United States formally withdrew its
intent of ratification of the Rome Statute and refused to join the
International Criminal Court (ICC), which was established in 2002
by the Rome Statute. However, the Obama administration has rees-
tablished a working relationship with the ICC. The result, in part,
was that the wars in Afghanistan and Iraq went far worse than
expected—with a tremendous and painful financial and human
cost to both the United States and the civilian populations of our
enemies.

The story begins in 2002 when talks for a U.N. Security Council
resolution to authorize the invasion of Iraq broke down. After the
United States failed to convince the other permanent members
of the Security Council that Saddam Hussein's weapons of mass
destruction (WMD) program necessitated intervention, the United
States decided to act, even in the absence of a binding resolution
permitting military force. Although other countries supported the
invasion, most notably Britain, the weight of the Security Council
was against the United States.

The legal and political defense of the invasion was a two-pronged
assault. First, Bush argued that the action was *not* an example of
American unilateralism; rather, it was the action of a coalition of the
willing, a group of states that were willing to make the world a safer
place by ridding it of an unpredictable dictator who possessed dangerous weapons. Second, the Bush administration introduced the
novel argument that a Security Council resolution was not required
to authorize force against Iraq. Rather, Saddam Hussein was not
adequately cooperating with U.N. weapons inspectors, and Iraq
was in material breach of the Security Council resolutions that had
been passed after the first Iraq War (the Gulf War, 1990–1991). This
argument attempted to transform the invasion into an enforcement
action, an international sanction against a state that was violating
its previous international obligations imposed by the U.N. Security

Council. By relabeling the action, the administration hoped that the Security Council's refusal to issue a new resolution would be ignored. The argument failed to convince much of the U.N. membership, many of whom viewed the war as illegal.

The war, which began with an invasion of Iraq in March 2003, went badly (a historic understatement perhaps). Although there was evidence of degraded remnants of misplaced and abandoned chemical weapons, no prohibited weapons were found, much to the embarrassment of the Bush administration. True, Saddam Hussein was located, and then prosecuted and executed by the new Iraqi government. However—since February 2009, when President Obama announced that U.S. combat forces would be withdrawn, and through October 2011, when Obama proclaimed that the final U.S. forces would leave Iraq by the end of the year, bringing the U.S. mission in Iraq to an end—a stable and unified government has continued to elude the country. In 2014, militants belonging to the Islamic State of Iraq and the Levant (ISIL) began a military campaign to gain territory in both Iraq and Syria—further destabilizing the government of Iraq.

More important, in the eyes of some, the Iraq invasion provoked a massive international backlash against the United States, squandering all of the goodwill that had flowed to the United States after the 9/11 attacks. The international hostility toward the United States not only hampered the war in Iraq, but it also had spillover effects that contaminated the conduct of hostilities against al-Qaeda in Afghanistan. Had the United States never invaded Iraq—and poisoned the well of international support—the war in Afghanistan might have been fought with a much higher number of coalition partners. And, after defeating the Taliban, a much larger number of countries might have promised troops to help rebuild infrastructure and provide security. In the absence of this international support, the United States has struggled to rid the country of Islamic extremists.

This was just the beginning. The United States continued to demonstrate hostility toward the United Nations in matters having nothing to do with the war against Iraq. The Bush administration chose not to cooperate with the International Criminal Court (ICC) and, along with Israel and Sudan, went so far as to "unsign" the Rome Statute—an act of uncertain legal consequences under international law but an act of huge political and diplomatic signaling: *it doesn't matter how many state parties have ratified the Rome Statute, we won't play ball.*[1] And the U.S. estrangement from the International Court of Justice (ICJ) was already well underway before the Bush administration, but it certainly accelerated during the period from 2000 to 2008. In 1984, the United States withdrew its consent from jurisdiction before the ICJ for matters of general international law. And in 2005, the Bush administration withdrew from the ICJ with regard to all cases dealing with consular relations. Although the United States was arguably the driving force behind the creation of this judicial organ after World War II, it has, over the years, turned away from international adjudication.

The present chapter argues that this general trajectory is foolhardy and that it fails to accord with the demands of rationality. As we explained in previous chapters, the formation of an international legal norm also, implicitly, includes a reason to comply with it even when they become inconvenient. And participating in international institutions is the most prominent means by which a state can comply with international law. The New Realists, especially Posner and Vermeule, are deeply skeptical of international legal institutions, which they view as hostile to U.S. national interests and incapable of enforcing compliance from reluctant actors. But what the New Realists fail to understand is that flouting international law is *irrational*. Once one understands the proper contours of rationality, including *large-chunk* rationality and the *package deal* argument, it becomes clear that reengaging international institutions is not only rationally defensible but also rationally required.

Consequently, section 6.1 will address the abstract question of why Americans are so hostile to international legal regimes. Critics of the United Nations sometimes refer to international law as a form of *global legalism* and the idea that legal tools can solve problems and help govern the international community even in the absence of a world government. Section 6.1 addresses this critique and argues that the supposed tension between global legalism and rational choice is a false dichotomy. Properly understood, rationality counsels in favor of participating in international legal regimes, not defecting from them. Section 6.2 will explain why *large-chunk* rationality suggests that the United States would be well advised to comply with the international prohibition against the use of force, especially since the system is weighted toward the Security Council in which the United States exercises a veto and enjoys a disproportionate level of influence by virtue of its post-World War II status as an enforcer of geopolitical stability. Sections 6.3 and 6.4 will explain why the United States should join the International Criminal Court and reengage the ICJ, despite the perennial concerns regarding sovereignty that arise when the United States participates in international adjudicatory bodies. The simple fact remains that refusing to participate in international institutions is myopic.

6.1 Global Legalism versus Rational Choice: A False Dichotomy

Critics of global legalism are haunted by the specter of world government. In short, the argument works like this: liberal internationalists would prefer a world government that could solve problems at the global level and finally dissolve the tyranny of the nation-state. Since world government is either impracticable or impossible, liberal internationalists have settled on a second-best alternative: a system of international law that performs as much of the functions of world government as possible. However, much of the international legal system suffers from the same failures as the fanciful utopianism of world government. As Eric Posner wrote in *The Perils of Global Legalism*:

> What explains the rise of global legalism? The simple demand-side explanation is that the implausibility and failure of the world government, economic integration, ideological integration, and hegemony approaches to global collective action problems have left a gap that global legalism has filled. The world needs institutions that will solve global collective action problems and, if these other approaches have failed, international law itself has not been directly refuted.[2]

The idea here is *law without government*. For Posner, this is a con-tradiction, an unresolvable paradox upon which international law has been spinning like a top for decades.[3] The international legal system has none of the same features of a domestic government: a unified executive, a parliament, or a legislature with plenary pow-ers, or a judicial organ with compulsory jurisdiction. In the absence of a stable world government, global legalism attempts to fill the void by providing a conceptual system that imposes legal regulation on the conduct of nation-states. But since there is no world gov-ernment standing behind these legal regulations, international law represents an impotent solution—nothing more than law without government. The institutional weaknesses of international law boil down to, in Posner's own words, legislation without legislatures, enforcement without enforcers, and adjudication without courts.[4] So international law has all of the appearances of law without any of the institutional support to back it up. Posner aims to pull the veil back on this often overlooked fact.

According to Posner, the consequence of this basic, indisput-able fact is that states have no reason to comply with international law "when they prefer to free ride."[5] International law helps solve coordination problems, but anything more is pure idealism; when states find international law inconvenient, they will decline to fol-low it. Only a strong enforcement mechanism—of the sort found in a domestic legal order—will ensure that states comply with interna-tional law instead of ignoring it. Because international law has no such enforcement mechanism, international lawyers are laboring under the naïve fiction of global legalism.

Posner and other New Realists view this argument as not only consistent with—but also inspired by—rational choice theory. States acting out of rational self-interest have no reason to comply with inconvenient doctrines of international law because international law lacks the institutional mechanisms to demand compliance: leg-islatures, binding courts, and so forth. These institutional mecha-nisms work because they give rational agents a reason to comply with the law. The threat of sanctions changes the expected payoff of free riding or defecting from particular norms. For Posner, this general argument applies to states: "For the rational choice theorist, the answer is plain: states cannot solve global collective action problems by creating institutions that themselves depend on global collective action."[6] Consequently, global legalists are "not enthusiasts for rational choice theory and have grappled with this problem in other ways."[7]

The New Realists have the point exactly backward. It isn't the global legalists who fail to embrace rational choice theory. Far from it. Rather, Posner and the other New Realists are operating with an impoverished understanding of rationality, as the previous chapters have demonstrated. Rational states should comply with international law because compliance with a particular normative regime is implicit in the very reasoning process that leads to the formation of the norm in the first place. This argument requires further explanation.

Theorists are often inclined to think of rationality in atomic units. Under this view, the rational agent should maximize his opportunities at each moment in time. If compliance yields the highest payoff, he should comply; if defection produces a better outcome, he should defect. However, this view of rationality produces self-defeating results. In many situations, defection yields better results at that particular time, but it makes the life of the agent go worse overall. This version of rationality is both self-defeating and incoherent. Rational agents should select the strategy or plan that makes their life go better overall. If that plan is compliance, then the rational agent should ignore the temptation to defect and instead stick with a plan that makes his life go worse overall.

It sounds as if the argument is appealing exclusively to long-term benefits. And indeed, many scholars of international law have used rational choice theory to explain that the long-term benefits of complying with international law gives states a reason to follow international law even when defection seems like a plausible scenario. In such situations, states should take the long view and stick to compliance with international law. While this is certainly true, it may even be the case that states should comply with international law even when we narrow our focus to the situation at hand and ignore the long-term consequences.

The institutional weaknesses of international law allegedly stem from the state system. Posner is correct in pointing out that state sovereignty is partly to blame here; states are not inclined to agree to a world government, or any institutions that remotely resemble it, because doing so requires a substantial abrogation of state sovereignty.[8] A state's degree of hostility toward international law will often vary depending on that state's obsession with the concept of sovereignty (i.e., high in the case of the United States, somewhat less so for European states). It is no surprise then that the European states were willing to trade some of their sovereign prerogatives to gain the institutional advantages of the European Union.

Sovereignty means more than just voluntarism and consent; it also means that states enjoy sovereign equality—each state is *formally* equal before international law. This means that in terms of access to the formal mechanism of creating international law, the United States, China, and Myanmar are all on equal footing. Each are persons before the law, capable of negotiating and ratifying treaties, engaging in state practice to create customary international law, and litigating before international tribunals such as the International Court of Justice.[9] No one state is more important than any other, regardless of size and regardless of political organization. So it does not matter that Myanmar is small or that China is not a democracy. Their participation in the international legal process is formally equal. Does this delegitimize international law? Furthermore, does the sovereign equality of states doom international institutions, like the United Nations, that are based on the sovereign equality of nation-states?

This skepticism about the building blocks of international law demands a multipronged response. The response is complicated, because even committed internationalists have long had a contentious relationship with the concept of sovereignty. Louis Henkin famously implored international lawyers to banish the "S" word—*sovereignty*—from the discipline because it was doing more harm than good.[10] For Henkin, sovereignty was an excuse that states deployed to deflect external criticism of their behavior. More important, sovereignty provided a barrier to effective international responses to human rights abuses occurring within the sovereign territory of another state. Human rights activists deplored robust conceptions of sovereignty that operated as a trump that prevailed over competing concepts of individual human rights. Under this view, if anything is a trump, it ought to be individual human rights—not state sovereignty.

Internationalists are therefore in an odd position with regard to sovereignty. They want to defend it, but only with a version of sovereignty that they can live with. I suspect that some of this reluctance has inhibited the development of sophisticated defenses of sovereignty. The task is most likely to be undertaken by scholars with a detached, theoretical relationship to the concept.

In addition, the formal equality of nation-states is hardly surprising. It has analogs in the U.S. domestic system of government, and there, no one seriously suggests that it forms an impediment to the nation's legitimacy as a democratic state. The U.S. Constitution endows the states with sovereign equality, treating them as atomic units for purposes of Senate representation; each state, regardless of its population or geographic size, gets the same number of senators. Furthermore, states matter for purposes of amending the Constitution and for all issues that fall within the plenary power of the fifty U.S. states. Although the federal government is sovereign for all external matters (foreign relations and military affairs) and areas that fall within the federal government's enumerated powers in the Constitution, the remaining political power is reserved for the states (and the people themselves). As Justice Kennedy said, the Founding Fathers "split the atom of sovereignty . . . . It was the genius of their idea that our citizens would have two political capacities, one state and one federal, each protected from incursion by the other."[11]

This is more than just an analogy. The two points are causally connected because the sovereign equality of the U.S. states (say Vermont and California) stems from the sovereign equality of nation-states under international law. When the colonies won their freedom from Britain they became independent sovereign entities under the international system. They then freely chose to join together to form the United States, first through the Articles of Confederation and later through the U.S. Constitution. This new arrangement allowed the states to retain much of the sovereignty that they had won in the Revolution. But the key point here is that this hard-won sovereignty was in fact a creature of an international system that recognized the sovereign equality of nation-states (which each colony became after winning independence from Britain).

The sovereign equality of Vermont and California does not provide a reason to distrust the legitimacy of the U.S. system. An individual citizen of Vermont has more political power and influence than an individual citizen of California, who is just one drop within the very large sea. True, each gets one vote in the presidential election, and each gets the same proportionate influence in Congress. But in other areas, like the U.S. Senate and their individual capacity to influence state legislation, the Vermonter has greater power and influence; he or she is, comparatively speaking, a large fish in a small sea. Put another way, each senator from California represents a large number of Californians whose voices are diminished in the Senate, while each senator from Vermont represents a small number of Vermonters whose voices are amplified in the Senate. Bicameralism, with one popular chamber and one state chamber, represented the compromise that mediated between the two possible loci of political power: the individual and the state. The U.S. House of Representatives is based on the individual. The U.S. Senate is based on the state. And no federal law can be passed without agreement in both domains.

The sovereign equality of states under the international system can be defended on intellectual grounds. States are collective entities, endowed with legal and moral personhood under the international legal system. This is an ancient principle, going back as far as Emmerich de Vattel, if not further, and it establishes that states act with the requisite unity of purpose to qualify as group agents.[12] It is precisely for this reason that states become both the subjects and objects of international law and international relations. States are capable of engaging in relations with each other, by signing treaties and engaging in other forms of diplomatic relationships. If the status of states as group agents was a mere fiction, or illusory, none of this would be possible. Furthermore, states engage in coherent rational action: they select among available preferences; deliberate about alternative courses of action; and engage in means-end reasoning. All of this makes states both capable of forming international legal norms and of being bound by them; they are loci of moral and legal concern.[13]

None of this means that the international system is illegitimate; it simply means that states are the building blocks from which international institutions are created, and their interests matter. It does follow, however, that international institutions are not directly analogous to domestic political institutions; it is unreasonable to expect that one will look like the other. The United Nations is not the U.S. federal government; the U.N. General Assembly is neither Congress nor a parliament; the ICJ is neither the U.S. Supreme Court nor even the European Court of Human Rights. Although it might be tempting to view the basic structure of the U.N. Charter as setting up a tripartite system with horizontal separation of powers, there are important differences.

Finally, one should not exaggerate the degree to which the sovereign equality of states structures the basic contours of international institutions. Although each member of the United Nations is a full and equal member of the institution, the power to make binding law is concentrated in the Security Council, with veto power reserved for the five permanent members. Their entitlement to the veto power stems not from the sovereign equality of states but from their position as world superpowers after the conclusion of World War II—factors that have nothing to do with sovereign equality or legal personality as Vattel understood it. These are institutional concessions to the states that sacrificed the most during World War II and were therefore most likely to retain the capacity to ensure international peace and security. Why states that are not on the Security Council have a reason to join (and stay) with the United Nations is an interesting question, and one that we will develop more fully in the next section.

Before continuing, a brief discussion is in order regarding the nature of this chapter's argument. It is prescriptive, not descriptive. The argument is not meant to be an explanation of state behavior. It is not meant to explain why states join the United Nations; why states join the International Criminal Court; why states comply with requests to arrest suspects and turn them over to The Hague; or why states submit their disputes to the ICJ for resolution and why they comply with their judgments.

Such arguments always run into the problem of accommodating the exceptions when states fail to cooperate with the U.N.; when states refuse to sign the Rome Statute; and when states withdraw their consent to ICJ jurisdiction.

Rather, the argument here is normative: states ought to join these institutions, not just in situations where doing so has obvious benefits but also in situations where defection might be tempting. The theoretical foundation for this argument was laid in chapter 4, which concluded that rational agents should comply with normative constraints if and only if a strategy of compliance is part of a rationally defensible plan that makes the agent's life go better over all. This was true in cases where the agent's long-term interest required taking the long view, but it is also true in single-shot cases where the plan spans a single interaction. Those interactions encompass two central moments: forming the intention to comply with the constraint and following through on the constraint even when the benefit has already accrued and all that remains is the burden. Since a rational plan includes both of these elements (we called this the *package-deal argument*), it may sometimes be the case that rational agents should follow the rationally defensible plan, even if rationality appears to suggest that at any moment, they should defect from their prior agreements or commitments. The prime example we used was the toxin puzzle, a thought experiment designed to show that narrow-minded concentration on the agent's best response *at a single moment in time* risks confusing the forest for the trees where rationality is concerned. Forming the intention to drink the toxin is rationally justified because it is one part of a rational plan that makes the agent's life go better over all.

The present chapter will apply this theoretical insight to international institutions. The question is whether a state, as a rational agent, should follow through on its international commitments once the benefits of the agreements have already accrued and only the burdens remain. International legal institutions represent a particular subset of this question. Is it rational to join? Prior scholars have invoked long-term national interests to explain why participation in international institutions is rationally justified.[14] But the argument above, if true, is far more powerful and radical. It suggests that a rational state should follow through on its international commitments even in isolated scenarios without taking into consideration the long-term interest. Forming the international agreement means following through as well, because both parts (norm formation and rational follow-through) comprise a package-deal that makes the life of the state go better overall. And this package-deal argument does not depend on multiple iterations of the game; it applies even in more localized temporal contexts.

The following sections will therefore address engagement and compliance with the U.N., the ICJ, and the ICC. Each entity involves a different set of normative considerations and a different set of incentives that led to their creation. What unites them is a fundamental truth that selecting a strategy of compliance with the post-World War II U.N. legal institutions is rationally justified under the package-deal argument. Before continuing, however, we should address whether domestic law ought to be configured to cure the alleged "legitimacy deficit" of international law and protect U.S. sovereignty.

6.2 Does Globalization Need Taming?

Critics of global legalism are inclined to view international institutions as potential threats to U.S. sovereignty—a familiar and old refrain. International institutions delegate decision-making away from U.S. political institutions that are endowed with legitimacy by the U.S. Constitution. Transferring decision-making authority to international institutions—such as the ICC, the World Trade Organization, or other free-trade arbitral tribunals—is contrary to the structure and intention of the U.S. Constitution, which allocates powers vertically between the states and the federal government and horizontally between the three federal branches of government; international institutions were never included in this calculation. Consequently, delegating decision-making authority to international institutions upsets this carefully choreographed balance of power, and it does so in ways that have no political legitimacy since international institutions include many illiberal nation-states.

Concerns about sovereignty led the United States Senate to delay ratification of key human rights treaties for decades. This included the Genocide Convention, which the United States signed in 1948 but the Senate refused to ratify until 1988.[15] Much of the delay in the 1950s and 1960s stemmed from isolationist senators from the South concerned that international human rights commitments might require the United States to pass civil rights legislation, which they opposed. Some treaties were never ratified, such as the Convention to Eliminate all Forms of Discrimination Against Women (CEDAW).[16] In addition to the United States, the only non-parties to CEDAW are Sudan, South Sudan, Somalia, Iran, Palau, and Tonga, making the United States an outlier among the international community.[17] Because of the heightened super-majority requirement for senate ratification, a small number of senators stalled ratification. As a consequence of this institutional obstacle, formal treaties waned in importance, replaced by international agreements that required congressional agreement but not a Senate super-majority.[18]

In TAMING GLOBALIZATION, Julian Ku and John Yoo argue that international law suffers from a fundamental democracy deficit and is alienated from the popular sovereignty that resides with the American people.[19] Their argument represents a much more subtle version of the anti-delegation arguments that isolationists offered in past decades. In this new version, domestic legal mechanisms tame the effects of international law by limiting its scope and flattening its reach. These mechanisms include the non-self-execution of treaties (requiring Congress to pass a separate implementing law), the right of presidents to offer new and divergent interpretations of international legal agreements (after the Senate has already ratified them), and even state (as in New York or California) participation in foreign policy. Each of these mechanisms prevents international law from running too far ahead of the government's authority. "Our approach," Yoo and Ku conclude, "ensures that as our government's reach extends upward, it does not lose touch with the people to which it is responsible."[20]

Yoo and Ku's analysis rests on two conceptions of sovereignty.[21] First, there is the traditional Westphalian conception of sovereignty[22] that we have already discussed. States have authority over their own affairs, and this sovereign authority makes them legal subjects of international law, capable of engaging in international legal relations but also making them subject to its regulations. This is precisely the conception of sovereignty that Louis Henkin found so dangerous—it could be understood to provide the state with exclusive authority to run its internal affairs, unfettered by the prying eyes of the international community. The modern human rights movement is predicated on the idea that such a strict reading of sovereignty must be too rigid.

The second conception of sovereignty is more internal, and it is often embodied by the phrase *popular sovereignty*.[23] Unlike in prior centuries where the monarch or ruler was viewed as the sovereign, in its formative years, the United States was built around the radical notion that the people themselves are sovereign. As such, the political order is grounded by the sovereignty of the people, who created the federal government as an expression of their sovereignty but can dissolve it if they wish. In the United States, government does not rule over the people; the people created the government as an expression of their own sovereignty.

Critics of internationalism fret over international institutions because such institutions risk losing touch with popular sovereignty. Judges at the International Court of Justice are not selected by the American people nor are the other representatives on the Security Council. Even worse, customary international law is formed from the state practice of foreign governments, who are certainly not elected by the American people. It is safe to say that almost no international legal norms (with the exception of treaties ratified by the U.S. Senate) are direct expressions of U.S. popular will. Yoo and Ku use this as their argument for why international law should slow down, and why domestic law should place obstacles in its way.[24]

The first method involves non-self-executing treaties, which cannot be directly applied as domestic law in the absence of separate implementing legislation passed by Congress.[25] Diplomats negotiating the treaty provisions can include specific language that makes clear that the treaty will not have domestic effect until further implementing legislation is passed, or the federal courts can adopt a presumption in favor of reading treaties as non-self-executing. As a canon of treaty interpretation, courts using this method will assume, all other things being equal, that a treaty is non-self-executing unless there is clear evidence to the contrary. This does not change the binding nature of the international agreement, but it does limit the applicability of the treaty in domestic legal contexts, such as litigation before federal courts.

What justifies a general presumption favoring non-self-executing treaties? Indeed, all things are rarely equal, and in the past, courts have looked closely at context to determine whether a particular treaty regime contemplated further legislative action or whether it was crafted with an eye toward immediate effect in the domestic area. Yoo and Ku's argument here is that requiring implementing legislation in more cases shifts the decision-making to more representative institutions.[26] Instead of treaties that are negotiated by the executive branch and ratified by the Senate, implementing legislation must be passed by both houses of Congress and presented to the president for signature. And while state interests reign in the Senate, the House is governed exclusively by popular will. So the shift toward non-self-executing treaties better protects the popular sovereignty that is threatened by international legal agreements.[27]

The second method involves judicial and legislative deference to presidential interpretations of international law.[28] This is especially controversial. In 1983, more than a decade after the United States signed the Anti-Ballistic Missile (ABM) Treaty, President Reagan concluded that the treaty did not prohibit the U.S. military from developing the Strategic Defense Initiative (SDI) (dubbed "Star Wars").[29] This interpretation directly contradicted the Senate's interpretation of the treaty, and Senate leaders loudly complained about the president's attempt to reinterpret the treaty. From their point of view, by smuggling the change in as a reinterpretation of the treaty (and an unconvincing one at that), Reagan was trying to unilaterally change the treaty that the Senate had ratified.[30] The treaty had specifically proclaimed that the development of land, sea, air, or space-based missile defense programs was prohibited.[31] So the better reading of the treaty was that the United States was violating its obligations by developing SDI. Consequently, the Senate argued that judicial or legislative deference to executive interpretations of treaty language was not appropriate. The Senate's understanding of the treaty at the time of ratification was equally important, if not more so.

One can understand why the New Realists would conclude that courts should defer to executive (re-)interpretations of international law. First, they claim that federal courts are ill suited to grappling with the complexities of foreign affairs and should defer to the political branches.[32] This suggests that courts should defer to presidential understandings of customary international law. While courts can take years or decades to resolve litigation and issue opinions, presidents can respond to the exigencies of the moment and issue new interpretations of customary international law when the situation demands it.[33] Yoo and Ku are inclined to think of this as analogous to *Chevron* deference in administrative law, where courts defer to agency interpretations of implementing legislation and regulations that fall within their zone of competence.[34]

Their views about popular sovereignty also generate an argument about presidential primacy in treaty interpretation. Treaties are crafted by the president and ratified by the Senate. Between the president and the Senate, the president is the more representative branch of government since the president is directly elected by popular vote while the Senate represents the interests of the states. In practice, some internationalists might be sympathetic to this argument. In fact, the Senate's counter-majoritarian status has proved deeply problematic for ratification of basic treaty commitments; the isolationism of a small number of southern Senators (hardly a majority) is a major reason the United States has not ratified more treaties. In that sense, internationalists might be in favor of moving the ratification power to the House of Representatives, which is far more democratic. However, this option is not on the table. What *is* on the table is whether courts and legislatures will defer to presidential interpretations of treaties and other international legal norms. And this proposal only promotes popular sovereignty in the most formal sense. While the president is popularly elected, he is only a single individual, whose interbranch deliberations are shielded from public scrutiny. In contrast, Senate deliberations are public and bring a large number of stakeholders to the table for negotiation and reconsideration. The idea that deference to executive branch interpretations of international law will promote popular sovereignty rings hollow. It only resolves the interbranch rivalry between the president and the Senate in foreign relations in favor of the president—an outcome that strengthens unilateral executive authority and weakens the separation of powers.

A third mechanism involves maintaining and reinforcing state (e.g., New York or California) autonomy in the wake of international law compliance.[35] Here, it is important to understand that upholding international legal obligations is usually considered imperative regardless of the obstacles of the domestic system. Consider the extensive litigation in both international and domestic cases over the U.S. failure to uphold its obligations under the Vienna Convention on Consular Relations.[36] The Convention requires domestic law enforcement officials to allow foreign citizens, in criminal custody, the right to speak with a consular official from their home nation.[37] For many years, local police in the United States were not in the habit of informing suspects of their rights under the Vienna Convention. Although *Miranda* warnings were so common that they grew into the fabric of popular culture—through police procedurals on television—no one thought to modify the standard *Miranda* warning to notify suspects of their international rights under the Vienna Convention.

Once these violations became widely known, international tribunals were tasked with determining what should be done with inmates on death row who never received their Vienna Convention notifications. Although it was arguably a violation, it was unclear what the legal consequences should be because of two major complications. First, many defense lawyers had failed to raise the issue at trial, so state courts considered the issue waived as a matter of law under state procedural default rules. Second, most of these convictions fell under state law rather than federal law, and it was the federal government that represented the United States before international tribunals.

On the first point, the ICJ flatly concluded that state procedural default rules should not prevent the United States from fulfilling its Vienna Convention obligations.[38] In other words, the very application of the state procedural default rules violated the Convention if they were used to bar meaningful recovery for Vienna Convention violations. On the second point, the ICJ concluded that the defendants should not have been executed while the merit phase of the proceedings was pending. The ICJ had issued "provisional measures" designed to preserve the status quo while the state parties had a chance to litigate the issue fully before the World Court. When the U.S. federal government received notice of the ICJ provisional measures, the text of the decision was forwarded to the governor of Arizona[39] (who declined to stay the execution), a response that the ICJ found to be inadequate.

Unfortunately, the president had no authority to interfere in a state criminal justice matter. Whether a particular governor wanted to stay an execution or issue a clemency was a matter for the governor to decide and was not subject to reversal by the president. This discretion was part of the basic sovereignty that the individual states retain in the American system of federalism, according to the U.S. Supreme Court in *Medellin*, which concluded that the demands of international law were insufficient to override state government's authority over police matters under the vertical separation of power implied by federalism.[40] In short, the United States violated international law, and there was nothing the president could do about it because the federal government is a government of enumerated powers.[41]

Yoo and Ku want to harness state autonomy as an institutional avenue to tame international legal obligations.[42] Like *Medellin*, where federalism prevented the United States from complying with international law, Yoo and Ku see the states as a last line of defense against institutional overreaching by the international system. Although international law can do many things, the Constitution prevents it from abrogating the sovereignty of the fifty states, which retain their plenary power in areas not explicitly delegated to the federal government.

Of course, the answer is not so simple. In some areas, the Constitution does abrogate the sovereignty of the individual states. For example, in *Missouri v. Holland*, the Supreme Court ruled that the federal government could sign and ratify treaties that regulated conduct that could not otherwise be regulated through a domestic statute.[43] In *Missouri*, the treaty regulated migratory birds—a subject that Congress could not regulate under its enumerated powers through a domestic statute. However, the Supreme Court concluded that doing so via a treaty was not an impermissible end run around the Constitutional constraints of federalism.

Other Supreme Court holdings have limited the treaty power when it conflicts with the Constitution. In *Reid v. Covert*, for instance, the Court upheld the jury trial rights of an American defendant who had been prosecuted for murder on an overseas military base.[44] A bilateral agreement between the United States and Germany provided military jurisdiction for crimes committed on the base. However, the Court concluded that the treaty was an insufficient basis for abrogating the jury trial right of the defendant. Unlike *Missouri*, however, the treaty-power restrictions vindicated in *Reid* flowed from the Bill of Rights, not the structural implications of our federal system.[45] This suggests that the limits of *Missouri* apply in cases where individual rights—not state rights and the horizontal separation of powers—are at issue.

This leaves *Medellin*, where the Supreme Court did limit the ability of international law to penetrate the local state system and upset the delicate balance between state and federal governments that the framers carefully calibrated. As such, *Medellin* is the perfect exemplar of federalism's power to tame international law. The defendants in the case wanted the federal courts to grant automatic effect to the ICJ *Avena* decision that called for the executions to be halted.[46] Concluding that the relevant treaties, including the U.N. Charter, the Optional Protocol to the Vienna Convention, and the ICJ Statute, were all non-self-executing, the Court refused to give automatic effect to the *Avena* judgment.[47] This conclusion stood in marked contrast with the language of article 94(1) of the U.N. Charter, which plainly states that "[e]ach Member of the United Nations undertakes to comply with the decision of the International

Court of Justice in any case to which it is a party."[48] However, the Court gave more weight to article 94(2), which states that parties who fail to comply with ICJ judgments may be referred to the Security Council, "which may, if it deems necessary, make recommendations or decide upon measures to be taken to give effect to the judgment."[49] The Court concluded that ICJ judgments can only be enforced by the Security Council's authority to issue binding resolutions, an advantageous legal interpretation for permanent members of the Council that enjoy a veto.[50]

The Court had another way to vindicate the ICJ's decision. President Bush had issued a memorandum demanding that state courts give effect to the *Avena* decision.[51] President Bush's intervention in support of the defendants cuts against the broad narrative of President Bush as hostile to international arrangements. However, the president's memorandum must be viewed in its local context—the president was asserting executive authority over all matters relating to foreign relations, of which consular relations and ICJ decisions would naturally fall. So the administration's position was not that federal courts should give automatic effect to ICJ judgments but rather that the president alone had the authority to decide whether ICJ judgments should become binding law in the United States. Having reviewed the relevant interests of the United States, in particular, concerns about foreign countries extending reciprocal consular notification to U.S. citizens, Bush decided that compliance with the ICJ decision was in the best interest of the United States. Consequently, his view attempted to expand presidential authority against the rights of state courts to handle criminal prosecutions.

The Supreme Court rejected this expansive interpretation of executive authority, holding that it could be found in the Take Care Clause, in congressional acquiescence, or in an independent international-dispute resolution power sounding in the foreign relations power of the president.[52] *Medellin* therefore involves the union of two essential constraints on international law, both of which are championed by Yoo and Ku: a general presumption that treaties are non-self-executing and federalist structural restrictions on our federal officials' ability to accept and apply international law when it seeks to preempt state law. This principle is not universal: the Supreme Court upheld the right of presidents to enforce international disputes in *Dames & Moore v. Regan* as well as *Garamendi*.[53] In the former case, the president had the authority to terminate cases filed in federal court as a condition of the Algiers Accords, which ended the Hostage Crisis and created the U.S.-Iran Claims Tribunal as an international dispute mechanism (though not one that the hostages could avail themselves of). Similarly, in *Garamendi*, the Supreme Court vindicated the power of the president to preempt California state insurance regulations that interfered with the president's ability to resolve Holocaust-era banking and insurance claims at the international level.[54]

Yoo and Ku believe that *Garamendi* and *Medellin* leave ample room for state autonomy in foreign affairs and, in so doing, provide state officials with the legal tools to slow down federal enactment of international law.[55] The problem with this approach is that it sacrifices the unity associated with federal control over foreign affairs. With each individual state exercising autonomy over matters of foreign affairs, the United States would be pulled in fifty different (and potentially competing) directions. The tensions between the various state approaches would also harm the country's ability to engage in relations with foreign nations. Foreign nations will be reluctant to engage in negotiations with the United States if they fear that their agreements will be subject to the whim of individual states, or possibly even abrogated due to the domestic demands of the federal system. These were precisely the types of concerns that motivated President Bush's desire to implement the ICJ *Avena* decision. Furthermore, the point is conceptual: international legal personality requires the ability to engage in foreign relations; if state autonomy is reinforced and augmented, at a certain point, the legal personality of the state becomes a mere fiction, and the nation's external posture becomes compromised. Foreign states would start treating the United States as a mere conglomerate of individual states that ought to be approached individually, rather than as a coherent nation that can be dealt with at the federal level. Disunity becomes an obstacle to a nation's own goals that it hopes to achieve through foreign relations.

Ku and Yoo recognize the potential pitfalls of state autonomy, but they conclude that the risk of disunity can be cured with executive action at the federal level.[56] This represents a retreat from the basic principle underlying their argument: the primacy of state autonomy. Taken to its logical conclusion, Ku and Yoo should vindicate state autonomy and conclude that *Garamendi* was wrongly decided and that California should have prevailed against the federal government before the Supreme Court. The bulk of their argument is that "for areas of law and policy within their traditional control, states possess information and information-processing expertise that are superior to those of federal courts."[57] State insurance questions are arguably within the traditional domain of state governments; vindicating the exclusive authority of the state would have tamed international law.

However, Ku and Yoo fail to distance themselves from the result in *Garamendi* because the interests of California were preempted not by the courts but by the president—a crucial difference for them. If the president or Congress determines that state autonomy risks harming the national interest, the political branches can preempt state autonomy with federal action. In contrast, Yoo and Ku object to federal judicial interference with state autonomy on the grounds that federal courts do not have the institutional competence to preempt state autonomy and select a better path that advances the state's interests.[58]

Under this approach, *Garamendi* involved an acceptable exercise of federal preemption because the preemption originated in the executive branch. Similarly, the Supreme Court should have upheld the administration's position in *Medellin* since President Bush made a specific executive finding that compliance with the Vienna Convention was essential to the nation's interests. The real engine of the argument, then, is not the autonomy of state governments on matters that fall within their traditional powers, but rather the comparative institutional incompetency of the judicial branch. What at first appeared like an argument sounding in the vertical separation of powers comes down to an old argument about the horizontal separation of powers and an assault on the judicial branch's competence to interpret and apply international law. Just like Posner and

Vermeule's complaint that the federal courts are "amateurs playing at security policy,"[59] Yoo and Ku's argument is based on little more than a fetish for executive action and a global and abstract skepticism of judicial branch involvement. Ironically, this is precisely the same argument that might be deployed against state autonomy in the foreign affairs realm, since it is unlikely that local state officials would have the international expertise or orientation to trace the foreign affairs consequences of their actions.

The state autonomy argument is also vulnerable to the objection that federal courts resolve federalism disputes between the states and the federal government in other contexts, such as the Dormant Commerce Clause.[60] No one suggests that federal courts should be stripped of their power to strike down local state actions that infringe upon areas that fall within federal authority. Why the asymmetry for matters of foreign affairs but not in other contexts? Ku and Yoo can only conclude that "asking federal courts to police state activities in foreign affairs has a different functional balance,"[61] an argument that fails to convince, especially since Ku and Yoo are forced to concede that federal courts have many institutional advantages, including the pull toward unity and coherence based on their appellate structure and the vesting of the judicial power in the Supreme Court.[62]

6.3 The United Nations

Between 2000 and 2008, the United States was reluctant to engage and partner with the United Nations, a decision that had profound consequences for the country. Although there are many areas of legal regulation where the U.N. takes a central role, the use of force is an ideal case study, especially since it represents a legal norm that goes to the very heart of the U.N. system: identifying and repairing breaches to international peace and security. Furthermore, if there is one area where the United States ought to easily engage with the U.N., it is in the area of peace and security, which falls within the primary jurisdiction of the U.N. Security Council—an institution with which the United States has outsized influence on account of its veto power.

When the Bush administration decided that Saddam Hussein was dangerous and should be removed from power, Secretary of State Colin Powell addressed the Security Council, providing detailed evidence regarding weapons of mass destruction, including the development of chemical weapons by Hussein's Baathist regime. However, the rest of the Security Council (primarily Russia and France) remained unconvinced by the argument and refused to sign on to a resolution that would authorize the use of force against Hussein. At that time—March 2003—the United States' posture toward the United Nations shifted. The era of U.N. multilateral force against Iraq—which President George H. W. Bush and Secretary of State James Baker had so carefully constructed for the first Gulf War, was now completely over. It was replaced with snide remarks made by Secretary of Defense Donald Rumsfeld about "old Europe" (a shot at France and Germany) and the "new Europe" (a compliment to emerging partners such as Poland).[63] The international coalition of the first Gulf War was now replaced with a "coalition of the willing" that would deploy military force without U.N. approval.[64] The era of U.N. Security Council authority was regarded as a quaint relic of the legal past.

The United States should reengage with the United Nations and the legal framework that it represents. Rationality demands it. Although the Obama administration has participated much more willingly in the affairs of the U.N. Security Council, it has also stated its willingness to act unilaterally if necessary. With the standard that we have identified, an agent should fulfill a normative commitment if doing so is one part of a rationally defensible plan that makes his life go better overall. Complying with the use-of-force framework in the U.N. Charter is one such rationally defensible plan. The following analysis will explain why.

The key structure of the Charter regime on the use of force is outlined in articles 2 and 51 of the U.N. Charter. Article 2(1) prohibits the use or threat of force by member states, although this commitment is widely understood to embody customary law; the prohibition on illegal use of force goes as far back as the Kellogg-Briand Pact and may even be implicit in the very notion of Westphalian sovereignty.[65] Article 51 carves out from the Article

2 prohibition on illegal force "the inherent right of individual or collective self-defence if an armed attack occurs against a Member of the United Nations."[66] Scholars often overlook the reference to the inherent right of self-defense, which in the equally authoritative French version of the Charter is rendered as *droit naturel*. In other words, article 51 protects the preexisting natural right to collective and individual self-defense, and nothing in article 2 of the Charter can be interpreted to supplant that natural right.[67] The only other avenue for the lawful exercise of military force is the Security Council's enforcement power under article 42, which allows the Security Council to authorize member states to "take such action by air, sea, or land forces as may be necessary to maintain or restore international peace and security."[68]

The result is a legal framework that elevates the Security Council as a clearinghouse for all decisions regarding the lawfulness of military action, with the one exception being the natural right of self-defense. This framework has served the United States remarkably well since its inception. Although critics often complain that the ability of the United States and other major world powers to veto U.N. Security Council resolutions allows these powers to act with impunity, this is certainly not a complaint that the United States might offer.[69] If anything, the current use-of-force regime is weighted toward the interests of the United States rather than against.

The United States might complain that vetoes—or threatened vetoes—from Russia or China could prevent the United States from launching military strikes in situations where military action is badly needed. This was allegedly the situation in Syria in 2013 when the United States failed to secure Security Council authorization for a military intervention against Assad's regime.[70] China and Russia were against intervention, leaving the United States to pursue the intervention against the wishes of the Security Council, and the effort floundered at both the international and domestic level. At the international level, leading states were skeptical that Assad's use of chemical weapons—clearly illegal under customary international law—would trigger a right of intervention from the world community.[71] Domestically, the American public failed to see the utility in the strike, especially since the rebels on whose behalf the United States would have intervened included a sizable percentage of Islamic extremists and al-Qaeda fighters hoping to turn Syria into an Islamic state. Those who wanted an intervention would be forgiven for thinking that the Security Council—and the Charter rules on the use of force—were the real obstacle to intervention.

There are multiple responses here. Most important, the rules on the use of force are rationally defensible because the United States—like any other state—retains the right to use force in self-defense when an armed attack occurs against them. The United States was only blocked from intervening in Syria because no such viable claim of self-defense was available. Lawyers argued about the Responsibility to Protect—a burgeoning legal principle that some lawyers falsely believe supports unilateral intervention in the absence of U.N. Security Council authorization.[72] Other officials, including John Kerry, argued that violating the ban on chemical weapons triggered a right of intervention, a principle nowhere stated in the Chemical Weapons Convention—an instrument that Syria never signed.[73] Had the Syrian intervention represented a true case of U.S. self-defense (or even collective self-defense), the U.N. Charter by its bare terms would have permitted military action even without Security Council authorization. So by agreeing to the U.N. Charter system on the use of force, states gain the protection of a system whereby other states will be prohibited from exercising force (thus representing a huge benefit to peace and stability), while at the same time retaining the right to engage in unilateral self-defense if other states fail to comply with the prohibition. In other words, states gain the protection of the global prohibition on the use of force but need not sacrifice their own right to exercise self-defense when the prohibition is breached. The only exception to this rule is Security Council-authorized enforcement actions, and in this regard, it is perhaps laudable that Security Council authorizations for the use of military force are few and far between. The result, from the perspective of the rational agent, is a rationally defensible strategy that far exceeds the expected payoff from an international system where the Security Council does not exist.

Critics might point out that the problem stems from the actual content of the right of self-defense. Perhaps the law of self-defense unfairly advantages aggressive states and fails to protect weak victim states.[74] For example, the ICJ has inexplicably limited the right of self-defense to cases of attack from foreign states, thus eliminating the possibility that attacks from non-state actors might trigger the right of self-defense. Second, the Charter does not permit the use of force to defend against future attacks because the language of article 51 requires that the right be triggered when an "armed attack occurs."

On the issue of attacks against non-state actors, prohibiting self-defense in response to threats from non-state actors makes no sense either legally or conceptually.[75] First, article 51 says absolutely nothing about the origin of the unlawful attack. In fact, the provision deliberately uses the passive voice in the phrase "if an armed attack occurs," rather than saying "if another state launches an armed conflict"—a phrase that would have justified the exclusion of non-state situations had it been used in the final drafting of the Charter. The ICJ's decision is therefore inconsistent with the language of article 51, and indeed, the ICJ's conclusion on this point cited no legal authority at all for the proposition that armed attacks must come from a foreign state.[76] Apparently, the ICJ still believes that states are the only viable subjects and objects of international law—a quaint and unrealistic view. Furthermore, other international organs clearly disagree with the ICJ's opinion here. After the 9/11 terrorist attacks, the U.N. Security Council issued a resolution concluding that the 9/11 attacks triggered the United States' right of self-defense, a position that is flatly inconsistent with the ICJ views on non-state actors.[77] So the ICJ's view on the matter has not carried the day, nor is it representative of the current state of the law, though it is perhaps correct to describe the issue as unsettled. It would appear that the Security Council's view of the right to self-defense is the better and more persuasive position.

Second, on the issue of future attacks, it is true that article 51 requires that an armed attack occur. However, most scholars and most states have interpreted article 51 to permit self-defense against imminent attacks.[78] Occasionally, these are described as preemptive strikes, although the terminology is used inconsistently and ought to be avoided.[79] The basic issue here is imminence; if the attack is imminent or underway, need the victim state wait until the bombers are in the air before responding? The vast majority of scholars believe not, and state practice supports this view. What *is* controversial is whether a preventive war of self-defense is permissible, that is, preventing a foreign state from even developing the capacity to attack.[80] Bush administration officials advocated for this view of self-defense in arguing that the United States could exercise force against Saddam Hussein to prevent him from attacking innocent states in the future.[81] This argument was controversial and failed to attract widespread international support, although it is perhaps consistent with Israel's unilateral bombing of Iraq's Osirak nuclear reactor in 1981—a military strike that is best described as preventive in nature.[82] In general, there is little evidence that international law supports preventive self-defense.

In contrast, self-defense against imminent attacks is well supported in international law and carefully tracks the rules regarding self-defense in domestic criminal law.[83] Although there have been attempts to displace the imminence requirement in both international and domestic criminal law, those efforts have proven futile because imminence supports the principles of transparency and publicity that must be met before force is appropriate.[84] In other words, the attack must be manifest in some way so that third parties can properly judge the intentions of the aggressor and determine that the "attack" is not simply in the overly sensitive eyes of the victim.[85] It is clear that the overwhelming weight of the international law of self-defense supports adequate intervention, and the "doctrines" that might cripple appropriate exercises of self-defense are often deeply contested norms that can and should be dismissed as incorrect statements of the law.

6.4 The International Court of Justice

If the opinions of the ICJ are merely persuasive and nonbinding against third parties, one wonders why engagement with the World Court is so important—especially since, as the previous section demonstrated, the ICJ has occasionally made pronouncements of international law that are either unsupported by positive law or controversial among the leading publicists in the field. In any other context, this would read like the case against the ICJ, not a legal or political argument in support of its existence and continued relevance in the modern world.

In fact, despite its shortcomings, the ICJ fulfills an acute need in the international system, and states have reason to comply with its judgments even if they cannot be certain that its decisions will be favorable or will accord with their interests. There is, as in any adjudicatory body, an aspect of unpredictability—an essential characteristic resulting from open-minded jurists who think through the questions and render meaningful decisions. The results are not preordained (though they are constrained by the law itself) such that no litigant can predict the outcome with absolute certainty. So why participate in such a system? The answer, in short, is that the system is supported by large-chunk rationality at its purest.

The United States championed the creation of the ICJ when the basic framework for the U.N. system was hammered out at Dumbarton Oaks in Washington, D.C., in the summer of 1944.[86] Indeed, the United States had long been a supporter of a proposed world court, going back to the turn of the twentieth century when the United States championed the idea at the 1907 Hague Conference.[87] FDR supported the court as part of the new United Nations, whose structure was formally codified in the U.N. Charter and related documents that were drafted in San Francisco in 1945. In accordance with past practice, the United States has always had the right to appoint a justice to the World Court, an entitlement that very few states enjoy.[88]

The New Realist's skepticism of the ICJ is not new. Realists of one stripe or another have always challenged the court. After President Wilson negotiated the creation of the League of Nations, the U.S. Senate refused to ratify the treaty that created its judicial organ, which was then known as the Permanent Court of International Justice. In the absence of Senate ratification of the treaty, the United States refused to participate in proceedings before that court between the world wars. In a sense, the Realist objection to the World Court, and indeed to the U.N. in general, has never fully evaporated, leaving a wide gulf between U.S. skepticism of international institutions and European participation in them. As Sean Murphy explains, the schism is at least partly explained by the relative security of the American nation (isolated and protected from invasion by two oceans) and a European continent desperate to avoid repeating the mistakes of the past.[89]

The Europeans have recognized that their collective security is improved by their reciprocal participation in international institutions, even if that requires sacrificing some trappings of sovereignty. This calculation is a perfect example of constrained maximization.

Although realism has always chastened U.S. enthusiasm for the court, its modern estrangement from the institution began in earnest in 1984, when Nicaragua filed suit against the United States over covert paramilitary activities performed by U.S.-supported Contra forces.[90] By the time the court rendered its decision in 1986, the United States had already decided to withdraw from the court's plenary jurisdiction (though doing so did not prevent the court from issuing a decision on the merits of Nicaragua's complaint). The decision was a watershed in its substance, adding much-needed content to the customary rules on state responsibility; the court held that military actions could be attributed to a foreign state when it has effective control over the forces.[91] Although the possibility of an adverse decision on the merits provided one reason for the United States to withdraw from the court's plenary jurisdiction, at least part of the decision to do so can be attributed to the highly controversial nature, within the domestic political sphere, of Reagan's policy of supporting the Contras. Congressional scrutiny was already causing enough problems for the Reagan administration such that additional scrutiny from an international judicial body was most unwelcome, especially since it might provide fuel for congressional critics.[92]

Perhaps the single biggest reason for the United States to support the work of the ICJ is that its power is so limited (and its infringement of state sovereignty is correspondingly small). The biggest popular misconception of the ICJ is that its "compulsory" jurisdiction is compulsory, that is, that it has the power to summon reluctant states before it to account for their behavior. Nothing could be further from the truth. The court's so-called compulsory jurisdiction is based entirely on consent, so that only states that have accepted the court's jurisdiction are permitted to file suit in the court to resolve general matters of international law; this is more properly described as the court's plenary jurisdiction. Moreover, the court's plenary jurisdiction is reciprocal so that a consenting state may only file suit against other consenting states that have agreed to submit themselves to the court's plenary jurisdiction. To date, seventy states have accepted the court's jurisdiction.

The court has other nonplenary sources of jurisdiction. States can agree to ad hoc jurisdiction to resolve a particular dispute with another nation.[93] However, in keeping with its reluctance to support the court's operations, the United States has not used the court's ad hoc jurisdiction since 1981 (in a dispute with Canada).[94] The court may also gain jurisdiction from enforcement clauses in specific treaties, which confer jurisdiction on the court to resolve disputes among a treaty's signatories. A notable example is the Genocide Convention, whose jurisdictional grant to the ICJ allowed the court to hear the genocide case between Bosnia and Serbia.[95] However, the United States pulled out of the Genocide Convention's protocol granting jurisdiction to the ICJ, and so when Serbia sued the United States at the ICJ complaining about its bombing campaign during the Balkan Wars, the case was dismissed for lack of jurisdiction.[96] Similarly, the United States has withdrawn its consent to jurisdiction arising under the Vienna Convention on Consular Relations, the very jurisdiction that gave rise to the *Avena* case and similar decisions that criticized the U.S. failure to grant consular notification for foreign nationals in custody for capital offenses.

It would be wrong to jump to the conclusion that the United States is hostile to all forms of international adjudication. In the absence of ICJ as a viable forum for the resolution of general disputes under its plenary jurisdiction, a large number of specialized tribunals were created, with U.S. consent or participation, to address controversies in specific areas. The World Trade Organization includes a dispute resolution system, as does the North American Free Trade Agreement; foreign investment disputes can be resolved through arbitration at the International Centre for the Settlement of Investment Disputes. One might be tempted to dismiss these examples as mere arbitration panels, though a thorough examination of ICJ jurisdiction reveals that the World Court's procedures share many of the essential characteristics of international arbitration.

Although the United States helped conceive of the World Court and consented to its plenary jurisdiction in 1946, it has not followed through on that international commitment. The failure of other major world powers, including China and Russia, to accept the court's plenary jurisdiction is surely partly to blame. The standard Realist view (whether old or new) is that the strong states ignore the court because they have nothing to gain from it; weaker states join the court because international judgments in their favor could produce a strategic or rhetorical advantage that might strengthen their hand in the game of foreign relations. Again, as Murphy notes, litigants managed to convince the World Court to strongly critique U.S. military activities in the *Oil Platforms Case*, and likewise condemn Israeli actions in the *Wall* case.[97] In both cases, the interests of weaker groups were strengthened by the outcomes. In *Oil Platforms*, Iran sued the United States for destroying oil platforms in 1987 and 1988; the Court concluded that the U.S. military action could not be justified by self-defense. Although the Court refused to order reparations, the decision strengthened Iran's diplomatic posture. In the *Wall* Case, the ICJ issued an advisory opinion concluding that Israel's construction of a security wall around Palestinian occupied territory violated international law—a decision that harmed Israel in the court of world opinion. So, from that perspective, the United States has much to lose from participating in ICJ cases.

These calculations ask the wrong questions. The U.S. withdrawal from the ICJ must be viewed within the totality of the U.S. disengagement from international institutions. The United States has not only embraced but indeed magnified its credentials as the standard-bearer for exceptionalism. When combined with its skepticism toward U.N. Security Council control over use-of-force decisions (a strange tactic given the U.S. veto power there) and its refusal to resign or ratify the Rome Statute for the International Criminal Court, the U.S. withdrawal from ICJ jurisdiction has drawn a portrait (perhaps unfairly) of the United States as an international scofflaw. This is especially true among our European partners. The result is not damage just to reputation but also to the institutions themselves—institutions that help constrain other states just as much as they might constrain the United States. The single pertinent question is whether participation in these institutions (and compliance with their norms) makes the life of the United States go better overall, that is, whether a world with legal institutions is part of a rationally defensible plan.

6.5 The International Criminal Court

The narrative of estrangement continued with the creation of the ICC. The United States (along with Britain, France, and Russia) gave birth to the modern era of international tribunals by creating the International Military Tribunal at Nuremberg, which was then followed by twelve highly influential prosecutions before a domestic criminal tribunal convened by the American government in Nuremberg. Although the project of international criminal justice then lay fallow for half a century, the United States pushed for its resurrection after the atrocities in the Balkans and Rwanda; the result was the Security Council-backed tribunals for Yugoslavia (ICTY) and Rwanda (ICTR). The ICTY was created not just with U.S. acquiescence but with U.S. leadership as one component of the U.S.-led peace process that culminated in the Dayton Peace Accords. The United States also participated in the drafting process of the Rome Statute of the International Criminal Court, though President Clinton was keenly aware that Senate ratification was all but impossible for any tribunal that might indict and prosecute U.S. citizens. Despite this fact, Clinton signed the Rome Statute during his last night in office, giving symbolic resonance to American support for international justice.

President Bush effectively unsigned the treaty.[98] Although signing an international treaty (in the absence of ratification) does not obligate the signatory to fulfill the commitments expressed in the treaty, signatories are under a minimal obligation not to frustrate the object and purpose of the treaty. Apparently, this was reason enough to reverse the Clinton signature, so Ambassador Bolton issued a new declaration effectively "unsigning" the treaty.[99] President Bush then signed legislation authorizing all necessary military force to recover U.S. nationals destined for trial before the ICC, the so-called "Hague Invasion Act."[100]

When the Assembly of State Parties of the ICC assembled in Kampala, Uganda, for its first review conference, the chief subject of discussion was the crime of aggression. The original Rome Statute excluded jurisdiction over the crime of aggression until such time as the state parties could agree to a definition of the crime—a definition that didn't arrive until the conference in Kampala, more than a decade later.[101] Strangely, the United States was a major player in the Kampala negotiations even though the United States was not a state party to the ICC and was present only under observer status. The resulting compromise not only included a definition of aggression but also crafted a unique triggering mechanism that allowed the court to exercise jurisdiction in special circumstances. The triggering mechanism served U.S. interests (as well as Russia and China) because it severely limited the ICC's jurisdiction over cases of aggression to situations where the Security Council had already determined that an act of aggression had occurred.[102] Given the U.S. veto on the Security Council, the triggering mechanism allowed the United States to exert considerable influence over the ICC's jurisdiction on aggression even though the United States was not a member of the court.[103]

At the same time, the administration was supporting the court in other areas as well. In response to the Darfur Crisis, the United States abstained from a Security Council resolution that invoked its Chapter VII authority to refer the situation to the ICC.[104] Although the United States did not vote in favor of the resolution, its willingness to allow the resolution to pass without veto was heralded as a major advance for international justice.[105] Similarly, the Obama administration actively lobbied for a Security Council referral of the Libya situation to the ICC—a referral that arguably helped isolate the government of Colonel Gaddafi and hastened the coalescing of the international community against him.[106] A similar process played out over Syria, where the United States would have supported referral of President Assad to the ICC if only Russia and China had not threatened to veto such a move. Both Russia and China made it abundantly clear that they were unwilling to authorize a referral to the ICC so long as the civil war was still ongoing, and the two nations were certainly opposed to a resolution authorizing a military intervention against the Syrian regime.[107]

In the United States, the New Realists have launched a sustained attack against the ICC. Eric Posner called it the "Absurd International Criminal Court" in the *Wall Street Journal*, declaring it a failure in expending too much money ($100 million) and completing too few cases.[108] He also concluded that it failed on consequentialist grounds, inflaming tensions in Kenya, interfering with the peace process in Uganda, and failing to solve the Darfur crisis.[109] And John Yoo, in reviewing David Scheffer's memoir about his time as an American diplomat setting up the Yugoslavian and Rwandan tribunals, declares that tribunals are a mere afterthought and that only military force can prevent atrocities.[110]

These criticisms miss the mark because they misunderstand the rationale behind international tribunals like the ICC. They are designed to end impunity, that is, to punish perpetrators for violating international law.[111] The primary reason to punish perpetrators is that impunity represents an a priori evil, one that must be stamped out from the world's war zones.[112] Even if only partially—even minimally—effective, the pursuit is still worthwhile. It is true, of course, that ICC referrals are based on the Security Council's authority to restore international peace and security, so it is imperative that the court have some positive effect on regional instability. However, there is no requirement for this effect to be direct and immediate; the ICC may improve the situation on the ground in various inchoate and indirect ways, promoting the rule of law and establishing legal norms that crimes against humanity, war crimes, and genocide represent jus cogens violations of international law. It is wrong, and empirically erroneous, to think that despots will change their behavior given the prospect at trial in The Hague.[113] (Indeed, a trial in the comfort of The Hague might be preferable to death at the hands of an enemy.) But this type of direct deterrence is not the only consequence that would justify the court's operation. If the court can persuade victim communities to refrain from launching deadly acts of vengeance, and instead to submit their grievances to a court of law, then there will be positive benefits to regional peace and security.[114]

The New Realist hysteria that the ICC would erode U.S. sovereignty generates more heat than light. The Rome Statute already includes a deferral clause in article 16 that allows the Security Council to defer any investigation or prosecution for twelve months, subject to renewal ad infinitum.[115] Although this would not prevent investigations against the United States that were supported by other Security Council members (who could veto a deferral resolution), the provision would prevent the nations in the developing world from strategically triggering ICC jurisdiction in a manner that would annoy Russia, China, and the United States as a collective group. In addition, the Rome Statute provision on complementary jurisdiction limits the ICC to a forum of last resort. Finally, the United States has signed more than 100 bilateral agreements with foreign nations extracting promises not to transfer or deliver Americans to The Hague.[116] These agreements are not only tolerated but are also explicitly recognized by article 98 of the Rome Statute, which prevents the court from requesting surrender of any defendant "which would require the requested State to act inconsistently with its obligations under international agreements. . . ."[117] The totality of these systematic constraints is that the ICC already defers to national sovereignty to the maximum extent consistent with the very idea of an international criminal tribunal.

United States support for the ICC, up to and including signing and ratifying the Rome Statute, would provide a major boost to the court and would invigorate the toolbox of diplomats and international lawyers trying to end impunity for international crimes. Its impact on U.S. sovereignty would be minimal, even hypothetical more than actual, and would do little to harm U.S. strategic interests. It would, however, require the United States to finally forgo its rhetoric of exceptionalism and concede that all individuals, even U.S. citizens, are potential subjects of international criminal jurisdiction. This is unlikely to happen anytime soon, regardless of which party is in power in the White House. But if domestic political will allowed it, the United States could finally follow through on its commitment to international justice that it made first in 1945 at Nuremberg and then in the mid-1990s with the creation of the ad hoc tribunals.

6.6 Conclusion

The attack on international law, and its resulting isolationism, ought to be reversed. Skepticism regarding international law generates more than just theoretical anxiety; it also supports political actors who want the United States to withdraw from international institutions or ignore their legal rulings. Under the naïve view, going it alone advances the national interest of the state—a rational "defection" from the law. As this chapter has shown, this initially plausible argument is mistaken. Living in a world with meaningful legal and institutional constraints can maximize national self-interest. This chapter sketched a roadmap for maximizing this self-interest by following through on international commitments. Reengaging international institutions will begin the process of operationalizing the central insight of this book: harmonizing self-interest and legal obligation as mutually reenforcing.

Conclusion

The argument in this book has a tripartite structure. The first goal of the book was to systematically describe the assault on international law, with particular emphasis on how academic arguments about the nature of international law have affected the work of the executive and judicial branches of government. The assault not only questioned the legitimacy of international law based on a questionable theory of what counts as real law but also devised doctrines and theories to limit the scope of its application in federal courts (chapter 1) and provide avenues for the president to ignore it (chapter 2). At the heart of this attack was the mistaken assumption that national self-interest (and American commitment to acting in its self-interest) was somehow fatal to the project of international law.

It should be noted, however, that the book's argument did not include a strong causal claim. Chapters 1 and 2 did not argue that the academic and intellectual attacks on international law caused the Bush administration, in particular in its first term, to veer so far away from international law. Indeed, that might have happened anyway. Rather, the argument is that the intellectual attack on international law gave the Bush administration's foreign policy the veneer of academic respectability, and made it comparatively easier for the administration to pursue these policies. If the intellectual arguments about international law had not been laid at the foundation, the Bush administration would have had to work harder to justify its policies. As it happens, the attack on international law did that work for them.

The second goal of the book was to demonstrate why the New Realist assumptions about rationality are wrong. In chapters 3 and 4, the book demonstrated that the supposed tension between self-interest and obligation is a red herring and that acting out of self-interest is entirely consistent with the basic principles of international law. At the heart of this argument was a deep claim about the nature of rationality. I suggested that states accept constraints on their behavior as part of a strategy of constrained maximization. The theory not only suggested that states should comply with international law as justified by long-term interests but also made the much more radical claim that following through and adhering to international law is rational, even when the state is tempted to defect and ignore its previous promises. In these cases, acting out of self-interest and acting out of obligation go hand in hand. The attack on international law has consistently obscured this reality by turning self-interest and obligation into mutually exclusive categories. Although other scholars (particularly in international relations) have also asserted that national self-interest can include compliance with international law, this book was unique in excavating the deep theory of rationality implicit in this point.

The third part of the book was an exercise in applied theory. Rather than simply reside at the deep level of theory, it was essential to demonstrate that this vision of international law as rational constraint could be operationalized on the ground. Consequently, we considered as a case study the laws of war (chapter 5), showing how adherence to the laws of war is consistent with both national self-interest and legal obligation. Although the laws of war do constrain state behavior, they also license the wholesale killing of one's enemies (provided some conditions are met), thus demonstrating that compliance with the laws of war is not a barrier to fighting international terrorism or other emerging security threats. At least some of the New Realist program simply assumes that there will be a security trade-off for states that comply with international law. Chapter 5 exploded this myth by reconstructing the basic principles of international humanitarian law and showing how their structure provides an excellent example of constrained maximization. Finally, the book's exercise in applied theory ended with a plea for reengaging with international institutions (chapter 6). Engagement with the United Nations, the ICC, and the ICJ are all justified by the strategy of constrained maximization, because following through on a legal commitment is justified even if there are costs associated with following the rule. The rationality of these commitments cannot be evaluated by considering the execution of the promise in total abstraction. Rather, one must evaluate everything together (joining the United Nations and then following its rules, for example) as a package deal. Chapter 6 demonstrated that international legal institutions are calibrated at a modest level (providing minimal but meaningful reciprocal constraints) that can be adopted and followed as part of a coherent rational strategy. As with intending and then drinking the toxin, it is rational to join international institutions and then follow their rules.

International law is a polarizing topic. Some scholars and politicians are predisposed against it and are inclined to view it with suspicion—an external obstacle to American sovereignty and self-government by the people. To them, much in this book will be anathema. Others are disposed in favor of international law, and to them, many of the arguments in this book will sound like preaching to the choir. Hopefully, most readers are somewhere in between, trying to determine when and how a sovereign state should constrain itself through a system of international law. Why accept the constraints when a world without constraints beckons like a siren's song? The answer, of course, is that rationality both permits and demands fidelity to constraints. The strategy of straightforward maximization produces isolation and even global xenophobia—a situation that will only intensify as the rest of the world increases its engagement with and participation in international institutions.

NOTES

INTRODUCTION

1   *See* John Yoo, *The Continuation of Politics by Other Means: The Original Understanding of War Powers*, 84 CALIFORNIA LAW REVIEW 167 (1996). For a more recent expression of this argument, see Robert J. Delahunty & John C. Yoo, *The President's Constitutional Authority to Conduct Military Operations Against Terrorist Organizations and the Nations that Harbor or Support Them*, 25 HARVARD JOURNAL OF LAW & PUBLIC POLICY 487, 492 (2002) ("The centralization of authority in the President alone is particularly crucial in maters of national defense, war, and foreign policy, where a unitary executive can evaluate threats, consider policy choices, and mobilize military and diplomatic resources with a speed and energy that is far superior to any other branch.").

2   Memorandum from Office of the Assistant Attorney Gen. to Alberto R. Gonzales, Counsel to the President (Aug. 1, 2002) [hereinafter Bybee Memorandum].

3   Bybee Memorandum, pp. 5–6.

4   Memorandum from John Yoo, Deputy Assistant Attorney General & Robert J. Delahunty, Special Counsel, to William J. Haynes II, General Counsel, Department of Defense 1 (Jan. 9, 2002) [hereinafter Yoo Memorandum]. Gonzales then drafted a memo that reiterated Yoo's conclusions. Memorandum from Alberto R. Gonzales, Attorney General, to George W. Bush, President of the United States (Jan. 25, 2002).

5   Yoo Memorandum, pp. 2, 3, 14 ("Afghanistan's status as a failed state is ground alone to find that members of the Taliban militia are not entitled to enemy POW status under the Geneva Conventions.").

6   Patrick F. Philbin, *Legality of the Use of Military Commissions to Try Terrorists*, Memorandum to White House Counsel Alberto Gonzales (Nov. 6, 2001).

7   John Yoo, Memorandum for the Attorney General (Nov. 2, 2001) (redacted). The Yoo memorandum was eventually replaced by a new document authored by Jack Goldsmith. *See* Jack Goldsmith, Memorandum for the Attorney General (May 6, 2004) (redacted).

8   *See* JACK GOLDSMITH, THE TERROR PRESIDENCY 22 (2007).

9   *Id.* at 23.

10   *Id.*

11   *Id.* at 24 ("Yoo saw Ashcroft much more than Jay Bybee did, but he took his instructions mainly from Gonzales, and he sometimes gave Gonzales opinions and verbal advice without fully running matters by the Attorney General. This arrangement was an understandable affront to Ashcroft, who worried about the advice Yoo was providing in the Attorney General's name. So when the White House wanted to elevate Yoo to lead the office, Ashcroft put his food down and vetoed Yoo for the job.").

12   *Id.* at 25 ("It is unclear whether Ashcroft really believed this or whether he said it to kill Yoo's chances for other reasons.").

13   *Id.*

14   *Id.* at 144–46. *See also id.* at 149 (quoting a senior government lawyer as saying that the memo "reads like a bad defense counsel's brief, not an OLC opinion.").

15   *Id.* at 149.

16   For a discussion of this issue, see Trevor Morrison, *Stare Decisis in the Office of Legal Counsel*, 110 COLUMBIA LAW REVIEW 1448 (2010). There is even an OLC memorandum on the value of precedent in OLC memoranda, called "Best Practices for OLC Legal Advice and Written Opinions." *See id.* at 1453.

17   *See* JOHN YOO, WAR BY OTHER MEANS 186 (2006).

18   GOLDSMITH, *supra* note 8, at 161.

19   Daniel Levin, Memorandum for the Attorney General, Legal Standards Applicable under 18 U.S.C. §§ 2340–2340A (Dec. 30, 2004).

20   GOLDSMITH, *supra* note 8, at 161.

21   For example, Professor Grimmelmann at NYU Law School refers to Goldsmith as a hero and even compares him to Sir Thomas More in *A Man For all Seasons*. Specifically, Grimmelmann says that Goldsmith "is an honorable man and committed to the rule of law." *See* James Grimmelmann, *Jack Goldsmith, Hero*, THE LABORATORIUM BLOG (Sept. 8, 2007, 8:50 PM), http://laboratorium.net/archive/2007/09/08/jack_goldsmith_hero_1. *See also* Jeffrey Rosen, The Conscience of a Conservative, N.Y. TIMES, Sept. 9, 2007.

22   GOLDSMITH, *supra* note 8, at 71.

23   *See* Marcella Bombardieri, *Harvard Hire's Detainee Memo Stirs Debate*, BOSTON GLOBE, Dec. 9, 2004.

24   YOO, WAR BY OTHER MEANS, at 186.

25 Eric Posner is the son of the famous appeals court Judge Richard Posner. Judge Posner is considered the father of the modern law and economics movement, which took both the academy and judiciary by storm in the 1980s with a style of legal analysis that emphasized how legal rules should be designed with economic analysis to produce efficient outcomes. Judge Posner also lectures at Chicago Law School and has written dozens of books analyzing everything from why African American women are heavier than their white counterparts (not enough potential male partners to make it worthwhile for them to diet), to why the U.S. Constitution permits the federal government to curtail civil liberties in order to protect the nation from terrorist attacks (the Constitution is not a suicide pact). *See* RICHARD POSNER, OVERCOMING LAW 15 (1995); RICHARD POSNER, NOT A SUICIDE PACT: THE CONSTITUTION IN A TIME OF NATIONAL EMERGENCY (2006).

26 *See* ERIC A. POSNER & ADRIAN VERMEULE, TERROR IN THE BALANCE: SECURITY, LIBERTY, AND THE COURTS 185 (2007).

27 *See* ERIC A. POSNER & ADRIAN VERMEULE, THE EXECUTIVE UNBOUND: AFTER THE MADISONIAN REPUBLIC 32 (2010).

28 *Id.* at 106.

29 *See* Robert J. Delahunty & John Yoo, *Executive Power v. International Law*, 30 HARVARD JOURNAL OF LAW & PUBLIC POLICY 73 (2007); Jack Goldsmith & Eric Posner, *A Theory of Customary International Law*, UNIVERSITY OF CHICAGO LAW REVIEW (1999).

30 POSNER & VERMEULE, *supra* note 27, at 180–81.

31 *See* JACK GOLDSMITH & ERIC POSNER, THE LIMITS OF INTERNATIONAL LAW 185 (2005).

32 The first wave of realism in the international relations literature (often referred to as classical realism) then spurred a neo-realism offshoot beginning around 1979–1980 that focused on the anarchic structure of the international system. *See, e.g.,* KENNETH WALTZ, THEORY OF INTERNATIONAL POLITICS (1979).

33 *See* KENNETH WALTZ, THEORY OF INTERNATIONAL POLITICS (1979). For an important discussion of neo-realism in international relations, *see* LEA BRILMAYER, AMERICAN HEGEMONY: POLITICAL MORALITY IN A ONE-SUPERPOWER WORLD 33 (1994).

CHAPTER ONE

1 The Paquete Habana, 175 U.S. 677 (1900).

2 *Id.* at 700 ("[i]nternational law is part of our law, and must be ascertained and administered by the courts of justice of appropriate jurisdiction as often as questions of right depending upon it are duly presented for their determination.")

3   Curtis Bradley & Jack L. Goldsmith, *Customary International Law as Federal Common Law: A Critique of the Modern Position*, 110 HARVARD LAW REVIEW 815, 816–17 (1997).

4   Erie R.R. Co. v. Tompkins, 304 U.S. 64 (1938).

5   *Erie*, 304 U.S. at 78.

6   Bradley & Goldsmith, *supra* note 3, at 821.

7   *See* Philip Jessup, *The Doctrine of Erie Railroad v. Tompkins Applied to International Law*, 33 AMERICAN JOURNAL OF INTERNATIONAL LAW 740 (1939).

8   *Id.* at 742.

9   *Id.* at 743.

10 U.S. Term Limits, Inc. v. Thornton, 514 U.S. 779, 838 (1995) (Kennedy, J., concurring).

11 Banco Nacional de Cuba v. Sabbatino, 376 U.S. 398 (1964).

12 *See* Fausto de Quadros & John Henry Dingfelder Stone, *Act of State Doctrine*, *in* MAX PLANCK ENCYCLOPEDIA OF PUBLIC INTERNATIONAL LAW (2012).

13 *Sabbatino*, 376 U.S. at 423–24.

14 *Id.* at 422.

15 *Id.* at 425.

16 Bradley & Goldsmith, *supra* note 3, at 836 (citing United States v. Belmont, 301 U.S. 324 (1937)).

17 Bradley & Goldsmith, *supra* note 3, at 860.

18 *Id.* at 823–34.

19 *Id.* at 827.

20 Federal Judiciary Act of September 24, 1789, sec. 34, 28 U.S.C. § 725. *See also* 28 U.S.C. § 1652.

21 Bradley & Goldsmith, *supra* note 3, at 854.

22 Kuhn v. Fairmont Coal Co., 215 U.S. 349, 370–372 (1910); *see also* Black & White Taxicab Co. v. Brown & Yellow Taxicab Co., 276 U.S. 518, 532–536 (1928).

23 Bradley & Goldsmith, *supra* note 3, at 852.

24 *Id.* at 853–54.

25 Southern Pacific Co. v. Jensen, 244 U.S. 205, 222 (1917) (Holmes, J., dissenting).

26 Bradley & Goldsmith, *supra* note 3, at 855.

27 *Id.* at 853.

28 J.L. AUSTIN, THE PROVINCE OF JURISPRUDENCE DETERMINED 15 (1832).

29 H.L.A. HART, THE CONCEPT OF LAW 79 (2nd ed. 1994).

30 *Id.* at 81.

31 *Id.*

32 *Id.* at 94.

33 *Id.* at 95.

34 *Id.* at 101–03.

35 *Id.* at 213–37.

36 *Id.* at 216 ("Both forms of doubt arise from an adverse comparison of international law with municipal law").

37 HART, *supra* note 29, at 217.

38 *See* Oona A. Hathaway & Scott J. Shapiro, *Outcasting: Enforcement in Domestic and International Law*, 121 YALE LAW JOURNAL 252 (2011).

39 Bradley & Goldsmith, *supra* note 3, at 852.

40 *See* Southern Pacific Co. v. Jensen, 244 U.S. 205, 22 (1917) (Holmes, J., dissenting) (emphasis added).

41 I am not relying on Arthur Weisburd's argument, rejected by Bradley and Goldsmith, that customary international law emanates from an aggregation of the "joint lawmaking activity of many sovereigns." *See* Arthur Weisburd, *State Courts, Federal Courts, and International Cases*, 20 YALE JOURNAL OF INTERNATIONAL LAW 1, 51 (1995), *cited in* Bradley & Goldsmith, *supra* note 3, at 853. Rather, I am arguing that the international community represents a Holmesian "quasi-sovereign" insofar as it crafts legal norms that require compliance. The lack of a centralized enforcement mechanism can only deny the international community the status of "quasi-sovereign" if one accepts the discredited Austinian theory of sovereignty based on the command theory.

42 *See* JEAN-JACQUES ROUSSEAU, THE SOCIAL CONTRACT, book IV, ch. 2 (1762). *Cf.* HANS KELSEN, PRINCIPLES OF INTERNATIONAL LAW 316–17 (1952) (discussing international law in the absence of consent and drawing analogy to Rousseau's distinction between *volonté générale* and *volonté de tous*).

43 Bradley & Goldsmith, *supra* note 3, at 836.

44 *See In Memoriam: Louis Henkin*, 49 COLUMBIA JOURNAL OF TRANSNATIONAL LAW 1 (2010); RESTATEMENT (THIRD) OF FOREIGN RELATIONS LAW OF THE UNITED STATES (1987).

45 Bradley & Goldsmith, *supra* note 3, at 836.

46 *Id.*

47 Filartiga v. Pena-Irala, 630 F.2d 876 (2d Cir. 1980).

48 *Filartiga*, 630 F.2d at 881.

49 Bradley & Goldsmith, *supra* note 3, at 836.

50 *Filartiga*, 630 F.2d at 886–87.

51 *See, e.g.*, Harlan Grant Cohen, *Supremacy and Diplomacy: The International Law of the U.S. Supreme Court*, 24 BERKELEY JOURNAL OF INTERNATIONAL LAW 273, 285 (2006) ("Scholars have long battled over the status of customary international law under the Constitution. Justice Souter resolves the debate. Customary international law is federal common law."); William S. Dodge, *Customary International Law and the Question of Legitimacy*, 120 HARVARD LAW REVIEW FORUM 19, 23 (2007). ("Congress controls the

jurisdiction of the federal courts and could restrict their jurisdiction over questions of customary international law. Alternatively, Congress could override substantive rules of customary international law by enacting a statute to the contrary.")

52   *See* William R. Casto, *The* Erie *Doctrine and the Structure of Constitutional Revolutions*, 62 TULANE LAW REVIEW 907, 933–35 (1988).

53   *Erie*, 304 U.S. at 74–75.

54   U.S. Term Limits, Inc. v. Thornton, 514 U.S. 779, 838 (1995) (Kennedy, J., concurring).

55   *See, e.g.*, Ryan Goodman & Derek P. Jinks, Filartiga's *Firm Footing: International Human Rights and Federal Common Law*, 66 FORDHAM LAW REVIEW 463, 469 (1997). *See also* William S. Dodge, *Bridging* Erie: *Customary International Law in the U.S. Legal System after* Sosa v. Alvarez-Machain, 12 TULSA JOURNAL OF COMPARATIVE & INTERNATIONAL LAW 87, 88 (2004).

56   542 U.S. 692 (2004).

57   *Id.* at 698.

58   *Id.*

59   United States v. Alvarez-Machain, 504 U.S. 655 (1992); United States v. Verdugo-Urquidez, 494 U.S. 259 (1990).

60   United States v. Verdugo-Urquidez, 494 U.S. 259, 267 (1990) ("There is likewise no indication that the Fourth Amendment was understood by contemporaries of the Framers to apply to activities of the United States directed against aliens in foreign territory or in international waters.").

61   Sosa v. Alvarez-Machain, 542 U.S. 692, 699 (2004).

62   *Id.* at 725 ("[C]ourts should require any claim based on the present-day law of nations to rest on a norm of international character accepted by the civilized world and defined with a specificity comparable to the features of the 18th-century paradigms we have recognized.").

63   *Id.* at 715 (citing 4 WILLIAM BLACKSTONE, COMMENTARIES ON THE LAWS OF ENGLAND 68 (1769)).

64   *Id.* at 725.

65   542 U.S. at 729–30.

66   *Id.* at 730.

67   *Id.*

68   *See* Curtis A. Bradley, Jack L. Goldsmith & David H. Moore, Sosa, *Customary International Law, and the Continuing Relevance of* Erie, 120 HARVARD LAW REVIEW 869 (2007).

69   *Id.* at 893.

70   *Sosa v. Alvarez-Machain*, 542 U.S. at 741 (Scalia, J., concurring).

71   *Id.* at 743.

72   For a discussion of these cases, see GEORGE P. FLETCHER, TORT LIABILITY FOR HUMAN RIGHTS ABUSES 161–71 (2008).

73   *See, e.g.,* Khulumani v. Barclay Nat'l Bank Ltd., 504 F.3d 254 (2d Cir. 2007).

74   *See, e.g.,* Kiobel v. Royal Dutch Petroleum Co., 621 F.3d 111 (2d Cir. 2010); Herero People's Reparations Corp. v. Deutsche Bank, 370 F.3d 1192, 1193, 1195 (D.C. Cir. 2004); Flomo v. Firestone Nat'l Rubber Co., 643 F.3d 1013 (7th Cir. 2011).

75   *See Flomo,* 643 F.3d at 1018 ("We have to consider *why* corporations have rarely been prosecuted criminally or civilly for violating customary international law; maybe there's a compelling reason.").

76   The issue is discussed in Andrew Clapman, *Extending International Criminal Law Beyond the Individual to Corporations and Armed Opposition Groups,* 6 JOURNAL OF INTERNATIONAL CRIMINAL JUSTICE 899 (2008).

77   *See* Brief of Respondents in Opposition, on Petition for a Writ of Certiorari to the United States Court of Appeals for the Second Circuit, Kiobel v. Shell Petroleum Co., No. 10-1491, 2011 WL 3584741 (Aug. 12, 2011).

78   *See Kiobel,* 621 F.3d at 122.

79   *Compare* Kevin Jon Heller, *Talisman Energy—Amateur Hour at the International Law Improv,* OPINIO JURIS (Oct. 6, 2009), *available at* http://opiniojuris. org/2009/10/06/talisman-energy-amateur-hour-at-the-international-law-improv/, *with* Presbyterian Church of Sudan v. Talisman Energy, 582 F.3d 244, 258 (2d Cir. 2009).

80   *See, e.g.,* Liu Bo Shan v. China Constr. Bank Corp., 421 F. App'x 89 (2d Cir. 2011). *But see In Re* South African Apartheid Litig., 617 F. Supp. 2d 228 (S.D.N.Y. 2011).

81   Kiobel v. Royal Dutch Petroleum Co., 621 F.3d 111 (2d Cir. 2010).

82   Kiobel v. Royal Dutch Petroleum Co., 642 F.3d 379 (2d Cir. 2011) (denying rehearing en banc).

83   Transcript of Oral Argument at 1–7, Kiobel v. Royal Dutch Petroleum Co., No. 10-1491 (U.S., Feb. 28, 2012), *available at* http://www.supremecourt.gov/ oral_arguments/argument_transcripts/10-1491.pdf.

84   *See* Brief for Chevron Corporation, Dole Food Company, Dow Chemical Company, Ford Motor Company, GlaxoSmithKline plc, and the Procter & Gamble Company as Amici Curiae Supporting Respondents, Kiobel v. Royal Dutch Petroleum Co., 6 (Feb. 3, 2012) [hereinafter Goldsmith Amicus Brief].

85   *Id.* at 8.

86   *Id.* at 3.

87   *Id.* at 21.

88   *Id.* at 3.

89   *See* Eric Engle, Private Law Remedies for Extraterritorial Human Rights Violations 154 (2006) (unpublished Ph.D. dissertation, University of Bremen), *available at* http://aei.pitt.edu/7547/1/doktorarbeit.pdf.

90   Goldsmith Amicus Brief at 5.

91   Kiobel v. Royal Dutch Petroleum Co., 133 S. Ct. 1659, 1669 (2013).

92   Morrison v. Nat'l Australia Bank Ltd., 130 S. Ct. 2869 (2010).

93   *Kiobel*, 133 S. Ct. at 1669 (Kennedy, J., concurring).

94   *Kiobel*, 133 S. Ct. at 1671 (Breyer, J., concurring).

95   Anthony J. Colangelo, Kiobel: *Muddling the Distinction Between Prescriptive and Adjudicative Jurisdiction*, 28 MARYLAND JOURNAL OF INTERNATIONAL LAW 65, 71–72 (2013).

96   *Id.*

97   *Kiobel*, 133 S. Ct. at 1670.

98   For an in-depth discussion of the content of these memoranda, see Jens David Ohlin, *The Torture Lawyers*, 51 HARVARD INTERNATIONAL LAW JOURNAL 193 (2010).

99   *See* Memorandum from John Yoo, Deputy Assistant Secretary General, & Robert J. Delahunty, Special Counsel, Memorandum to William J. Haynes II, General Counsel, Department of Defense (Jan. 9, 2002) [hereinafter Yoo Memo]; Memorandum from Jay S. Bybee, Assistant Attorney General, Memorandum to Alberto R. Gonzales, Counsel to the President, and William J. Haynes II, General Counsel of the Department of Defense 32 (Jan. 22, 2002).

100   Yoo Memo at 35.

101   *Id.* at 35 n.108.

102   *Id.*

103   *Id.* at 36.

104   *Id.* at 38.

105   *Id.*

106   *Id.* at 42.

107   David J. Barron & Martin S. Lederman, *The Commander in Chief at the Lowest Ebb—Framing the Problem, Doctrine, and Original Understanding*, 121 HARVARD LAW REVIEW 689 (2008).

108   Youngstown Sheet & Tube Co. v. Sawyer, 343 U.S. 579, 635–37 (1952) (Jackson, J., concurring).

109   Barron & Lederman, *supra* note 107, at 714.

110   *Id.* at 706.

111   *See* Scott Shane & Benjamin Weiser, *Administration Considers Moving Site of 9/11 Trial*, N.Y. TIMES, Jan. 29, 2010.

112   *See* Charlie Savage, *Secret U.S. Memo Made Legal Case to Kill a Citizen*, N.Y. TIMES, Oct. 8, 2011.

113   *Id.*

114   *See* Mark Mazzetti, Charlie Savage & Scott Shane, *How a U.S. Citizen Came to Be in America's Cross Hairs*, N.Y TIMES, Mar. 9, 2013. *See also* Kevin Jon Heller, *Let's Call Killing al-Awlaki What It Is—Murder*, OPINIO JURIS (Apr. 8, 2010), *available at* http://opiniojuris.org/2010/04/08/lets-call-killing-al-awlaki-what-it-is-murder/.

115   Authorization for the Use of Military Force (AUMF), Pub. L. No. 107–40, § 2(a), 115 Stat. 224, 224 (2001). In response to some of these concerns, the Attorney General sent a letter to the Judiciary Committee outlining the legal rationale for the strikes. *See* Letter from Eric H. Holder Jr., to Sen. Patrick Leahy, Judiciary Committee Chairman (May 22, 2013).

116   *See* Michael D. Shear & Scott Shane, *Congress to See Memo Backing Drone Attacks on Americans*, N.Y. TIMES, Feb. 6, 2013.

117   *See* DEPARTMENT OF JUSTICE WHITE PAPER, LAWFULNESS OF A LETHAL OPERATION DIRECTED AGAINST A U.S. CITIZEN WHO IS A SENIOR OPERATIONAL LEADER OF AL-QA'IDA OR AN ASSOCIATED FORCE, at 3, *available at* http://msnbcmedia.msn.com/i/msnbc/sections/news/020413_DOJ_White_Paper.pdf.

118   *Id.* at 10.

119   *See* Authorization for the Use of Military Force (AUMF), Pub. L. No. 107–40, § 2(a), 115 Stat. 224, 224 (2001).

120   *See* Curtis A. Bradley & Jack L. Goldsmith, *Congressional Authorization and the War on Terrorism*, 118 HARVARD LAW REVIEW 2047, 2108 (2005).

121   *Id.* at 2112.

122   *See* Michael Bothe, *The Law of Neutrality*, *in* THE HANDBOOK OF INTERNATIONAL HUMANITARIAN LAW 571, 580 (Dieter Fleck ed., 2d ed. 2009).

123   For a discussion of this issue, see Rebecca Ingber, *Untangling Belligerency from Neutrality in the Conflict with Al-Qaeda*, 47 TEXAS INTERNATIONAL LAW JOURNAL 75, 96 (2011).

124   Military Commissions Act of 2006, 10 U.S. Code § 948a (2006).

125   Military Commissions Act of 2009, 10 U.S. Code § 948a (2009).

126   *See* Respondents' Memorandum Regarding the Government's Detention Authority Relative to Detainees Held at Guantanamo Bay, *In Re* Guantanamo Bay Detention Litig., Misc. No. 08-442 (TFH) (D.D.C. Mar. 13, 2009), at 2.

127   *Id.*

128   *See* Al-Bihani v. Obama, 590 F.3d 866, 872 (D.C. Cir. 2010).

129   Bradley & Goldsmith, *Congressional Authorization and the War on Terrorism*, 118 HARVARD LAW REVIEW 2047, 2108 (2005). They borrowed the term from the U.S. Defense Department order creating the Combatant Status Review Tribunals (CSRT). *See* Memorandum from the Deputy Secretary of Defense to the Secretary of the Navy 1 (July 7, 2004). *See also* Boumediene v. Bush, 583 F. Supp. 2d 133, 134–35 (D.D.C. 2008) (using the associated forces concept in definition of enemy combatant and noting that the term first appeared in the Defense Department's CSRT order before its inclusion in the Military Commission Act of 2006).

130   Al-Bihani v. Obama, 619 F.3d 1 (D.C. Cir. 2010).

131   *Id.* at 2.

132   *Id.*

133   *Id.* at 17. Kavanaugh also cited other articles. *See* Ernest A. Young, *Sorting Out the Debate over Customary International Law*, 42 VIRGINIA JOURNAL OF INTERNATIONAL LAW 365, 393–94 (2002); Bradford R. Clark, *Federal Common Law: A Structural Reinterpretation*, 144 UNIVERSITY OF PENNSYLVANIA LAW REVIEW 1245, 1279–81 & n.169 (1996); John F. Manning, *Textualism and the Equity of the Statute*, 101 COLUMBIA LAW REVIEW 1, 99 n.382 (2001).

134   Murray v. The Charming Betsy, 6 U.S. (2 Cranch) 64, 118 (1804) ("It has also been observed that an act of Congress ought never to be construed to violate the law of nations if any other possible construction remains. . . .").

135   Hamdi v. Rumsfeld, 542 U.S. 507 (2004).

136   Hamdi v. Rumsfeld, 542 U.S. at 521.

137   *See* Al-Bihani v. Obama, 619 F.3d 1, 54 (D.C. Cir. 2010) (Williams, J., concurring) ("Use of international law as a one-way ratchet seems to me illogical.").

138   Bradley & Goldsmith, *Congressional Authorization and the War on Terrorism*, 118 HARVARD LAW REVIEW 2047, 2094 (2005). According to Bradley and Goldsmith: "[I]f the international laws of war can inform the powers that Congress has implicitly granted to the President in the AUMF, they logically can inform the boundaries of such powers." *Id.* For Kavanaugh, this argument upsets appropriate judicial deference to executive action in the national security context. *See* Al-Bihani, 619 F.3d at 44 (citing Dep't of Navy v. Egan, 484 U.S. 518 (1988), Haig v. Agee, 453 U.S. 280 (1981), Dames & Moore v. Regan, 453 U.S. 654 (1981), Youngstown Sheet & Tube Co. v. Sawyer, 343 U.S. 579 (1952), and United States v. Curtiss-Wright, 299 U.S. 304 (1936)).

139   552 U.S. 491 (2008).

140   *Al-Bihani*, 619 F.3d at 10.

141   In a brisk counterattack, Senior Circuit Judge Williams represented the lone standard-bearer willing to stand up for international law on the D.C. Circuit. In a concurring opinion, Judge Brown took Williams to task for supporting judicial aggrandizement, an Orwellian usurpation of the legislative role and an attempt to "dictate to Congress what it is supposed to think." According to Judge Brown, Judge Williams's conclusion that the judiciary should be involved in policing the executive branch operations during wartime—using international legal principles—represents "a hazy but ominous hermeneutics" at odds with the Constitution. *Al-Bihani*, 619 at 4. Brown then denies that international law should ever be granted equal footing with legislative history or dictionary definitions when engaging in statutory interpretation. This is an incredible claim, since some Supreme Court justices already (albeit controversially) look to international sources to cash out the content

of constitutional provisions. And the issue here is simply statutory provision. Furthermore, where the congressional statute uses concepts or terms that originate in international law—such as the law of war or the use of force—then recourse to these domains represents not an ambitious interpretive tool but simple due diligence into the provenance of these concepts. To blithely denigrate the use of international law as "ominous hermeneutics" is to insist that these concepts are purely domestic in origin and that they can and should be untethered from their international origins.

CHAPTER TWO

1   For an example of the argument, see ERIC A. POSNER & JACK L. GOLDSMITH, THE LIMITS OF INTERNATIONAL LAW 39 (2006) ("A state's compliance with the co-operative strategy in the bilateral prisoner's dilemma has nothing to do with acting from a sense of legal obligation. States do not act in accordance with a rule that they feel obliged to follow; they act because it is in their interests to do so.").

2   *See* ERIC A. POSNER & ADRIAN VERMEULE, THE EXECUTIVE UNBOUND: AFTER THE MADISONIAN REPUBLIC 4 (2010) ("the major constraints on the executive, especially in crises, do not arise from law or from the separation-of-powers framework defended by liberal legalists, but from politics and public opinion"). *See also id.* at 113–14 (noting that mechanisms of self-constraint are more important than Madisonian separation of powers).

3   POSNER & VERMEULE, *supra* note 2, at 14.

4   *Id.* at 152–53.

5   *Id.* at 12 ("Public opinion, not Madisonian deliberation, rules the day.").

6   *Id.* at 14–15.

7   *See* Richard H. Pildes, *Law and the President,* 125 HARVARD LAW REVIEW 1381 (2012).

8   *Id.* at 1409.

9   *Id.* at 1410.

10   *Id.*

11   *Id.*

12   POSNER & VERMEULE, *supra* note 2, at 135.

13   *Id.* at 113.

14   *Id.* at 79.

15   *Id.*

16   Pildes, *supra* note 7, at 1408–09.

17   *See generally* LARRY D. KRAMER, THE PEOPLE THEMSELVES: POPULAR CONSTITUTIONALISM AND JUDICIAL REVIEW 107 (2005) (concluding that "[i]n a world of popular constitutionalism, government officials are regulated, not the regulators, and final interpretive authority rests with the people themselves").

18 For a survey of the different connections between judicial developments and public opinion, see Nathaniel Persily, Jack Citrin & Patrick J. Egan, eds., PUBLIC OPINION AND CONSTITUTIONAL CONTROVERSY (2008). *See also* Larry Alexander & Lawrence B. Solum, *Popular? Constitutionalism?*, 118 HARVARD LAW REVIEW 1594 (2005).

19 BRUCE ACKERMAN, WE THE PEOPLE: FOUNDATIONS (1991).

20 POSNER & VERMEULE, *supra* note 2, at 82 (noting the "sponginess" of popular constitutionalism).

21 *Id.* at 82–83.

22 *Id.* at 83.

23 *See, e.g.*, Larry D. Kramer, POPULAR CONSTITUTIONALISM, CIRCA 2004, 92 CALIFORNIA LAW REVIEW 959 (2004).

24 *See* ACKERMAN, *supra* note 19, at 6–7.

25 J.L. AUSTIN, THE PROVINCE OF JURISPRUDENCE DETERMINED 15 (1832).

26 United States v. Nixon, 418 U.S. 683 (1974).

27 The counterfactual question has been posed many times. *See, e.g.*, STEVEN J. BRAMS, GAME THEORY AND THE HUMANITIES: BRIDGING TWO WORLDS 133 (2011).

28 *See* H. L. A. HART, THE CONCEPT OF LAW (3d ed. 2012). *See also* Pildes, *supra* note 7, at 1410.

29 *Id.* at 95–97.

30 *Id.* at 108. For a good discussion on this topic, see Stephen Perry, *Hart on Social Rules and the Foundations of Law: Liberating the Internal Point of View*, 75 FORDHAM LAW REVIEW 1171, 1202 (2006) (noting that there is no definite answer to the question of how much of the population needs to adopt this shared attitude about the validity of the law); Scott Shapiro, *What is the Rule of Recognition (and Does It Exist)?*, *in* THE RULE OF RECOGNITION AND THE U.S. CONSTITUTION 235, 250 (Matthew Adler & Kenneth Himma eds., 2009). Shapiro's account relies heavily on Bratman's account of shared agency. *See* MICHAEL BRATMAN, INTENTION, PLANS, AND PRACTICAL REASON (1987).

31 HART, *supra* note 28, at 214.

32 Marbury v. Madison, 5 U.S. (1 Cranch) 137, 177 (1803).

33 *See* Matthew D. Adler, *Popular Constitutionalism and the Rule of Recognition: Whose Practices Ground U.S. Law?*, 100 NORTHWESTERN UNIVERSITY LAW REVIEW 719 (2006).

34 *Id.* at 721.

35 *Id.* at 722.

36 HART, *supra* note 28, at 61. *See also* Adler, *supra* note 33, at 719.

37 *See* Adler, *supra* note 33, at 725.

38 POSNER & VERMEULE, *supra* note 2, at 3–5, 14–15.

39 John Yoo, *War, Responsibility, and the Age of Terrorism*, 57 STANFORD LAW REVIEW 793 (2004).

40 See, e.g., Jide Nzelibe & John Yoo, *Rational War and Constitutional Design*, 115 YALE LAW JOURNAL 2512 (2006).

41 POSNER & VERMEULE, *supra* note 2, at 8–10.

42 *See generally* JOHN YOO, THE POWERS OF WAR AND PEACE: THE CONSTITUTION & FOREIGN AFFAIRS AFTER 9/11 (2006).

43 *Id.* at 144.

44 *Id.* at 145.

45 *Id.* at 160.

46 *Id.* at 159.

47 *Id.*

48 *See, e.g.,* POSNER & VERMEULE, *supra* note 2, at 33; William E. Scheuerman, *The Economic State of Emergency*, 21 CARDOZO LAW REVIEW 1869, 1887 (2000).

49 POSNER & VERMEULE, *supra* note 2, at 34–41.

50 *See generally* Carl Schmitt, THE CRISIS OF PARLIAMENTARY DEMOCRACY (Ellen Kennedy trans., 1985) (1923).

51 POSNER & VERMEULE, *supra* note 2, at 42.

52 *Id.*

53 *Id.*

54 *Id.*

55 *Id.*

56 *Id.* at 42–43.

57 Schmitt was heavily influenced by Hobbes and wrote a book about him. *See* Carl Schmitt, THE LEVIATHAN IN THE STATE THEORY OF THOMAS HOBBES: MEANING AND FAILURE OF A POLITICAL SYMBOL (George Schwab & Erna Hilfstein trans., 1996) (1938).

58 THOMAS HOBBES, LEVIATHAN 111 (J. C. A. Gaskin ed., 1996) (1651).

59 *Id.* at 125 (pt. 2, ch. 19, para. 6).

60 *Id.*

61 *Id.* (pt. 2, ch. 19, para. 7).

62 *See* Thomas Hobbes, BEHEMOTH: OR THE LONG PARLIAMENT 113–14 (Stephen Holmes ed., 1990) (1889).

63 *Id.* at 3–4.

64 HOBBES, *supra* note 58, at 125 (pt. 2, ch. 19, para. 8).

65 *Id.*

66 *Id.* at 124–25 (pt. 2, ch. 19, para. 4).

67 *Id.*

68 *Id.*

69 Consider the case of the North Korean government, which has a "military first" policy.

70 HOBBES, *supra* note 58, at 125 (pt. 2, ch. 19, para. 5).

71 *Id.*

72 POSNER & VERMEULE, *supra* note 2, at 43.

73   *Id.* at 27 ("As a strictly comparative matter, however, the contrast is strik-
     ing: the executive can act with much greater unity, force, and dispatch than
     can Congress, which is chronically hampered by the need for debate and
     consensus among large numbers").

74   *Id.* at 43–44.

75   *Id.* at 44.

76   This antipathy to collective action shows up in other works. *See* POSNER
     & DAVID WEISBACH, CLIMATE CHANGE JUSTICE 101 (2012) ("the idea that
     nation-state can be moral agents is highly unappealing, as it relies on
     notions of collective responsibility that have been rejected by mainstream
     philosophers as well as institutions such as criminal law and tort law").

77   *See generally* CHRISTIAN LIST & PHILIP PETTIT, GROUP AGENCY: THE
     POSSIBILITY, DESIGN, AND STATUS OF CORPORATE AGENTS (2011).

78   *See generally* CAROL ROVANE, THE BOUNDS OF AGENCY: AN ESSAY IN
     REVISIONARY METAPHYSICS (1997).

79   *See, e.g.*, Seumas Miller & Pekka Makela, *The Collectivist Approach to
     Collective Moral Responsibility*, 36 METAPHILOSOPHY 634 (2005) (support-
     ing individualist account of responsibility).

80   *See* Lewis A. Kornhauser & Lawrence G. Sager, *The One and the
     Many: Adjudication in Collegial Courts*, 81 CALIFORNIA LAW REVIEW 1, 10–13
     (1993); Philip Pettit, *Collective Persons and Powers*, 8 LEGAL THEORY 443
     (2002).

81   Pettit, *id.* at 444.

82   *Id.* at 446.

83   *See* DEREK PARFIT, REASONS AND PERSONS 214–16 (1984) (arguing that in the
     reductionist view, psychological connections within an individual can vary
     by degree). *Cf.* Jeanette Kennett & Steve Matthews, *The Unity and Disunity
     of Agency*, 10 PHILOSOPHY, PSYCHIATRY, & PSYCHOLOGY 305 (2003).

84   *See* ROVANE, *supra* note 78, at 181.

85   *Id.* at 141.

86   *See* introduction at 3-8.

87   POSNER & VERMEULE, *supra* note 2, at 43–44.

88   *Id.* at 31.

89   SCHMITT, *supra* note 50, at 31–32.

90   *Id.* at 42–45.

91   *Id.* at 46.

92   *See* CARL SCHMITT, POLITICAL THEOLOGY: FOUR CHAPTERS ON THE CONCEPT
     OF SOVEREIGNTY 7–12 (George Schwab trans., 1985) (1922).

93   *Id.* at 6–10.

94   For a discussion, see WILLIAM E. SCHEUEMAN, CARL SCHMITT: THE END OF
     LAW 74 (1999).

95 CARL SCHMITT, CONSTITUTIONAL THEORY 187 (Jeffrey Seitzer trans., 2008) (1928) (discussing the political concept of law).

96 SCHEUEMAN, *supra* note 94, at 169.

97 *Id.* at 134. *See also* Vivian Grosswald Curran, *Rethinking Hermann Kantorowicz, in* RETHINKING THE MASTERS OF COMPARATIVE LAW 61, 81 (Annelise Riles ed., 2001).

98 SCHEUEMAN, *supra* note 94, at 16 (discussing Schmitt's 1933 work *State, Movement, Folk*).

99 *See generally* JAMES SUROWIECKI, THE WISDOM OF CROWDS (2005).

100 See Francis Galton, *Vox Populi*, NATURE, Mar. 7, 1907.

101 JOHN STUART MILL, ON LIBERTY (1999) (1869). For a critical discussion of this issue, see Miriam Solomon, *Groupthink versus the Wisdom of Crowds: The Social Epistemology of Deliberation and Dissent*, 44 SOUTHERN JOURNAL OF PHILOSOPHY 28–42 (2006).

102 *Compare* Hélène Landemore, *Democratic Reason: The Mechanisms of Collective Intelligence in Politics, in* COLLECTIVE WISDOM: PRINCIPLES AND MECHANISMS 251 (Hélène Landemore & Jon Elster eds., 2012) *with* Adrian Vermeule, *Collective Wisdom & Institutional Design, in* COLLECTIVE WISDOM, *supra*, at 338, 339.

103 See Carl Hulse, *Pentagon Prepares a Futures Market on Terror Attacks*, N.Y. TIMES, July 29, 2003.

104 *See* VICTOR M. HANSEN & LAWRENCE MEIR FRIEDMAN, THE CASE FOR CONGRESS: SEPARATION OF POWERS AND THE WAR ON TERROR 19 (2009).

105 *See* Jon Elster, *The Optimal Design of a Constituent Assembly, in* COLLECTIVE WISDOM, *supra* note 102, at 148.

106 *Id.* at 170.

107 *See* CHRISTIAN LIST & PHILIP PETTIT, GROUP AGENCY: THE POSSIBILITY, DESIGN, AND STATUS OF CORPORATE AGENTS (2013).

108 *Id.* at 46.

109 ERIC A. POSNER & ADRIAN VERMEULE, TERROR IN THE BALANCE: SECURITY, LIBERTY, AND THE COURTS 3 (2007).

110 *Id.*

111 *Id.* at 21–22.

112 *Id.* at 15–16.

113 *Id.* at 31 (emphasis added).

114 *Id.* at 131–34.

115 *Id.* at 132.

116 *Id.* at 133.

117 For a discussion, see Eric A. Posner & Adrian Vermeule, *Accommodating Emergencies, in* THE CONSTITUTION IN WARTIME: BEYOND ALARMISM AND COMPLACENCY 55, 57 (Mark Tushnet ed., 2005) (decrying both the Ratchet Theory and the Panic Theory). The Panic theory states that "during an

emergency people panic, and when they panic they support policies that are unwise and excessive." *Id.*

118   POSNER & VERMEULE, *supra* note 109, at 149.

119   *Id.* at 132.

120   *See* JEREMY WALDRON, TORTURE, TERROR, AND TRADEOFFS: PHILOSOPHY FOR THE WHITE HOUSE 15 (2010).

121   POSNER & VERMEULE, *supra* note 109, at 47.

122   POSNER & VERMEULE, *supra* note 2, at 106.

123   SCHMITT, *supra* note 92, at 6–13. For a discussion, see OREN GROSS & FIONNUALA NÍ AOLÁIN, LAW IN TIMES OF CRISIS: EMERGENCY POWERS IN THEORY AND PRACTICE 162–69 (2006).

124   POSNER & VERMEULE, *supra* note 2, at 91.

125   *Id.*

126   POSNER & VERMEULE, *supra* note 9, at 38.

127   *Id.* at 39.

128   *Id.*

129   POSNER & VERMEULE, *supra* note 2, at 91.

130   *Id.* at 97.

131   *Id.* at 103.

132   *Id.* at 105.

133   *Id.* at 106.

134   JACK GOLDSMITH, POWER AND CONSTRAINT: THE ACCOUNTABLE PRESIDENCY AFTER 9/11 (2012).

135   *See* GEORGE W. BUSH, DECISION POINTS 173 (2010) ("My most solemn responsibility as president was to protect the country. I approved the use of the interrogation techniques. The new techniques proved highly effective.").

136   GOLDSMITH, *supra* note 134, at 19.

137   *Id.* at xii–xiii.

138   Barack Obama, Televised Presidential Address (Mar. 28, 2011) ("And so nine days ago, after consulting the bipartisan leadership of Congress, I authorized military action to stop the killing and enforce UN Security Council Resolution 1973. We struck regime forces approaching Benghazi to save that city and the people within it. We hit Gaddafi's troops in neighboring Ajdabiya, allowing the opposition to drive them out. We hit his air defenses, which paved the way for a No Fly Zone. We targeted tanks and military assets that had been choking off towns and cities and we cut off much of their source of supply. And tonight, I can report that we have stopped Gaddafi's deadly advance.").

139   Authority to Use Military Force in Libya, Memorandum from Caroline D. Krass, Principal Deputy Assistant Attorney General (Apr. 1, 2011) [hereinafter Krass Libya Memorandum], at 8.

140   *Id.*

141   Deployment of United States Armed Forces to Haiti, 28 Op. Att'y Gen. 30 (Mar. 17, 2004), *available at* http://www.justice.gov/sites/default/files/olc/opinions/2004/03/31/op-olc-v028-p0030_0.pdf.

142   Proposed Deployment of United States Armed Forces into Bosnia, 19 Op. O.L.C. 333 (Nov. 30, 1995), *available at* http://www.justice.gov/sites/default/files/olc/legacy/2014/01/29/op-olc-19.pdf.

143   Krass Libya Memorandum, at 11–12.

144   Statement by Harold Hongju Koh before the Senate Foreign Relations Committee Regarding Authorization for Use of Military Force after Iraq and Afghanistan (May 21, 2014), at 12, *available at* http://www.foreign.senate.gov/imo/media/doc/Koh_Testimony.pdf.

145   *Id.* at 12.

146   *See, e.g.,* Mary Ellen O'Connell, *U.S. Strains Credibility on Its Libya Role,* CNN.com, June 21, 2011 ("The international law definition of hostilities comports with common sense. As Sen. Dick Durbin, D-Illinois, put it on 'Meet the Press' last weekend: 'It doesn't pass a straight-face test in my view that we're not in the midst of hostilities (in Libya).'").

147   *See, e.g.,* Scott Horton, *Rules for Drone Wars: Six Questions for Philip Alston,* HARPER'S BLOG (June 9, 2010, 2:12 pm) ("In a speech which assiduously made no mention of the CIA, he didn't address, for example, the scope of the armed conflict in which the United States asserts it is engaged, the criteria for individuals who may be targeted and killed, the existence of any substantive or procedural safeguards to ensure the legality and accuracy of killings, or the existence of accountability mechanisms. In fighting to promote the rule of law, the United States needs also to follow it."), *available at* http://harpers.org/blog/2010/06/rules-for-drone-wars-six-questions-for-philip-alston/.

148   *See* Francis Lieber, Instructions for the Government of Armies of the United States in the Field, General Order No. 100 ("Lieber Code"), art. 20 (Apr. 24, 1863).

149   *See* POSNER & VERMEULE, *supra* note 2, at 86–88.

150   Youngstown Sheet & Tube Co. v. Sawyer, 343 U.S. 579, 610–11 (1952) (Frankfurter, J., concurring).

151   *See* Curtis A. Bradley & Trevor W. Morrison, *Historical Gloss and the Separation of Powers,* 126 HARVARD LAW REVIEW 412, 441–42 (2012).

152   *See* Jack L. Goldsmith, *What Happened to the Rule of Law?,* N.Y. TIMES, Aug. 31, 2013.

153   *Id.*

154   *Id.*

155   *See* Jack. L. Goldsmith, *Why Doesn't President Obama Seek Congressional Approval for Syria?,* LAWFARE (Aug. 28, 2013, 8:25 am), *available at* http://www.lawfareblog.com/2013/08/why-doesnt-president-obama-seek-congressional-approval-for-syria/.

156   Goldsmith, *supra* note 152.

157   *See* Saira Mohamed, *Taking Stock of the Responsibility to Protect*, 48 STANFORD JOURNAL OF INTERNATIONAL LAW 319 (2012).

158   On co-belligerency, see Ido Blum & Valentina Azarov, *Belligerency, in* MAX PLANCK ENCYCLOPEDIA OF INTERNATIONAL LAW (2001).

159   GOLDSMITH, *supra* note 134, at xi.

160   *Id.* at xii.

161   *Id.* at 235 (the accountability process includes "lawyer scrutiny, reporting requirements, inspector general and congressional investigations, Accountability Board proceedings, prosecutorial and ethics investigations, civil trials, FOIA processing and disclosures, public criticism and calumnity, and elections, all of which impose carious forms of psychological, professional, reputational, financial, and political costs on those held accountable.").

CHAPTER THREE

1   *See* THOMAS C. SCHELLING, THE STRATEGY OF CONFLICT 3–20 (2d ed. 1980) (discussing the "retarded science of international strategy").

2   *Cf.* JOEL P. TRACHTMAN, THE ECONOMIC STRUCTURE OF INTERNATIONAL LAW 4–5 (2008) (discussing how the social science methodologies of modeling and empirical testing can generate and validate predictions and hypotheses).

3   *See* SCHELLING, *supra* note 1, at 7 (noting that "[w]hat is impressive is . . . how vague the concepts still are, and how inelegant the current theory of deterrence is"); *see also id.* at 213–14 (explaining the prisoner's dilemma); *id.* at 225–26 (using the prisoner's dilemma to explain coordination and cooperation regarding warning systems).

4   *See* WILLIAM POUNDSTONE, THE PRISONER'S DILEMMA (1992).

5   *See, e.g.,* Kenneth W. Abbott, *Modern International Relations Theory: A Prospectus for International Lawyers*, 14 YALE JOURNAL OF INTERNATIONAL LAW 335, 337–38 (1989); John K. Setear, *An Iterative Perspective on Treaties: A Synthesis of International Relations Theory and International Law*, 37 HARVARD INTERNATIONAL LAW JOURNAL 139 (1996).

6   *See, e.g.,* John K. Setear, *Responses to Breach of a Treaty and Rationalist International Relations Theory: The Rules of Release and Remediation in the Law of Treaties and the Law of State Responsibility*, 83 VIRGINIA LAW REVIEW 1, 8, 74–75 (1997).

7   *See, e.g.,* Peter J. Katzenstein, *Introduction: Alternative Perspectives on National Security, in* THE CULTURE OF NATIONAL SECURITY: NORMS AND IDENTITY IN WORLD POLITICS 13, 17–26 (Peter J. Katzenstein ed., 1996) (discussing the effects of cultural-institutional context and political identity in state action); *see also* ALEXANDER WENDT, SOCIAL THEORY OF INTERNATIONAL POLITICS 198 (1999) (defining national interest to

include physical survival, autonomy, economic well-being, and collective self-esteem).

8   *See, e.g.,* THOMAS M. FRANCK, FAIRNESS IN INTERNATIONAL LAW AND INSTITUTIONS 42–45 (1995) (suggesting that states may act a certain way because of their beliefs about what membership in the community of nations entails); THOMAS M. FRANCK, THE POWER OF LEGITIMACY AMONG NATIONS 25 (1990) (arguing that nations obey rules because they perceive the rules to have a high degree of legitimacy); LOUIS HENKIN, HOW NATIONS BEHAVE: LAW AND FOREIGN POLICY 46–48 (2d ed. 1979) (rejecting the cynical view that state compliance only occurs in cases of rational expected outcomes); Harold Hongju Koh, *Why Do Nations Obey International Law?*, 106 YALE LAW JOURNAL 2599, 2602–03 (1997) (noting that "international law norms now help construct national identities and interests" and analyzing the process of "interaction, interpretation, and internalization of international [legal] norms").

9   *See, e.g.,* JACK L. GOLDSMITH & ERIC A. POSNER, THE LIMITS OF INTERNATIONAL LAW (2005); Eric A. Posner, *Do States Have a Moral Obligation to Obey International Law?*, 55 STANFORD LAW REVIEW 1901 (2003). The current wave is "new" because it harkens back to a first wave of prominent skeptics of international law. *See generally* HANS J. MORGENTHAU, POLITICS AMONG NATIONS: THE STRUGGLE FOR POWER AND PEACE (2d ed. 1954) (updating a first edition that discussed the obsolescence of the sovereign nation state and warned against the illusory hopes for the newly established United Nations).

10 GOLDSMITH & POSNER, *supra* note 9, at 184 (concluding that "[w]hen states cooperate in their self-interest, they naturally use the moralistic language of obligation rather than the strategic language of interest. But saying that the former is evidence of moral motivation is like saying that when states talk of friendship or brotherhood they use these terms, which are meant to reflect aspirations for closer relations, in a literal sense"). Goldsmith and Posner thereby presume that the language of morality and the language of interest are mutually exclusive categories—a proposition they never explicitly defend. *See also id.* at 100 (distinguishing the view that states comply with international law because it is the right thing to do from the view that states comply when it is in their self-interest).

11 *Id.* at 36–37 (arguing that in treaty contexts, states may achieve "shallow multistate cooperation" and that, in the context of customary international law, "genuine multistate cooperation is unlikely to emerge"); *see also id.* at 87 (asserting skepticism that "genuine multinational collective action problems can be solved by treaty").

12 *Id.* at 87 (describing how cooperation in pairs creates a multilateral regime).

13 *Id.* at 88 (describing the "strong pattern in international law" whereby threats of retaliation are nearly always the responsibility of the victims

of violations and concluding that the "enforcement of multilateral treaty regimes is usually bilateral").

14 *See id.* at 87–88.

15 *Id.* at 66 (arguing that theorists inflate context-specific and temporally limited behavioral patterns, coincidences of interest, and situations of coercion into exogenous rules of customary law).

16 *Id.* at 36 (discussing the costs associated with the multilateral model, including increased costs of monitoring and the risk of undetected free-riding).

17 Not everyone agrees that reciprocity is the most relevant concept for understanding international legal obligations. In an important article, Lea Brilmayer concludes that reciprocity is "unsuitable" and even "pernicious" as a framework for understanding human rights obligations, which she believes should be conceptualized as pledges. *See* Lea Brilmayer, *From 'Contract' to 'Pledge': The Structure of Human Rights Agreements,* 77 BRITISH YEARBOOK OF INTERNATIONAL LAW 163, 187–88 (2006).

18 GOLDSMITH & POSNER, *supra* note 9, at 32–35 (describing coordination problems).

19 *Id.* at 60 (recalling that the three-mile territorial sea rule was insisted upon by states with powerful navies but that even these powerful states were often unable to make credible threats to enforce the rule).

20 *See, e.g.,* GOLDSMITH & POSNER, *supra* note 9, at 150–51 (discussing reciprocal compliance in the context of GATT).

21 *See id.* at 100.

22 *Id.* at 185 (arguing that a moral obligation to comply with international law is illusory).

23 *Id.* at 205–06.

24 *Id.* at 209–15.

25 *See also* Jack Goldsmith, *Liberal Democracy and Cosmopolitan Duty,* 55 STANFORD LAW REVIEW 1667, 1675–82 (2003) (discussing the limitations on ascribing strong cosmopolitan sentiments and duties to liberal democratic governments).

26 For a particularly trenchant example, see Robert Hockett, *The Limits of Their World,* 90 MINNESOTA LAW REVIEW 1720 (2006) (reviewing GOLDSMITH & POSNER, THE LIMITS OF INTERNATIONAL LAW).

27 *See, e.g.,* Thomas M. Franck, *The Power of Legitimacy and the Legitimacy of Power: International Law In an Age of Power Disequilibrium,* 100 AMERICAN JOURNAL OF INTERNATIONAL LAW 88, 90 (2006) ("Not surprisingly, however, the claim [of law's fecklessness] resonates strongly in the halls of American governance.").

28 For a classic example, see MARY ELLEN O'CONNELL, THE POWER AND PURPOSE OF INTERNATIONAL LAW: INSIGHTS FROM THE THEORY AND PRACTICE OF ENFORCEMENT (2008).

29 *See, e.g.,* ANDREW T. GUZMAN, HOW INTERNATIONAL LAW WORKS: A RATIONAL CHOICE THEORY 13 (2008) (providing an explanation of international law's effectiveness from a rational choice perspective).

30 Although Guzman uses game theory models expertly to demonstrate the effectiveness of international law, *id.,* he does not directly dwell on the issue that I have raised here, that is, whether the assumption of self-interest implicit in the prisoner's dilemma undermines international law's essential normativity. Guzman has pursued his analysis in a number of important essays. *See, e.g.,* Andrew T. Guzman, *A Compliance-Based Theory of International Law,* 90 CALIFORNIA LAW REVIEW 1823 (2002) [hereinafter Guzman, *A Compliance-Based Theory*] (presenting a theory of international law in which compliance occurs in a model of rational, self-interested states); Andrew T. Guzman, *Reputation and International Law,* 34 GEORGIA JOURNAL OF INTERNATIONAL & COMPARATIVE LAW 379 (2006) [hereinafter Guzman, *Reputation and International Law*] (describing expected loss of reputation as one mechanism of ensuring compliance); Andrew T. Guzman, *Saving Customary International Law,* 27 MICHIGAN JOURNAL OF INTERNATIONAL LAW 115 (2005) [hereinafter Guzman, *Saving Customary International Law*] (mapping out a theory of customary international law based on a model of rational choice); *see also* Jeffrey L. Dunoff & Joel P. Trachtman, *Economic Analysis of International Law,* 24 YALE JOURNAL OF INTERNATIONAL LAW 1 (1999) (exploring the actual and potential application of law and economics to international law).

31 *See, e.g.,* GOLDSMITH & POSNER, *supra* note 9, at 100. Other commentators have noted the lack of support for this assumption. *See, e.g.,* George Norman & Joel P. Trachtman, *The Customary International Law Game,* 99 AMERICAN JOURNAL OF INTERNATIONAL LAW 541, 541–42 (2005). The argument presented by Goldsmith and Posner relies on the proposition that customary international law is based on *opinio juris* and that acting in self-interest precludes acting out of a sense of legal obligation. *See* GOLDSMITH & POSNER, *supra* note 9, at 14–15. The answer to this skeptical challenge lies in properly understanding *opinio juris* as "the intent of states to propose or accept a rule of law that will serve as the focal point of behavior, implicate an important set of default rules applicable to law but not to other types of social order, and bring into play an important set of linkages among legal rules." Norman & Trachtman, *supra,* at 542. *See also* José E. Alvarez, *A BIT on Custom,* 42 N.Y.U. JOURNAL OF INTERNATIONAL LAW & POLITICS 17, 43 (2009) ("That states have or may have had 'economic' reasons to conclude a treaty does not exclude other normative effects produced by these treaties' entry into force, subsequent practice under them, or efforts to enforce them.").

32 GOLDSMITH & POSNER, *supra* note 9, at 87–88.

33 *Cf.* Eyal Benvenisti, *Customary International Law as a Judicial Tool for Promoting Efficiency, in* THE IMPACT OF INTERNATIONAL LAW ON INTERNATIONAL COOPERATION: THEORETICAL PERSPECTIVES 85, 92–94 (Eyal Benvenisti & Moshe Hirsch eds., 2004) (describing the use of customary international law for shifting to a new, more efficient equilibrium); Charles Lipson, *Why Are Some International Agreements Informal?, in* INTERNATIONAL LAW AND INTERNATIONAL RELATIONS 293, 297–98 (Beth A. Simmons & Richard H. Steinberg eds., 2006) (discussing how tacit understandings and implicit rules may create a Nash equilibrium).

34 *See* DOUGLAS G. BAIRD, ROBERT H. GERTNER & RANDAL C. PICKER, GAME THEORY AND THE LAW 39–41 (1994).

35 *See* KAUSHIK BASU, PRELUDE TO POLITICAL ECONOMY: A STUDY OF THE SOCIAL AND POLITICAL FOUNDATIONS OF ECONOMICS 114–16 (2000) (describing the problem of choosing between multiple Nash equilibria); *see also* BAIRD ET AL., *supra* note 34, at 39–40 (discussing a classical example of a focal point); SCHELLING, *supra* note 1, at 110–12 (discussing focal points).

36 *Cf.* Avery Katz, *The Strategic Structure of Offer and Acceptance: Game Theory and the Law of Contract Formation*, 89 MICHIGAN LAW REVIEW 215 (1990) (discussing game theory in the context of contract breach).

37 *See* Norman & Trachtman, *supra* note 31, at 542, 571.

38 *See, e.g.*, Guzman, *A Compliance-Based Theory, supra* note 30 (presenting a theory of international law in which compliance occurs in a model of rational, self-interested states); Setear, *supra* note 6, at 1 (examining the international legal rules that govern responses to treaty breaches from the perspective of rationalist theories of international relations).

39 However, *pace* Goldsmith and Posner, the parties' self-interested compliance does not preclude their acting out of *opinio juris. See* Norman & Trachtman, *supra* note 31, at 541–42; *see also* Alvarez, *supra* note 31, at 44.

40 *See* GOLDSMITH & POSNER, *supra* note 9, at 87 (arguing that the free rider problem is worse when an agreement involves large numbers of states).

41 *See* BASU, *supra* note 35, at 114 (discussing problem of multiple Nash equilibria).

42 *See* HERBERT GINTIS, GAME THEORY EVOLVING: A PROBLEM-CENTERED INTRODUCTION TO MODELING STRATEGIC INTERACTION 109 (2d ed. 2009).

43 *See, e.g.*, Andrew T. Guzman, *Public Choice and International Regulatory Competition*, 90 GEORGETOWN LAW JOURNAL 971, 975 (2002) (discussing how choice of law and issues of public choice affect the substantive law adopted by states).

44 *See id.* at 984 (noting that there are "problems with international cooperation that make it inferior to well-functioning domestic systems").

45 *See* MICHAEL J. GLENNON, LIMITS OF LAW, PREROGATIVES OF POWER: INTERVENTIONISM AFTER KOSOVO 3 (2001) ("It is widely agreed that the most important rules are rules governing use of force. . . .").

46 *See id.*

47 *See generally id.* at 17–19 (describing the U.N. Charter and the Security Council's role in authorizing the use of force).

48 *See* YORAM DINSTEIN, WAR, AGGRESSION AND SELF-DEFENCE 83 (4th ed. 2005) (describing the pact as a "watershed" moment in the development of *jus ad bellum*).

49 *See* MARY ELLEN O'CONNELL, INTERNATIONAL LAW AND THE USE OF FORCE: CASES AND MATERIALS 114–17 (2005).

50 GLENNON, *supra* note 45, at 17–19.

51 *Cf.* Jules Lobel & Michael Ratner, *Bypassing the Security Council: Ambiguous Authorizations to Use Force, Cease-Fires and the Iraqi Inspection Regime*, 93 AMERICAN JOURNAL OF INTERNATIONAL LAW 124, 154 (1999) (discussing the Council's impotence and failure to act in this area).

52 *See, e.g.*, JOHN WESTLAKE, CHAPTERS ON THE PRINCIPLES OF INTERNATIONAL LAW 115 (1894); HENRY WHEATON, ELEMENTS OF INTERNATIONAL LAW 90 (8th ed. 1866); THEODORE D. WOOLSEY, INTRODUCTION TO THE STUDY OF INTERNATIONAL LAW 184 (5th ed. 1879).

53 *See* O'CONNELL, *supra* note 49, at 240 (discussing the fact that the United Nations Charter prohibits force generally while leaving a limited exception for self-defense).

54 *But see* Sean D. Murphy, *The Doctrine of Preemptive Self-Defense*, 50 VILLANOVA LAW REVIEW 699, 702 (2005) (noting some uncertainty about "whether preemptive self-defense is permissible under international law, or whether it is permissible but only under certain conditions").

55 It is certainly true that not all states comply with the prohibition regarding the use of force. However, Henkin must surely be right that "almost all nations observe almost all principles of international law and almost all of their obligations almost all of the time." *See* HENKIN, *supra* note 8, at 47 (emphasis omitted). If there is any doubt regarding the veracity of the maxim, one need only ask what the world would look like today if the prohibition regarding the use of force was not followed most of the time.

56 *Cf.* SCHELLING, *supra* note 1, at 119 (suggesting that game theory can be more extensively used to analyze nonzero-sum games of strategy).

57 *See, e.g.*, GOLDSMITH & POSNER, *supra* note 9, at 184 (arguing that states use moralistic and legalistic rhetoric merely to disguise purely self-interested motives).

58 *Id.* at 225 ("International law is a real phenomenon, but international law scholars exaggerate its power and significance.").

59 *See, e.g.*, GLENNON, *supra* note 45; Lobel & Ratner, *supra* note 51.

60 *See, e.g.*, Hockett, *supra* note 26; Norman & Trachtman, *supra* note 31, at 541–42.

61 DAVID GAUTHIER, MORALS BY AGREEMENT (1986).

62 Many moral philosophers have pursued similar themes, but without explic-
    itly invoking game theory as a methodological tool. *See, e.g.,* THOMAS
    NAGEL, THE POSSIBILITY OF ALTRUISM (1970); T.M. SCANLON, WHAT WE OWE
    TO EACH OTHER (1998).

63 *See generally* JOHN RAWLS, A THEORY OF JUSTICE (1971) (describing and
    elaborating upon the conception of justice that is implicit in the contract
    tradition).

64 GAUTHIER, *supra* note 61, at 9 ("Morality does not emerge as the rabbit
    from the empty hat . . . . [I]t emerges quite simply from the application of
    the maximizing conception of rationality to certain structures of interac-
    tion."); *see also* Jody S. Kraus & Jules L. Coleman, *Morality and the Theory
    of Rational Choice, in* CONTRACTARIANISM AND RATIONAL CHOICE: ESSAYS
    ON DAVID GAUTHIER'S MORALS BY AGREEMENT 254, 255 (Peter Vallentyne
    ed., 1991) (arguing that rationality cannot provide the substantive content
    of morality).

65 GAUTHIER, *supra* note 61, at 9 ("Reason overrides the presumption against
    morality.").

66 *See id.* at 10 (emphasizing that his theoretical focus is on why it is rational
    for individuals to agree to constraining principles ex ante as well as to com-
    ply with such agreed constraints ex post).

67 This is one way of understanding Hobbes's theory: collective rationality
    and mutual benefit demand a social contract, but individuals might pre-
    fer free riding, thus requiring the leviathan to enforce individual compli-
    ance. For further discussion of the relationship of collective rationality
    to the social contract in Hobbes's theory, see PHILIP PETTIT, MADE WITH
    WORDS: HOBBES ON LANGUAGE, MIND, AND POLITICS (2008). *See generally*
    DAVID P. GAUTHIER, THE LOGIC OF LEVIATHAN: THE MORAL AND POLITICAL
    THEORY OF THOMAS HOBBES (1969) (describing and expanding and critically
    reflecting upon Hobbes's moral and political theory).

68 For more recent projects pursuing the same line, see generally KEN BINMORE,
    GAME THEORY AND THE SOCIAL CONTRACT II: JUST PLAYING (1998) (using
    game theory to discuss morality and social reform).

69 GAUTHIER, *supra* note 61, at v ("The present enquiry began . . . when, fum-
    bling for words in which to express the peculiar relationship between
    morality and advantage, I was shown the Prisoner's Dilemma.").

70 *Id.* at 177 (arguing that cooperation and constraint by all would "yield nearly
    optimal and fair outcomes").

71 *Id.* at 14–15.

72 *Id.* at 15.

73 *Id.* at 175–76.

74 *See* PETTIT, *supra* note 67, at 108 ("Hobbes's picture is that as [people] each
    contract to create a commonwealth, people know that should they later

defect, then the sovereign, drawing on the strength of the rest, will be there to punish them.").

75   The value of reputational gains and the costs associated with reputational losses will depend on the degree to which reputation is carried over from one legal context to another. *See, e.g.,* GUZMAN, *supra* note 29, at 100–11 (discussing the compartmentalizing of reputation); George W. Downs & Michael A. Jones, *Reputation, Compliance, and International Law,* 31 JOURNAL OF LEGAL STUDIES 95 (2002) (outlining empirical and theoretical reasons for believing that the actual effects of reputation are both weaker and more complicated than the standard view of reputation suggests); *see also* Edward T. Swaine, *Rational Custom,* 52 DUKE LAW JOURNAL 559, 618 (2002) (noting that "states do not, in fact, interact solely with respect to one rule or the other, and it is also possible to understand their interaction with respect both to an individual rule and to the system of customary international law").

76   GAUTHIER, *supra* note 61, at 176–77.

77   *Id.* at 176.

78   *See id.* at 174–75.

79   Gauthier himself published work regarding Hobbes's theory of international relations. *See, e.g.,* GAUTHIER, *supra* note 67, at 207–12 (discussing Hobbes's views on the state of nations and observing that the development of nuclear weapons is "bringing the state of nations nearer to the true Hobbesian state of nature"); *see also* David Gauthier, *Deterrence, Maximization, and Rationality, in* THE SECURITY GAMBLE: DETERRENCE DILEMMAS IN THE NUCLEAR AGE 100, 107 (Douglas MacLean ed., 1984) (drawing on Hobbes's theories of nature to defend the rationality of deterrent policies).

80   *See, e.g.,* ABRAM CHAYES & ANTONIA HANDLER CHAYES, THE NEW SOVEREIGNTY: COMPLIANCE WITH INTERNATIONAL REGULATORY AGREEMENTS 70 (1995) (discussing South Africa's status as an international pariah in the 1960s).

81   For a similar argument, see Peter J. Spiro, *A Negative Proof of International Law,* 34 GEORGIA JOURNAL OF INTERNATIONAL & COMPARATIVE LAW 445, 447 (2006).

82   *Cf.* GLENNON, *supra* note 45, at 60–64 (discussing desuetude).

83   *See also* CHARLES R. BEITZ, POLITICAL THEORY AND INTERNATIONAL RELATIONS 47–49 (1979) (noting that, in the face of considerable empirical evidence to the contrary, people continue to suggest that international relations resembles a Hobbesian state of nature).

84   *See, e.g.,* CHAYES & CHAYES, *supra* note 80, at 22–28 (proposing different methods of ensuring compliance); *see also* DAVID CORTRIGHT & GEORGE A. LOPEZ, THE SANCTIONS DECADE: ASSESSING UN STRATEGIES IN THE 1990S (2000) (analyzing the effectiveness of twelve cases of U.N. sanctions).

85   *See* ERIC A. POSNER, LAW AND SOCIAL NORMS (2000).

86   *Id.* at 187 (asserting that people rationally use the rhetoric of principle "in order to obtain strategic advantages in their interactions with others").

87   Posner cashes out the idea of an absolute principle as a claim regarding incommensurability. *See id.* at 192–98. In other words, if someone says that no amount of money will convince him to give up a much-needed vacation with his family, that person is implicitly saying that the value of money and the value of time with his family are incommensurable and cannot be compared. If they *could* be compared, according to Posner, there would be a price at which the amount of money would outweigh the value of the time with the family. *Id.* at 193–94. Posner concludes that incommensurability claims signal to others that one will not cheat. *Id.* at 197.

88   *Id.* at 195–97.

89   *Id.* at 190 (asserting, as an example, that "a rational person will sacrifice his reputation when the gains are sufficiently high").

90   *Id.* at 197.

91   *Id.* at 195.

92   *Id.* at 197–98. The notion that states are inherently unprincipled is a feature of neo-realism in international relations. For a discussion, see LEA BRILMAYER, AMERICAN HEGEMONY: POLITICAL MORALITY IN A ONE-SUPERPOWER WORLD 35 (1994).

93   *See, e.g.,* GOLDSMITH & POSNER, *supra* note 9, at 197.

94   *Id.* at 167–84 (discussing their "theory of international rhetoric").

95   *Id.* at 185.

96   *Id.* at 169 ("[S]tates provide legal or moral justifications for their actions, no matter how transparently self-interested their actions are.").

97   *Id.* at 172.

98   *Cf. id.* at 178–79 (discussing how leaders will address their speech to foreign leaders but intend their talk for domestic audiences).

99   *Id.* at 185.

100   *See* GAUTHIER, *supra* note 61, at 182–84.

101   *See, e.g.,* David Gauthier, *Commitment and Choice: An Essay on the Rationality of Plans, in* ETHICS, RATIONALITY, AND ECONOMIC BEHAVIOUR 217, 217–19 (Francesco Farina et al. eds., 1996) [hereinafter Gauthier, *Commitment and Choice*] (arguing that plans serve as a rational guide for subsequent actions); *see also* David Gauthier, *Intention and Deliberation, in* MODELING RATIONALITY, MORALITY, AND EVOLUTION 41, 53 (Peter A. Danielson ed., 1998) (discussing why an agent would rationally deliberate about plans).

102   *See* Gauthier, *Commitment and Choice, supra* note 101, at 219 (discussing how agents who adopt a plan restrict subsequent deliberation for actions that are compatible with that plan).

103   *Id.* at 219–21 (describing conditions for rational reconsideration).

104 *See generally* MICHAEL E. BRATMAN, INTENTION, PLANS, AND PRACTICAL REASON (1987) (providing a more elaborate discussion on the role of plans in understanding the relationship between rationality and action).

105 *Id.* at 64–65 (discussing plan stability in order to explain the rationality of an agent's reconsideration or nonreconsideration of a plan); *see also* Gauthier, *Commitment and Choice, supra* note 101, at 221 ("[A] full appreciation of the role that plans play in deliberation requires revisions in the orthodox view of economic rationality.").

106 BRATMAN, *supra* note 104, at 2–3.

107 *Compare* Gauthier, *Commitment and Choice, supra* note 101, at 221–22 ("[F]rom the standpoint of the economist . . . [a]n agent's reasons for an action are adequate just in case he prefers the expected outcome of that action no less than the expected outcome of any of its alternatives. The expected outcome of an action is the probability-weighted sum of the possible outcomes of the action."), *with* GAUTHIER, *supra* note 61, at 184–85.

108 Gauthier, *Commitment and Choice, supra* note 101, at 222.

109 *See id.* at 222–23 (discussing how the thesis that human beings are maximizing individuals can be applied to rational planning). For further discussion, see generally EDWARD F. MCCLENNEN, RATIONALITY AND DYNAMIC CHOICE: FOUNDATIONAL EXPLORATIONS (1990) (analyzing how to normatively justify principles of rationality).

110 Gauthier, *Commitment and Choice, supra* note 101, at 228 (challenging the view that "directly maximizing considerations are to be brought to bear on each particular choice"). Simply put, commitment to a plan "makes planning maximally efficacious in co-ordinating one's own actions . . . with those of others, so that one may best realize one's objectives." *Id.*

111 *See id.* at 242–43.

112 *See* Michael E. Bratman, *Following Through with One's Plans: Reply to David Gauthier, in* MODELING RATIONALITY, MORALITY, AND EVOLUTION, *supra* note 100, at 55 (arguing that rational deliberation and plan stability are linked by the concept of planning). Along with Gauthier, Bratman believes that deliberation about future actions "is justified by appeal to its expected long-run impacts." *See id.* at 59. Bratman concludes that reconsideration of a plan is rationally justified if the agent believes that a specific alternative will better achieve "the very same long-standing, stable and coherent desires and values." *Id.* at 61; *see also* Michael E. Bratman, *Planning and Temptation, in* MIND AND MORALS: ESSAYS ON COGNITIVE SCIENCE AND ETHICS 293, 294 (Larry May et al. eds., 1996) (suggesting that coordination is impossible without stable intentions and plans).

113 For a discussion of myopic choosers, see Edward F. McClennen, *Rationality and Rules, in* MODELING RATIONALITY, MORALITY, AND EVOLUTION, *supra* note 101, at 16. A formal model was first offered by R. H. Strotz in

Myopia and Inconsistency in Dynamic Utility Maximization, 23 REVIEW OF ECONOMIC STUDIES 165, 173 (1955).

114   Claire Finkelstein developed a version of this view in her essay, *Acting on an Intention, in* REASONS AND INTENTIONS 67, 83 (Bruno Verbeek ed., 2008).

115   *See, e.g.,* J. J. C. Smart, *Extreme and Restricted Utilitarianism, in* ETHICAL THEORY 286, 286–88 (James Rachels ed., 1998).

116   *Id.* at 286–87.

117   *Id.* at 287.

118   *See, e.g.,* GUZMAN, *supra* note 29, at 15–22.

119   *Cf.* GOLDSMITH & POSNER, *supra* note 9, at 7–10 (addressing the methodology of rational choice theory, but mostly addressing constructivist challenges).

120   *See* JOHN RAWLS, POLITICAL LIBERALISM 52 (expanded ed. 1996) ("Justice as fairness . . . does not try to derive the reasonable from the rational.").

121   *Compare* RAWLS, A THEORY OF JUSTICE, *supra* note 62, at 16 (noting that contract terminology conveys the idea that principles of justice are principles that would be chosen by rational persons and that "[t]he theory of justice is a part, perhaps the most significant part, of the theory of rational choice"), *with* John C. Harsanyi, *Morality and the Theory of Rational Behaviour, in* UTILITARIANISM AND BEYOND 39, 39 (Amartya Sen & Bernard Williams eds., 1982) (noting that Rawls's ethical theory, while based on intellectual traditions in moral philosophy, makes essential use of the modern Bayesian theory of rational behavior).

122   *See, e.g.,* ALAN GEWIRTH, REASON AND MORALITY (1978).

123   *See* JOHN RAWLS, JUSTICE AS FAIRNESS: A RESTATEMENT 29 (2001).

124   For a discussion of the structure of the naturalistic problem regarding rationality, see Ronald de Sousa, *Modeling Rationality: A Normative or Descriptive Task?, in* MODELING RATIONALITY, MORALITY, AND EVOLUTION, *supra* note 100, at 120 (defining normativism as the claim that "within all attempts to model actual reasoning processes there must be an ineliminable element of normativity").

125   *See* Christine M. Korsgaard, *Personal Identity and the Unity of Agency: A Kantian Response to Parfit*, 18 PHILOSOPHY & PUBLIC AFFAIRS 101, 109–15 (1989) (discussing how rational, unified agents make life plans).

126   Rational agents engage in means–ends reasoning when they conclude that because they have a reason to do x, and y is a means to achieve x, then they also have a reason to do y. So, for example, a highway traveler has a reason to eat dinner; since exiting the highway and stopping at a restaurant is a means to achieve dinner, then the agent has a reason to exit the highway. This is an elementary building block of practical reason. The transitive ordering of preferences implies that if an agent prefers A to B, and prefers

B to C, then, by definition, he prefers A to C. The law of noncontradiction suggests that if a belief set includes both A and not-A, then the agent
should revise one of his beliefs. So, for example, if the agent believes that
the light is both on and off, then one of these beliefs ought to be revised.

127   See ISAAC LEVI, THE COVENANT OF REASON: RATIONALITY AND THE
COMMITMENTS OF THOUGHT 1–19 (1997).

128   This view is arguably implicit in JOHN RAWLS, THE LAW OF PEOPLES: WITH
"THE IDEA OF PUBLIC REASON REVISITED" 32 (2001). See also HANS KELSEN,
PRINCIPLES OF INTERNATIONAL LAW 154 (1952) (discussing the relationship
of a state to the international community).

129   See also Philip Pettit, Collective Persons and Powers, 8 LEGAL THEORY 443
(2002) (discussing the organization of certain collectives).

130   For more on the irrelevancy of this distinction for purposes of the commitment to rationality, see CAROL ROVANE, THE BOUNDS OF AGENCY: AN
ESSAY IN REVISIONARY METAPHYSICS 132 (1998).

131   Cf. Carol Rovane, What Is an Agent?, 140 SYNTHESE 181 (2004) (discussing
group agents).

132   See ISAAC LEVI, HARD CHOICES: DECISION MAKING UNDER UNRESOLVED
CONFLICT 151 (1986) ("[E]ven students of market economies attribute
beliefs, desires, goals, values and choices to families, firms and, of course,
government agencies. . . .").

133   See generally Franck, supra note 27 (discussing international law in an age
of disparities of power).

134   See, e.g., GOLDSMITH & POSNER, supra note 9, at 116 (discussing how weaker
states can be coerced into compliance by more powerful states).

135   For a discussion of this problem, see BEITZ, supra note 83, at 41–44, 47–48.

136   For a general discussion of how underlying geopolitical realities can preclude establishing effective rules of international law, see GLENNON, supra
note 45.

137   Furthermore, strong states might have unique reasons to comply with
international norms: strong states are in a better position to bear the
costs of cooperation more easily than weak states, so they may be less
tempted to defect. In the alternative, strong states might also comply
because they view the costs of international compliance as necessary costs
for regime stability. Compare A. O. HIRSCHMAN, NATIONAL POWER AND
THE STRUCTURE OF FOREIGN TRADE (1945), with ROBERT O. KEOHANE,
AFTER HEGEMONY: COOPERATION AND DISCORD IN THE WORLD POLITICAL
ECONOMY 214 (1984). For an important liberal political conception of
American hegemony, see BRILMAYER, supra note 92, at 169.

138   See, e.g., GOLDSMITH & POSNER, supra note 9, at 66–75 (discussing patterns of state compliance—and lack thereof—with regards to the customary international law exempting fishing vessels from the right of capture

during times of war); *see also id.* at 116–17 (discussing strategic coercion, "often in violation of international law" by stronger states to make weaker states comply with human rights norms when such compliance is in the interest of the stronger states).

139   *Id.* at 90 ("[W]e have explained the logic of treaties without reference to notions of 'legality' or *pacta sunt servanda* or related concepts. As was the case with customary international law, the cooperation and coordination models explain the behaviors associated with treaties without reliance on these factors, or on what international lawyers sometimes call 'normative pull.' ").

140   *See, e.g.,* Brett Frischmann, *A Dynamic Institutional Theory of International Law,* 51 BUFFALO LAW REVIEW 679, 681 (2003) ("Despite the significant advancements made in the study of international cooperation, there remains a gap between the types of institutions that traditional game theory predicts should exist and the types of institutions found in reality."); Ryan Goodman & Derek Jinks, *Measuring the Effects of Human Rights Treaties,* 14 EUROPEAN JOURNAL OF INTERNATIONAL LAW 171 (2003) (analyzing a study that aims to quantify the effect of human rights treaty ratification on human rights violations); Michael P. Scharf, *International Law in Crisis: A Qualitative Empirical Contribution to the Compliance Debate,* 31 CARDOZO LAW REVIEW 45 (2009) (using qualitative empirical data to assess the influence of international law on the formation of U.S. foreign policy in times of crisis).

141   *See* GOLDSMITH & POSNER, *supra* note 9, at 186.

142   *Id.* at 187–88.

143   *Id.* at 188 (citing CHRISTOPHER KUTZ, COMPLICITY: ETHICS AND LAW FOR A COLLECTIVE AGE 253 (2000)).

144   *See* 2 JOHN LOCKE, TWO TREATISES OF GOVERNMENT §§ 119–122, at 347–49 (Peter Laslett ed., rev. ed. 1988) (1690).

145   *See* GOLDSMITH & POSNER, *supra* note 9, at 189.

146   *See id.* at 187–88.

147   *See id.* at 190–91.

148   *See id.* at 189.

149   *Id.* at 191.

150   *Id.*

151   The conclusion that the autonomy of states (and nations) has no intrinsic value can and should be resisted, though a full account is impossible here. *See, e.g.,* CHARLES TAYLOR, SOURCES OF THE SELF: THE MAKING OF THE MODERN IDENTITY (1989) (presenting a history of the modern identity); *see also* WILL KYMLICKA, STATES, NATIONS AND CULTURES (1997) (arguing that group rights are derived from enlightenment commitment to individual flourishing); Allen Buchanan, *Democracy and the Commitment*

to *International Law*, 34 GEORGIA JOURNAL OF INTERNATIONAL & COMPARATIVE LAW 305, 320 (2006) (discussing how those who embrace a cosmopolitan moral perspective should regard international law); Avishai Margalit & Joseph Raz, *National Self-Determination*, 87 JOURNAL OF PHILOSOPHY 439, 443 (1990) (discussing the moral justifications for national self-determination).

152   *See* KYMLICKA, *supra* note 151, at 35.

153   For a full defense of the value of collectivities, *see* GEORGE P. FLETCHER & JENS DAVID OHLIN, DEFENDING HUMANITY: WHEN FORCE IS JUSTIFIED AND WHY (2008).

154   *See id.* at 136–47.

155   *See* FRIEDRICH KARL VON SAVIGNY, SYSTEM DES HEUTIGEN RÖMISCHEN RECHTS, BAND 2, 236 (1840) (asserting that juridical persons are fictitious but are nevertheless entitled to rights by extension).

156   *Cf.* JACK GOLDSMITH, THE TERROR PRESIDENCY: LAW AND JUDGMENT INSIDE THE BUSH ADMINISTRATION (2007) (discussing the author's experiences as head of the Office of Legal Counsel of the U.S. Department of Justice from 2003 to 2004).

CHAPTER FOUR

1   JACK L. GOLDSMITH & ERIC A. POSNER, THE LIMITS OF INTERNATIONAL LAW (2005); Eric A. Posner, *Do States Have a Moral Obligation to Obey International Law?*, 55 STANFORD LAW REVIEW 1901 (2003).

2   *See, e.g.*, GOLDSMITH & POSNER, *supra* note 1, at 185.

3   *See* Michael E. Bratman, *Time, Rationality, and Self-Governance*, 22 PHILOSOPHICAL ISSUES 73, 82 (2012) ("plan states play certain fundamental, interrelated roles in a planning agent's psychic economy").

4   The deterrence paradox is also sometimes referred to as the deterrence dilemma. In this chapter, I use the two terms synonymously. Although there is some question of whether the deterrence paradox constitutes a paradox in the "classical" definition of a paradox, this question of classification is irrelevant for the present inquiry. *See* Daniel M. Farrell, *A New Paradox of Deterrence*, *in* RATIONAL COMMITMENT AND SOCIAL JUSTICE: ESSAYS FOR GREGORY KAVKA 22, 23 (Jules L. Coleman & Christopher W. Morris eds., 2007).

5   POSNER & GOLDSMITH, *supra* note 1, at 100.

6   Posner and Goldsmith extensively survey basic concepts in rational choice theory used by economics, but they generally ignore the philosophical literature on rationality. *See* POSNER & GOLDSMITH, *supra* note 1, at 36–88 & *passim*.

7   *See* Gregory S. Kavka, *The Toxin Puzzle*, 43 ANALYSIS 33–36 (1983).

8   *Id.* at 34.

9   The intuition is borrowed from Jerry Seinfeld.

10 Kavka, *supra* note 7, at 34 ("Unfortunately, your daughter the lawyer, who has read the contract carefully, points out that arrangement of such external incentives is ruled out").

11 *See* David Gauthier, *Rethinking the Toxin Puzzle, in* RATIONAL COMMITMENT AND SOCIAL JUSTICE: ESSAYS FOR GREGORY KAVKA 47, 57 (Jules L. Coleman & Christopher W. Morris eds., 2007).

12 *See generally* MICHAEL E. BRATMAN, INTENTION, PLANS, AND PRACTICAL REASON (1987).

13 *Id.* at 65.

14 The issue is also discussed in David Gauthier, *Commitment and Choice: An Essay on the Rationality of Plans, in* ETHICS, RATIONALITY, AND ECONOMIC BEHAVIOR 217, 221 (Francesco Farina et al. eds., 1996).

15 *See* Gauthier, *id.* at 219 (plans restrict subsequent deliberation).

16 BRATMAN, *supra* note 12, at 3.

17 *See* POSNER & GOLDSMITH, *supra* note 1, at 4–10.

18 In this sense, consider Gauthier, *supra* note 11, at 47, 48 ("Intending to drink the toxin is part of my best course of action. I can and still shall recognize this. Tomorrow afternoon I shall have no ground for doubting that intending to drink the toxin is part of my best course of action, and so I shall not then have good reason to change my course of action. Intending to drink the toxin, I shall drink it. My reason for drinking it will be that drinking it is part of the best course of action that I could embrace as a whole—best not only prospectively, but still best at the time of drinking.").

19 To be fair, the New Realists are not the only theorists who think this way.

20 *See* Claire Finkelstein, *Acting on an Intention, in* REASONS AND INTENTIONS 67, 83 (Bruno Verbeek ed., 2008).

21 *See* David Gauthier, *Assure and Threaten*, 104 ETHICS 690–721 (1994).

22 *See* Edward McClennen, *Constrained Maximization and Resolute Choice*, 5 SOCIAL PHILOSOPHY AND POLICY 95–118 (1988), *reprinted in* THE NEW SOCIAL CONTRACT: ESSAYS ON GAUTHIER 95–118 (Ellen Paul et. al eds., 1988).

23 *See generally* Edward F. McClennen, *Prisoner's Dilemma and Resolute Choice, in* PARADOXES OF RATIONALITY AND COOPERATION 94 (Richmond Campbell & Lanning Sowden, eds., 1985).

24 McClennen solves the problem with intrapersonal superiority between former and later selves, like a form of internal Pareto optimality. If neither your prior self nor your later selves are harmed by the change in plan, then it is rational to switch plans. *See* EDWARD F. MCCLENNEN, RATIONALITY AND DYNAMIC CHOICE: FOUNDATIONAL EXPLORATIONS 256–57 (1990); Edward F. McClennen, *Pragmatic Rationality and Rules*, 26 PHILOSOPHY & PUBLIC AFFAIRS 210–58 (1997). The issue is also discussed in CHRISTOPHER WOODARD, REASONS, PATTERNS, AND COOPERATION 57 (2007).

25   *See* Gauthier, *supra* note 11, at 56.

26   DAVID GAUTHIER, MORALS BY AGREEMENT 187 (1986).

27   This theory echoes how constructivists in international relations use the notion of national identity or habit to explain why states comply with international law. *See, e.g.*, Ted Hopf, *The Logic of Habit in International Relations*, 16 EUROPEAN JOURNAL OF INTERNATIONAL RELATIONS 539–561 (2010).

28   ARISTOTLE, NICOMACHEAN ETHICS, bk. II, ch. I (350 B.C.E.).

29   GAUTHIER, *supra* note 26, at 184–85.

30   *Id.* at 186.

31   *Id.* at 187.

32   *Id.* at 189.

33   Brian Skyrms, *The Shadow of the Future, in* RATIONAL COMMITMENT AND SOCIAL JUSTICE: ESSAYS FOR GREGORY KAVKA 12–21 (Jules L. Coleman & Christopher W. Morris eds., 2007).

34   *See also* ROBERT AXELROD, THE EVOLUTION OF COOPERATION 4 (1984) (discussing Hobbes); Kenneth Oye, ed., COOPERATION UNDER ANARCHY (1986).

35   *See* HOBBES, LEVIATHAN, bk. XV, ch. 4; Skyrms, *supra* note 33, at 12.

36   Skyrms, *supra* note 33, at 16–17.

37   *Id.* at 17.

38   *Id.*

39   Gauthier, *supra* note 11, at 57.

40   *Id.*

41   *Id.* at 56.

42   *See* Michael E. Bratman, *Toxin, Temptation, and the Stability of Intention, in* RATIONAL COMMITMENT AND SOCIAL JUSTICE: ESSAYS FOR GREGORY KAVKA 59–83 (Jules L. Coleman & Christopher W. Morris eds., 2007).

43   *Id.* at 66.

44   Edward F. McClennen, *Rationality and Rules, in* MODELING RATIONALITY, MORALITY, AND EVOLUTION 16 (Peter A. Danielson ed., 1998).

45   *Id.* at 24.

46   *Id.* (but noting that you "retain the option of reconsideration insofar as events turn out to be different from what you had anticipated").

47   This possibility is discussed in Joe Mintoff, *Minimally Constrained Maximization: An Outline, in* REASONS AND INTENTIONS 85, 111 (2008).

48   Bratman, *supra* note 42, at 62.

49   *Id.* at 66.

50   *Id.* at 66–67.

51   *See generally* GREGORY KAVKA, MORAL PARADOXES OF NUCLEAR DETERRENCE (1987).

52   The dilemma is addressed in Duncan MacIntosh, *Retaliation Rationalized: Gauthier's Solution to the Deterrence Dilemma*, 72 PACIFIC PHILOSOPHICAL QUARTERLY 9–32 (1991).

53 *See* Gauthier, *supra* note 21, at 711.

54 The objection is discussed in Joe Mintoff, *Rational Cooperation, Irrational Retaliation*, 74 PACIFIC PHILOSOPHICAL QUARTERLY 362–80 (1993).

55 *See* GAUTHIER, *supra* note 26, at 4.

56 *See* Gareth Williams, *The Problems of David Gauthier's Attempt to Derive Morality from Rationality*, 51 PHILOSOPHICAL NOTES 1–4 (1998).

57 KAVKA, *supra* note 51, at 19.

58 *See, e.g.*, Farrell, *supra* note 4, at 25–29.

59 Legality of the Threat or Use of Nuclear Weapons, Advisory Opinion, 1996 I.C.J. 226 (July 8).

60 *Id.* ¶ 97.

61 *Id.* at 328 (dissenting opinion of Vice President Schwebel).

62 *Id.* ("in some circumstances, the threat of the use of nuclear weapons—as long as they remain weapons unproscribed by international law—may be both lawful and rational").

63 *Id.* at 327 ("Can it seriously be maintained that Mr. Baker's calculated—and apparently successful—threat was unlawful?").

64 *See* Gregory S. Kavka, *Some Paradoxes of Deterrence*, 75 JOURNAL OF PHILOSOPHY 285, 285 (1978) ("The moral paradoxes of deterrence arise out of the attempt to determine the moral status of the defender's intention to retaliate in such cases. If the defender knows retaliation to be wrong, it would appear that this intention is evil. Yet such "evil" intentions may pave the road to heaven, by preventing serious offenses and by doing so without actually harming anyone.").

65 *Id.* at 288.

66 Farrell, *supra* note 4, at 38.

67 *See also* Mintoff, *supra* note 54, at 362–70 (arguing that reconsideration under limited circumstances is rational and constitutes a response to the deterrence objection).

68 *See* Gauthier, *supra* note 11, at 55.

69 *Compare* Gauthier, *supra* note 21, at 705–06, *with* David Gauthier, *Deterrence, Maximization, and Rationality*, 94 ETHICS 474, 494 (1984). *See also* Mintoff, *supra* note 54, at 616–17; Bratman, *supra* note 42, at 65.

70 Gauthier, *supra* note 21, at 692–93 (citing DAVID HUME, A TREATISE OF HUMAN NATURE 520–21 (1888)).

71 Gauthier, *supra* note 21, at 693.

72 For an extensive discussion, see BRIAN SKYRMS, THE STAG HUNT AND THE EVOLUTION OF SOCIAL STRUCTURE (2004).

73 *Id.* at 4.

74 *Id.* at 5.

75 Gauthier, *supra* note 21, at 695–96.

76 POSNER & GOLDSMITH, *supra* note 1, at 185.

77 *Id.* at 14–15.

78 *Id.* at 167–84.

79 *See, e.g., id.* at 14–15.

80 Other theorists have pointed out that Posner and Goldsmith's reliance on this alleged dichotomy is fallacious. *See, e.g.,* George Norman & Joel P. Trachtman, *The Customary International Law Game,* 99 AMERICAN JOURNAL OF INTERNATIONAL LAW 541, 541–42 (2005); Jose E. Alvarez, *A BIT on Custom,* 42 N.Y.U. JOURNAL OF INTERNATIONAL LAW & POLITICS 17, 43 (2009).

81 For the moment, I use these terms virtually interchangeably.

82 *See* Scott J. Shapiro & Oona A. Hathaway, *Outcasting: Enforcement in Domestic and International Law,* 121 YALE LAW JOURNAL 252 (2011).

83 GAUTHIER, *supra* note 26, at 2–10.

84 This is so because Gauthier's account of morality is based on contractarianism. So following through on agreements entails acting morally because all of morality is essentially an elaborate agreement to avoid the pitfalls of the state of nature.

85 *See* DEREK PARFIT, ON WHAT MATTERS, vol. 1, at 433–47 (2011).

86 DEREK PARFIT, REASONS AND PERSONS 241 (1984).

87 *Id.* at 217 (what matters is Relation-R).

88 *Id.* at 289.

89 Several philosophers have pursued this insight as the basis for a general theory of personal identity. *See, e.g.,* Christine Korsgaard, *Personal Identity and the Unity of Agency: A Kantian Response to Parfit,* 18 PHILOSOPHY & PUBLIC AFFAIRS 101–32 (1989); CAROL ROVANE, THE BOUNDS OF AGENCY: AN ESSAY IN REVISIONARY METAPHYSICS (1997).

90 I discuss this issue in Jens David Ohlin, *Is the Concept of the Person Necessary for Human Rights?,* 105 COLUMBIA LAW REVIEW 209 (2005).

91 Ohlin, *id.* at 228–29; EMMERICH DE VATTEL, THE LAW OF NATIONS § 12, at 3 (Joseph Chitty ed., 1853) (1758). *Compare with* ERIC A. POSNER & DAVID WEISBACH, CLIMATE CHANGE JUSTICE 101 (2010) (concluding that collective agency for nation-states is unappealing).

92 *See generally* KATERINA LINOS, THE DEMOCRATIC FOUNDATIONS OF POLICY DIFFUSION (2013); ANNE-MARIE SLAUGHTER, A NEW WORLD ORDER 50 (2004); Pierre-Hugues Verdier, *Transnational Regulatory Networks and Their Limits,* 34 YALE JOURNAL OF INTERNATIONAL LAW 113 (2009).

93 *See* CHRISTIAN LIST & PHILIP PETTIT, GROUP AGENCY: THE POSSIBILITY, DESIGN, AND STATUS OF CORPORATE AGENTS (2011).

94 Onerous legal procedures for amendment can serve as a way of entrenching a previous decision. *See, e.g.,* Christopher Serkin, *Public Entrenchment through Private Law: Binding Local Governments,* 78 UNIVERSITY OF CHICAGO LAW REVIEW 879, 887 (2011) (noting that as an informal method of

entrenching prior decisions, the Locrians in ancient Greece required "that the proponent of any legal change make his proposal with a noose around his neck.").

95   *Cf.* HOBBES, LEVIATHAN, pt. II, ch. 30 (concluding that the law of nations and the laws of nature were coextensive).

CHAPTER FIVE

1   *See generally* ANTHONY D'AMATO, THE CONCEPT OF CUSTOM IN INTERNATIONAL LAW (1971); MAARTEN BOS, A METHODOLOGY OF INTERNATIONAL LAW (1984).

2   Mark Weston Janis, *Individuals as Subjects of International Law*, 17 CORNELL INTERNATIONAL LAW JOURNAL 61 (1984).

3   *See* LOUIS HENKIN, THE AGE OF RIGHTS 37 (1990).

4   U.N. Charter art. 104 ("The Organization shall enjoy in the territory of each of its Members such legal capacity as may be necessary for the exercise of its functions and the fulfilment of its purposes."); NIGEL WHITE, THE UNITED NATIONS SYSTEM: TOWARD INTERNATIONAL JUSTICE 29 (2002) ("In these approaches the United Nations is subservient to the state; whereas the legal personality of a state is original and complete, the personality of the United Nations is derivative and incomplete, perhaps nonexistent if taken to the extreme.").

5   *See* RAY MURPHY, UN PEACEKEEPING IN LEBANON, SOMALIA AND KOSOVO: OPERATIONAL AND LEGAL ISSUES 246 (2007).

6   JAMES Q. WHITMAN, THE VERDICT OF BATTLE: THE LAW OF VICTORY AND THE MAKING OF MODERN WAR (2012).

7   *Id.* at 2 ("In particular, in past centuries, a pitched battle was often described as a momentous kind of trial or legal proceeding, a lawful way for two contending parties to settle their differences through a day of deliberate, staged collective violence."); *see also id.* at 3–8.

8   *See* INTERNATIONAL COMMITTEE OF THE RED CROSS (ICRC), CUSTOMARY INTERNATIONAL HUMANITARIAN LAW 3 (2005) (Rule 1, "Distinction between Civilians and Combatants").

9   *Id.* at 46 (Rule 14, "Proportionality in Attack"). *See also* Protocol Additional to the Geneva Conventions of 12 August 1949, and relating to the Protection of Victims of International Armed Conflicts art. 41, June 8, 1977, 1125 U.N.T.S. 3 [hereinafter Additional Protocol I], art. 51(5)(b).

10   Protocol Additional to the Geneva Conventions of 12 August 1949, and relating to the Protection of Victims of Non-International Armed Conflicts, June 8, 1977, 1125 U.N.T.S. 609 [hereinafter Additional Protocol II], art. 13 (3); Additional Protocol I, art. 51(3).

11   Additional Protocol I, art. 35(2).

12   *See generally* Convention relative to the Treatment of Prisoners of War, Geneva, July 27, 1929, art. 2.

13   *But see* FRITS KALSHOVEN & LIESBETH ZEGVELD, CONSTRAINTS ON THE
     WAGING OF WAR 2 (4th ed. 2011) (The "limits set by *jus in bello* do not pur-
     port to turn armed conflict into a socially acceptable activity like the medi-
     eval jousting tournament: their aim goes no further than to prevent wanton
     cruelty and ruthlessness and to provide essential protection to those most
     directly affected by the conflict."); ALEXANDER GILLESPIE, A HISTORY OF
     THE LAWS OF WAR vol. 3, at 7–13 (2011).

14   *See* MICHAEL WALZER, JUST AND UNJUST WARS: A MORAL ARGUMENT WITH
     HISTORICAL ILLUSTRATIONS 35 (1997) (concluding that "among soldiers
     who choose to fight, restraints of carious sorts arise easily and, one
     might say, naturally, the product of mutual respect and recognition"
     but also noting that chivalry play only a "small part in contemporary
     combat").

15   *Cf.* WHITMAN, *supra* note 6, at 21 (discussing the difference between rules of
     game and rules of law, where the former requires perfect obedience to the
     rules and the latter does not).

16   People v. Russell, 91 N.Y.2d 280, 693 N.E.2d 193 (1998).

17   *Russell*, 91 N.Y.2d at 286–87.

18   *Id.* at 288.

19   *Id.*

20   *Id.*

21   *Id.* at 289.

22   New York v. Abbott, 445 N.Y.S.2d 344 (App. Div. 1981); New York v. Fabian,
     586 N.Y.S.2d 468, 471 (App. Div. 1992); Alston v. State, 662 A.2d 247, 254 (Md.
     1995).

23   For a rich discussion of reciprocity, see MARK OSIEL, THE END OF
     RECIPROCITY: TERROR, TORTURE, AND THE LAW OF WAR 4 (2009) (asking
     whether international humanitarian law (IHL) should be primarily recipro-
     cal or nonreciprocal).

24   *See* ICRC, *supra* note 8, at 498 (Rule 140, "The Obligation to Respect and
     Ensure Respect for International Humanitarian Law Does Not Depend on
     Reciprocity").

25   *See* Shane Darcy, *The Evolution of the Law of Belligerent Reprisals*, 175
     MILITARY LAW REVIEW 184, 185–86 (2003).

26   *See* Darcy, *id.* at 188.

27   The 1929 Geneva Convention, art. 2, outlawed reprisals against prisoners of
     war ("Prisoners of war are in the power of the hostile Government, but not
     of the individuals or formation which captured them. They shall at all times
     be humanely treated and protected, particularly against acts of violence,
     from insults and from public curiosity. Measures of reprisal against them
     are forbidden.").

28   Prosecutor v. Kupreskic, Case No. IT-95-16-T, Judgment, ¶ 530 (Int'l Crim.
     Trib. for the Former Yugoslavia Jan. 14, 2000) ("It should be added that

while reprisals could have had a modicum of justification in the past, when they constituted practically the only effective means of compelling the enemy to abandon unlawful acts of warfare and to comply in future with international law, at present they can no longer be justified in this manner. A means of inducing compliance with international law is at present more widely available and, more importantly, is beginning to prove fairly efficacious: the prosecution and punishment of war crimes and crimes against humanity by national or international courts.").

29   *Id.* ¶ 529. However, the ICTY in *Kupreskic* also stated that the prohibition does not apply when civilians abuse their rights, when civilians are collateral damage, or when civilians may be the legitimate target of reprisals (when not in the hands of the adversary). *See id.* at ¶¶ 522, 527.

30   *See* KAI AMBOS, TREATISE ON INTERNATIONAL CRIMINAL LAW vol. 1, at 391 (2013) ("it is questionable whether the reprisal prohibition contained in AP I is indeed part of customary international law").

31   ICRC, *supra* note 8, at 521 (Rule 146) ("Although practice in favour of a specific ban on the use of reprisals against all civilians is widespread and representative, it is not yet uniform. The United States, which is not a party to Additional Protocol I, has indicated on several occasions that it does not accept such a total ban. . . .").

32   *Id.* (commentary to Rule 146).

33   *Id.* (citing U.N. Secretary-General, Message dated June 9, 1984 to the Presidents of the Islamic Republic of Iran and the Republic of Iraq).

34   *See* FRANCIS LIEBER, INSTRUCTIONS FOR THE GOVERNMENT OF ARMIES OF THE UNITED STATES IN THE FIELD, General Order No. 100, art. 20 (Apr. 24, 1863) [hereinafter Lieber Code].

35   *Cf.* WHITMAN, *supra* note 6, at 256.

36   Additional Protocol I, art. 48.

37   *See, e.g.,* SAHR CONWAY-LANZ, COLLATERAL DAMAGE: AMERICANS NONCOMBATANT IMMUNITY AND ATROCITY AFTER WORLD WAR II 226 (2006).

38   The one exception was a stray paragraph on disproportionality in the trial chamber judgment in *Gotovina*, and in any event, the conviction was overturned by the ICTY Appeals Court. *See* Prosecutor v. Gotovina, Case No. IT-06-90-A, Appeal Judgment, ¶ 82 (Int'l Crim. Trib. for the Former Yugoslavia Nov. 16, 2012) (overturning Trial Chamber's finding that the attack against the town of Martić was disproportionate).

39   This issue is explored in greater detail in Jens David Ohlin, *Targeting and the Concept of Intent,* MICHIGAN JOURNAL OF INTERNATIONAL LAW (2013).

40   The U.S. Model Penal Code refers to this as acting with purpose. *See* Model Penal Code § 2.02(2)(a). Continental jurists also use the phrase *dolus directus.*

41 *See* Model Penal Code § 2.02(2)(b).

42 *See* Model Penal Code § 2.02(2)(c) ("A person acts recklessly with respect to a material element of an offense when he consciously disregards a substantial and unjustifiable risk that the material element exists or will result from his conduct").

43 For a discussion, see MICHAEL BOHLANDER, PRINCIPLES OF GERMAN CRIMINAL LAW 63–64 (2009).

44 Ohlin, *supra* note 39, at 103.

45 *Cf.* Mohamed Elewa Badar, *The Mens Rea Enigma in the Jurisprudence of the International Criminal Court*, *in* THE DIVERSIFICATION AND FRAGMENTATION OF INTERNATIONAL CRIMINAL LAW 504, 511 (Larissa van den Herik & Carsten Stahn eds., 2012).

46 *See, e.g.*, Prosecutor v. Galić, Case No. IT-98-29-T, ¶43, (Dec. 5, 2003) 3; Prosecutor v. Blaskic, Case No. IT-95-14-T, Appeal Judgment, ¶ 180 (Mar. 3, 2000); Prosecutor v. Kordić & Čerkez, Case No. IT-95-14/2-T, Judgment, ¶¶ 322–325 (Feb. 26, 2001).

47 *See* THOMAS AQUINAS, SUMMA THEOLOGICA (2674–1275) ("I answer that, Nothing hinders one act from having two effects, only one of which is intended, while the other is beside the intention.").

48 Anthony Kenny, *The Principle of Double Effect*, *in* ESSAYS ON THE ARISTOTELIAN TRADITION 47, 47–48 (2001).

49 MICHAEL WALZER, JUST AND UNJUST WARS 257–83 (3d ed. 2000) (1977); F. M. KAMM, THE MORAL TARGET: AIMING AT RIGHT CONDUCT IN WAR AND OTHER CONFLICTS 41 (2012).

50 *See* Additional Protocol I, art. 51(3) ("Civilians shall enjoy the protection afforded by this section, unless and for such time as they take a direct part in hostilities.").

51 *See generally* WILLIAM H. BOOTHBY, THE LAW OF TARGETING (2012).

52 *See* ICRC, *supra* note 8, at 19–24.

53 For a good discussion of the transitory element, see Bill Boothby, *"And For Such Time As": The Time Dimension to Direct Participation in Hostilities*, 42 NYU JOURNAL OF INTERNATIONAL LAW & POLITICS 741, 764–65 (2010) (questioning customary status of the rule and concluding that the "for such time" requirement is limited to treaty members).

54 The opinion of the Israeli Supreme Court in *Targeted Killing* refers to this as a revolving door problem. *See* HCJ 769/02 Public Committee Against Torture in Israel v. Government of Israel 53(4) PD 459 [2006] (Isr.) ("Targeted Killings Case"). *See also* Nils Melzer, *Keeping the Balance Between Military Necessity and Humanity: A Response to the Four Critiques of the ICRC's Interpretive Guidance on the Notion of Direct Participation in Hostilities*, 42 NYU JOURNAL OF INTERNATIONAL LAW & POLITICS 831, 888 (2010).

55 *See* Michael N. Schmitt, *Deconstructing Direct Participation in Hostilities: The Constitutive Elements*, 42 NYU JOURNAL OF INTERNATIONAL LAW & POLICY 697, 727 (2010).

56 *Compare* Schmitt, *id.* at 727, *with* Melzer, supra note 54, at 865–66.

57 The issue is discussed in Jens David Ohlin, *Targeting Co-Belligerents*, *in* TARGETED KILLINGS: LAW & MORALITY IN AN ASYMMETRICAL WORLD 60, 73 (2012).

58 *See* Amos N. Guiora, *Determining a Legitimate Target: The Dilemma of the Decision-Maker*, 47 TEXAS INTERNATIONAL LAW JOURNAL 315, 334 (2012).

59 *See* ICRC, *supra* note 8, at 23 (Rule 6).

60 ICRC, INTERPRETIVE GUIDANCE ON THE NOTION OF DIRECT PARTICIPATION IN HOSTILITIES UNDER INTERNATIONAL HUMANITARIAN LAW (2009) [hereinafter ICRC INTERPRETIVE GUIDANCE].

61 The process was described in W. Hays Parks, *Part IX of the ICRC "Direct Participation in Hostilities" Study: No Mandate, No Expertise, and Legally Incorrect*, 42 NYU JOURNAL OF INTERNATIONAL LAW & POLICY 769 (2010).

62 *See* ICRC, *Customary International Law*, at 21 (Rule 6), ("To the extent that members of armed opposition groups can be considered civilians (see commentary to Rule 5), this rule appears to create an imbalance between such groups and governmental armed forces. Application of this rule would imply that an attack on members of armed opposition groups is only lawful for 'such time as they take a direct part in hostilities' while an attack on members of governmental armed forces would be lawful at any time. Such imbalance would not exist if members of armed opposition groups were, due to their membership, either considered to be continuously taking a direct part in hostilities or not considered to be civilians.").

63 *See* ICRC INTERPRETIVE GUIDANCE, *supra* note 60, at 33.

64 *Id.* at 36.

65 Some scholars criticized the ICRC report for failing to put the two on equal ground, since the report concluded that organized armed groups include members who do not serve a continuous combat function and are therefore not targetable. For a discussion of this issue, see Melzer, *supra* note 54, at 851–52.

66 Melzer, *id.* at 850.

67 *Id.* at 852.

68 For a personal anecdote along these lines, see Parks, *supra* note 61, at 804 n.96. The analysis is slightly more complicated if the cook in question is a civilian contractor and is not part of the U.S. Army.

69 *See, e.g.*, Al Bihani v. Obama, 594 F. Supp. 2d 35, 39–40 (D.C. Cir. 2010).

70 Al Warafi v. Obama, 704 F. Supp. 2d 32, 38 (D.D.C. 2010); Hamlily v. Obama, 616 F. Supp. 2d 63, 75 (D.D.C. 2009).

71 *See* Ohlin, *supra* note 57, at 74.

72 ICRC, *supra* note 60, at 25 ("Membership in irregular armed forces, such as militias, volunteer corps, or resistance movements belonging to a party to the conflict, generally is not regulated by domestic law and can only be reliably determined on the basis of functional criteria, such as those applying to organized armed groups in non-international armed conflict.").

73 It should be noted that the ICRC's INTERPRETIVE GUIDANCE, *supra* note 60, at 77–82, argues that there is a duty to capture rather than kill, although this issue is conceptually distinct from the question of who can be targeted.

74 *But see* Anthea Roberts & Sandesh Sivakumaran, *Lawmaking by Nonstate Actors: Engaging Armed Groups in the Creation of International Humanitarian Law*, 37 YALE JOURNAL OF INTERNATIONAL LAW 107, 109 (2012) ("As international humanitarian law now treats nonstate armed groups as subjects rather than mere objects of international law, it is worth questioning whether nonstate armed groups can and should be given a role in the creation of the international law that governs conflicts to which they are parties."). It should be noted that the Roberts and Sivakumaran approach is normative, not descriptive.

75 *Compare* Jens David Ohlin, *The Duty to Capture*, 97 MINNESOTA LAW REVIEW 1268, 1304 (2012), *with* David Luban, *Military Necessity and the Cultures of Military Law*, 26 LEIDEN JOURNAL OF INTERNATIONAL LAW 315, 340 (2013) (suggesting that necessity plays both a regulatory and licensing function).

76 *See* Marko Milanović, *Norm Conflicts, International Humanitarian Law, and Human Rights Law*, *in* INTERNATIONAL HUMANITARIAN LAW AND INTERNATIONAL HUMAN RIGHTS LAW 95, 98 (Orna Ben-Naftali ed., 2011).

77 *See* Prosecutor v. Tadić, Case No. IT-94-1-T, Judgment, ¶¶ 557–560 (Int'l Crim. Trib. for the Former Yugoslavia May 7, 1997).

78 *Id.* at ¶¶ 561–568.

79 *See* Prosecutor v. Tadić, Case No. IT-94-1-I, Decision on the Defence Motion for Interlocutory Appeal on Jurisdiction ¶¶ 128–137 (Int'l Crim. Trib. for the Former Yugoslavia Oct. 2, 1995).

80 *Id.* ¶¶ 67–68.

81 Milanović, *supra* not 76, at 125.

82 *See* MARKO MILANOVIĆ, EXTRATERRITORIAL APPLICATION OF HUMAN RIGHTS TREATIES 43 (2011).

83 The issue is extensively discussed in Jennifer C. Daskal, *The Geography of the Battlefield: A Framework for Detention and Targeting Outside the "Hot" Conflict Zone*, 161 UNIVERSITY OF PENNSYLVANIA LAW REVIEW (2012); JASON RALPH, AMERICA'S WAR ON TERROR: THE STATE OF THE 9/11 EXCEPTION FROM BUSH TO OBAMA 140 (2013).

84   *See, e.g.*, Mary Ellen O'Connell, *On Drone Killings, Brennan Doesn't Uphold our Values*, CNN.com, Jan. 14, 2003, *available at* http://www.cnn.com/2013/01/14/opinion/oconnell-brennan.

85   *Id.*

86   *Cf.* Nasser Arrabyee & Robert F. Worth, *Fighting Spreads in Yemen, Raising Fear of Civil War*, N.Y. TIMES, June 1, 2011.

87   *Compare* Robert Chesney, *Reactions to the ACLU Suit: There Is Armed Conflict in Yemen, and the US Is Party to It*, LAWFARE (July 18, 2012, 12:48 PM), *available at* http://www.lawfareblog.com/2012/07/reactions-to-the-aclu-suit-there-is-armed-conflict-in-yemen-and-the-us-is-party-to-it/, *with* Kevin Jon Heller, *Let's Call Killing al-Awlaki What It Is—Murder*, OPINIO JURIS (Aug. 8, 2010), *available at* http://opiniojuris.org/2010/04/08/lets-call-killing-al-awlaki-what-it-is-murder/.

88   *But see* Mary Ellen O'Connell, *Combatants and the Combat Zone*, 43 UNIVERSITY OF RICHMOND LAW REVIEW 845, 858 (2009).

89   For a discussion of this specific region, see Laurie R. Blank & Benjamin R. Farley, *Characterizing US Operations in Pakistan: Is the United States Engaged in an Armed Conflict?*, 34 FORDHAM INTERNATIONAL LAW JOURNAL 151, 189 (2011) ("Once identified as an armed conflict rather than as isolated acts of violence, the hostilities between the United States and the TTP can be characterized as an intervention into the ongoing non-international armed conflict between Pakistan and the TTP. That conflict remains a non-international armed conflict because the United States is intervening on the side of the state actor. Alternatively, the conflict between the United States and the TTP can be characterized as a separate parallel conflict, either a Common Article 3 conflict, using the broad standard established in *Hamdan*, or, at a minimum, a transnational armed conflict triggering the application of fundamental principles of the law of war that govern the conduct of any military operations.").

90   Prosecutor v. Tadić, Case No. IT-94-1, Decision on Defence Motion for Interlocutory Appeal, ¶ 70 (Int'l Crim. Trib. for the Former Yugoslavia Oct. 2, 1995).

91   For a similar argument, see Michael Lewis, *Drones and the Boundaries of the Battlefield*, 47 TEXAS INTERNATIONAL LAW JOURNAL 293, 312 (2012).

92   *See Tadić, supra* note 90, at ¶¶ 67–68.

93   *Id.* at ¶ 69.

94   For background, see *Drone Strikes Kill, Maim and Traumatize too Many Civilians, U.S. Study Says*, CNN.com, Sept. 25, 2012, *available at* http://www.cnn.com/2012/09/25/world/asia/pakistan-us-drone-strikes/ (citing International Human Rights & Conflict Resolution Clinic at Stanford Law School & Global Justice Clinic at NYU School of Law, *Living Under Drones: Death, Injury and Trauma to Civilians from US Drone Practices in Pakistan* (Sept. 2012), *available at* http://www.livingunderdrones.org/).

95 For a good discussion of the *Tadić* criteria, see Marco Sassòli, *The Role of Human Rights and International Humanitarian Law in New Types of Armed Conflict, in* PAS DE DEUX: INTERNATIONAL HUMANITARIAN LAW AND INTERNATIONAL HUMAN RIGHTS LAW 34, 54 (Orna Ben-Naftali ed., 2011).

96 Geneva Convention for the Amelioration of the Condition of the Wounded and Sick in Armed Forces in the Field art. 3, Aug. 12, 1949, 6 U.S.T. 3114, 75 U.N.T.S. 31; see also Geneva Convention for the Amelioration of the Condition of Wounded, Sick and Shipwrecked Members of Armed Forces at Sea art. 2, Aug. 12, 1949, 6 U.S.T. 3217, 75 U.N.T.S. 85; Geneva Convention Relative to the Treatment of Prisoners of War art. 2, Aug. 12, 1949, 6 U.S.T. 3316, 75 U.N.T.S. 135; Geneva Convention Relative to the Protection of Civilian Persons in Time of War art. 2, Aug. 12, 1949, 6 U.S.T. 3516, 75 U.N.T.S. 287. For a discussion of these and related issues, see Marko Milanović & Vidan Hadzi-Vidanovic, *A Taxonomy of Armed Conflict, in* RESEARCH HANDBOOK ON INTERNATIONAL CONFLICT AND SECURITY LAW 256–314 (Nigel White & Christian Henderson eds., 2013) (criticizing the reasoning in *Hamdan v. Rumsfeld*, 548 U.S. 557 (2006)); Natasha Balendra, *Defining Armed Conflict*, 29 CARDOZO LAW REVIEW 2461, 2468–70 (2008); Dino Kritsiotis, *The Tremors of Tadić*, 43 ISRAEL LAW REVIEW 262, 263 (2010).

97 For a more detailed version of this argument, see Ohlin, *Duty to Capture, supra* note 75, at 1279–80.

98 *See generally* Geoffrey S. Corn, *Geography of Armed Conflict: Why It Is a Mistake to Fish for the Red Herring*, 89 INTERNATIONAL LAW STUDIES 77 (2013).

99 *See* Prosecutor v. Tadić, Case No. IT-94-1-T, Judgment, ¶¶ 561–568 (Int'l Crim. Trib. for the Former Yugoslavia May 7, 1997).

100 *See* Emily Crawford, *International Armed Conflict, in* MAX PLANCK ENCYCLOPEDIA OF INTERNATIONAL LAW (2011) (citing Common Article 2 in the Geneva Conventions).

101 *See* Thilo Marauhn & Zacharie F. Ntoubandi, *Non-International Armed Conflict, in* MAX PLANCK ENCYCLOPEDIA OF INTERNATIONAL LAW (2011) ("There is no general definition of non-international armed conflicts in public international law. Treaty law has, however, established different thresholds for its application in non-international armed conflict.").

102 Hamdan v. Rumsfeld, 548 U.S. 557, 629 (2006).

103 *Id.* at 631.

104 *See* Linda Greenhouse, *Supreme Court Blocks Guantanamo Tribunals*, N.Y TIMES, June 29, 2006 ("The decision was such a sweeping and categorical defeat for the Bush administration that it left human rights lawyers who have pressed this and other cases on behalf of Guantanamo detainees almost speechless with surprise and delight, using words like 'fantastic,' 'amazing,' 'remarkable.' Michael Ratner, president of the Center for

Constitutional Rights, a public interest law firm in New York that represents hundreds of detainees, said, 'It doesn't get any better.'").

105   On divergent interpretations of the *Hamdan* decision, see Marko Milanović, *Lessons for Human Rights and Humanitarian Law in the War on Terror: Comparing Hamdan and the Israeli Targeted Killings Case*, 89 INTERNATIONAL REVIEW OF THE RED CROSS 373, 393 (2007).

106   *See* International Covenant on Civil and Political Rights art. 6, ¶ 1, opened for signature Dec. 19, 1966, 999 U.N.T.S. 171 (entered into force Mar. 23, 1976) [hereinafter ICCPR].

107   *See* Hamdi v. Rumsfeld, 542 U.S. 507 (2004); Rasul v. Bush, 542 U.S. 466 (2004).

108   *Compare* Ohlin, *supra* note 75, at 1283–84, *with* Kai Ambos & Josef Alkatout, *Has 'Justice Been Done'? The Legality of Bin Laden's Killing Under International Law*, 45 ISRAEL LAW REVIEW 341, 347–50 (2012). *See also* Jordan J. Paust, *Self-Defense Targetings of Non-State Actors and Permissibility of U.S. Use of Drones in Pakistan*, 19 JOURNAL OF TRANSNATIONAL LAW & POLICY 237, 260 (2009).

109   As it happens, in most cases, al-Qaeda fighters do not comply with the requirements of belligerency and are therefore not entitled to immunity.

110   *See* JEH C. JOHNSON, SPEECH AT OXFORD UNION: THE CONFLICT AGAINST AL QAEDA AND ITS AFFILIATES: HOW WILL IT END (Nov. 30, 2012) ("I do believe that on the present course, there will come a tipping point—a tipping point at which so many of the leaders and operatives of al Qaeda and its affiliates have been killed or captured, and the group is no longer able to attempt or launch a strategic attack against the United States, such that al Qaeda as we know it, the organization that our Congress authorized the military to pursue in 2001, has been effectively destroyed.").

111   *Id.* ("At that point, we must be able to say to ourselves that our efforts should no longer be considered an 'armed conflict' against al Qaeda and its associated forces; rather, a counterterrorism effort against individuals who are the scattered remnants of al Qaeda, or are parts of groups unaffiliated with al Qaeda, for which the law enforcement and intelligence resources of our government are principally responsible, in cooperation with the international community—with our military assets available in reserve to address continuing and imminent terrorist threats."). *See also* David Rose, *Why We Should Shut down Guantanamo*, THE DAILY MAIL, Aug. 3, 2013 (discussing views of William Lietzau, U.S. Deputy Assistant Defense Secretary for Detainee Affairs, that the "struggle with terrorism is not going to end. But we do have to end the legally cognizable armed conflict with Al Qaeda, a specific transnational group").

112   *See* MILANOVIĆ, EXTRATERRITORIAL APPLICATION OF HUMAN RIGHTS TREATIES, at 229–62.

113 *See* Isayeva v. Russia, 41 Eur. Ct. H.R. 847, 875 (2005); Ergi v. Turkey, 1998-IV Eur. Ct. H.R. 59 (1998). For a discussion, see William Abresch, *A Human Rights Law of Internal Armed Conflict: The European Court of Human Rights in Chechnya*, 16 EUROPEAN JOURNAL OF INTERNATIONAL LAW 741 (2005) (analyzing application of human rights law in the ECHR's Chechnya cases); Gabriella Blum, *The Dispensable Lives of Soldiers*, 2 JOURNAL OF LEGAL ANALYSIS 115, 132 n.39 (2010).

114 U.S. Department of State, Fourth Periodic Report of the United States of America to the United Nations Committee on Human Rights Concerning the International Covenant on Civil and Political Rights, Dec. 30, 2011.

115 The one exception is Guantanamo Bay, over which the U.S. government has de facto jurisdiction and control. *See* Boumediene v. Bush, 553 U.S. 723, 755 (2008). For analysis, see Anthony J. Colangelo, *"De Facto Sovereignty": Boumediene and Beyond*, 77 GEORGE WASHINGTON LAW REVIEW 623 (2009).

116 *See, e.g.*, ICCPR, *supra* note 106.

117 LOUIS HENKIN ET AL., HUMAN RIGHTS (2009).

118 The issue is discussed in MILANOVIĆ, *supra* note 76.

119 *See, e.g.*, Gloria Gaggioli & Robert Kolb, *A Right to Life in Armed Conflicts? The Contribution of the European Court of Human Rights*, 37 ISRAEL YEARBOOK OF HUMAN RIGHTS 115, 134–36 (discussing the right to life in IHL); Noëlle Quénivet, *The Right to Life in International Humanitarian Law and Human Rights Law*, in INTERNATIONAL HUMANITARIAN LAW AND HUMAN RIGHTS LAW: TOWARDS A NEW MERGER IN INTERNATIONAL LAW 331, 338–40 (Roberta Arnold & Noëlle Quénivet eds., 2008) (discussing grounds for deciding on the justification of the use of force in IHL).

120 *See* ICCPR, *supra* note 106, art. 6(1).

121 *See* MILANOVIĆ, *supra* note 76, at 106 (discussing ICJ analysis in the *Nuclear Weapons Case* of "arbitrary" deprivations of life).

122 Universal Declaration of Human Rights, G.A. Res. 217 (III) A, art. 2, U.N. Doc. A/RES/217(III) (Dec. 10, 1948) ("Everyone is entitled to all the rights and freedoms set forth in this Declaration, without distinction of any kind, such as race, colour, sex, language, religion, political or other opinion, national or social origin, property, birth or other status. Furthermore, no distinction shall be made on the basis of the political, jurisdictional or international status of the country or territory to which a person belongs, whether it be independent, trust, non-self-governing or under any other limitation of sovereignty.").

123 *See, e.g.*, ICCPR, *supra* note 106, art. 4(2) (limiting scope of derogations).

124 Legality of the Threat or Use of Nuclear Weapons, Advisory Opinion, 1996 I.C.J. 226, 240 (July 8) (*Nuclear Weapons Case*).

125   Legal Consequences of the Construction of a Wall in the Occupied Palestinian Territory, Advisory Opinion, 2004 I.C.J. 136, 178 (July 9).

126   See *Nuclear Weapons Case, supra* note 124, ¶¶ 25 et seq.

127   *But see* Jordan Paust, *Self-Defense Targetings of Non-State Actors and Permissibility of U.S. Use of Drones in Pakistan*, 19 JOURNAL OF TRANSNATIONAL LAW & POLICY 237, 274 n.94 (2009) (referring to *lex specialis* as "Latinized nonsense").

128   The concept of military necessity was first codified in the Lieber Code, *supra* note 34, arts. 14, 15, & 16.

129   *See, e.g.,* Mary Ellen O'Connell, *The Right to Life in War and Peace. See also* Richard V. Meyer, *The Privilege of Belligerency and Formal Declarations of War, in* TARGETED KILLINGS: LAW & MORALITY IN AN ASYMMETRICAL WORLD 183, 195 (Claire Finkelstein, Jens David Ohlin & Andrew Altman eds., 2012) (discussing criticisms based on the principle of necessity).

130   See Department of Justice, Lawfulness of a Lethal Operation Directed Against a U.S. Citizen Who Is a Senior Operational Leader of Al-Qa'ida or an Associated Force (2011), *available at* http://www.fas.org/irp/eprint/doj-lethal.pdf.

131   For a discussion, see Mehrdad Payandeh, *The United Nations, Military Intervention, and Regime Change in Libya*, 52 VIRGINIA JOURNAL OF INTERNATIONAL LAW 355, 385 (2012).

132   *See, e.g.,* McCann v. United Kingdom, 21 Eur. Ct. H.R. (ser. A) ¶ 215 (1995).

133   HCJ 769/02 Public Committee Against Torture in Israel v. Government of Israel 53(4) PD 459 [2006] (Isr.).

134   Lieber Code, *supra* note 34, arts. 14–16.

135   *Id.,* art. 14.

136   *Id.,* art. 15.

137   This point is skillfully explained in John Fabian Witt, Lincoln's Code 184 (2012).

138   Lieber Code, *supra* note 34, art. 16.

139   This issue is discussed extensively in Ryan Goodman, *The Power to Kill or Capture Enemy Combatants*, 24 EUROPEAN JOURNAL OF INTERNATIONAL LAW 819 (2013).

140   JEAN PICTET, DEVELOPMENT AND PRINCIPLES OF INTERNATIONAL HUMANITARIAN LAW 75 (1985). *See also* ICRC, *supra* note 60, at 82 n.221.

141   *See* NILS MELZER, TARGETED KILLING IN INTERNATIONAL LAW 289 (2009).

142   See Goodman, *supra* note 139, at 842.

143   For an argument to the contrary, see Goodman, *id.,* at 837.

144   Additional Protocol I, *supra* note 9, art. 35(2).

145   For a full discussion of the distinction between military necessity in IHL and necessity in human rights law, see Geoffrey S. Corn, Laurie R. Blank, Chris Jenks & Eric Talbot Jensen, *Belligerent Targeting and the Invalidity of*

a Least Harmful Means Rule, 89 INTERNATIONAL LEGAL STUDIES 536, 552 (2013) ("From the first codified articulation of military necessity until the present day, this principle has been understood to authorize the application of deadly combat power against any belligerent opponent under the operational authority of enemy leadership and physically capable of acting to effectuate that leader's will. This broad scope of authority is directly linked to the primary objective of engaging in armed conflict: to bring the enemy into prompt submission as rapidly and efficiently as possible.").

146 *See* Jens David Ohlin, *Recapturing the Concept of Necessity*, Cornell Legal Studies Research Paper No. 13-90 (Mar. 8, 2013), *available at* http://ssrn.com/abstract=2230486.

CHAPTER SIX

1 *See* Luke A. McLaurin, *Can the President "Unsign" a Treaty? A Constitutional Inquiry*, 84 WASHINGTON UNIVERSITY LAW REVIEW 1941 (2006).

2 ERIC A. POSNER, THE PERILS OF GLOBAL LEGALISM 26 (2012).

3 Neo-realists have long argued that normative constraints on state behavior are impossible in the absence of world government. For a discussion of the fallacy of this jurisprudential argument, see LEA BRILMAYER, AMERICAN HEGEMONY: POLITICAL MORALITY IN A ONE-SUPERPOWER WORLD 53 (1994) (arguing that under the neo-realist view there would be no basis for normative assessments of domestic political legitimacy either because "[s]tandards of legitimacy have to come from somewhere outside the government, but the jurisprudential argument denies that such sources exist").

4 *Id.* at 28–34.

5 *Id.* at 34.

6 *Id.* at 34–35.

7 *Id.*

8 *Id.* at 35.

9 *See, e.g.,* Convention on Rights and Duties of States, Dec. 26, 1933, 49 Stat. 3097, 3100, 165 L.N.T.S. 19, 25 (referring to state as a "person of international law"; declaring that "the federal state shall constitute a sole person in the eyes of international law"; and arguing that juridical equality of states does not "depend upon the power which it possesses to assure its exercise, but upon the simple fact of its existence as a person under international law").

10 Louis Henkin, *That "S" Word: Sovereignty, and Globalization, and Human Rights, Et Cetera*, 68 FORDHAM LAW REVIEW 1 (1999).

11 U.S. Term Limits, Inc. v. Thornton, 514 U.S. 779, 838 (1995) (Kennedy, J., concurring).

12 EMMERICH DE VATTEL, THE LAW OF NATIONS § 12, at 3 (Joseph Chitty ed., 1853) (1758) ("The law of nations is the law of sovereigns; free and independent

states are moral persons . . . ."); *see also* IMMANUEL KANT, THE METAPHYSICS OF MORALS 114 (Mary Gregor ed., 1996) (1797) (referring to the state "as a moral person . . . living in relation to another state in the condition of natural freedom").

13 *See also* JOHN RAWLS, THE LAW OF PEOPLES 32–33 (1999) (theory of international relations founded on second original position composed of rational agents, behind a veil of ignorance, representing liberal societies); CHARLES R. BEITZ, POLITICAL THEORY AND INTERNATIONAL RELATIONS 53 (1979).

14 *See, e.g.*, ANDREW T. GUZMAN, HOW INTERNATIONAL LAW WORKS: A RATIONAL CHOICE THEORY 13 (2008).

15 Convention on the Prevention and Punishment of the Crime of Genocide, Dec. 9, 1948, 78 U.N.T.S. 277. *See* Myres S. McDougal & Richard Arens, *The Genocide Convention and the Constitution*, 3 VANDERBILT LAW REVIEW 683 (1950).

16 Convention on the Elimination of All Forms of Discrimination against Women, Dec. 18, 1979, 1249 U.N.T.S. 13 (entered into force Sept. 3, 1981).

17 List of State Parties to the Convention on the Elimination of All Forms of Discrimination Against Women, *available at* http://treaties.un.org/Pages/ViewDetails.aspx?src=TREATY&mtdsg_no=IV-8&chapter=4&lang=en. In fairness to the United States, it should be noted that several state parties have filed reservations, understandings, or declarations that substantially constrict their obligations under CEDAW.

18 *See* John C. Yoo, *Laws as Treaties? The Constitutionality of Congressional-Executive Agreements*, 99 MICHIGAN LAW REVIEW 757 (2001).

19 *See* JULIAN KU & JOHN YOO, TAMING GLOBALIZATION: INTERNATIONAL LAW, THE U.S. CONSTITUTION, AND THE NEW WORLD ORDER (2012).

20 *Id.* at 255.

21 *Id.* at 40.

22 *Id.* at 40–47.

23 *Id.* at 47–50.

24 *Id.* at 47 ("We ask what, if any, elements of the nation-state will remain 'sovereign' amid these forces of global governance?").

25 *Id.* at 87–112.

26 *Id.* at 108–09.

27 *Id.* at 110.

28 *Id.* at 113–49.

29 For a description of this incident, see Ronald A. Lehmann, *Reinterpreting Advice and Consent: A Congressional Fast Track for Arms Control Treaties*, 98 YALE LAW JOURNAL 885 (1989).

30 Joseph R. Biden, Jr. & John B. Ritch III, *The Treaty Power: Upholding a Constitutional Partnership*, UNIVERSITY OF PENNSYLVANIA LAW REVIEW 1529, 1531 (1989) ("Designed and ratified to serve as the bedrock of nuclear

arms control, the ABM Treaty was now to be gutted by a unilateral Reagan 'reinterpretation.'"). For the competing view, see Abraham D. Sofaer, *The ABM Treaty and the Strategic Defense Initiative*, 99 HARVARD LAW REVIEW 1972 (1986).

31   Treaty Between the United States of American and the Union of Soviet Socialist Republics on the Limitation of Anti-Ballistic Missile Systems, art. V(1), Oct. 3, 1972 ("Each Party undertakes not to develop, test, or deploy ABM systems or components which are sea-based, air-based, space-based, or mobile land-based."). 23 U.S.T. 3435, 944 U.N.T.S. 13.

32   Ku and Yoo also argue that the federal judiciary is the most decentralized of the three branches and therefore has a comparative institutional disadvantage when it comes to foreign policy. KU & YOO, *supra* note 19, at 131.

33   *Id*. at 132.

34   *Id*. at 134.

35   *Id*. at 151–76.

36   Vienna Convention on Consular Relations, Apr. 24, 1963, 21 U.S.T. 77, 596 U.N.T.S. 261.

37   Vienna Convention, *id*., art. 46.

38   LaGrand Case (Ger. v. U.S.), 2001 I.C.J. 466 (June 27).

39   Germany v. United States of America, 2001 I.C.J. 466, 516 (June 27, 2001).

40   Medellín v. Texas, 552 U.S. 491 (2008).

41   *Id*. at 525 ("The President has an array of political and diplomatic means available to enforce international obligations, but unilaterally converting a non-self-executing treaty into a self-executing one is not among them.").

42   KU & YOO, *supra* note 18, at 154.

43   Missouri v. Holland, 252 U.S. 416 (1920).

44   Reid v. Covert, 354 U.S. 1 (1957).

45   The issue is discussed in KAL RAUSTIALA, DOES THE CONSTITUTION FOLLOW THE FLAG? THE EVOLUTION OF TERRITORIALITY IN AMERICAN LAW (2009).

46   Case Concerning Avena and Other Mexican Nationals (Mex. v. U.S.), 2004 I.C.J. 128 (Mar. 31).

47   *Medellín*, 552 U.S. at 507–08.

48   U.N. Charter art. 94(1).

49   *Medellín*, 552 U.S. at 508–09.

50   *Id*. at 510.

51   Memorandum from President George W. Bush to the Attorney General (Feb. 28, 2005).

52   *Medellín*, 552 U.S. at 525.

53   Dames & Moore v. Regan, 453 U.S. 654 (1981); Am, Ins. Ass'n v. Garamendi, 539 U.S. 396 (2003).

54   *Garamendi, id*.

55   KU & YOO, *supra* note 19, at 156.

56   *Id.* at 176.

57   *Id.* at 163.

58   *Id.* at 162.

59   ERIC A. POSNER & ADRIAN VERMEULE, TERROR IN THE BALANCE: SECURITY, LIBERTY, AND THE COURTS 31 (2007).

60   KU & YOO, *supra* note 19, at 165.

61   *Id.*

62   *Id.* at 164.

63   *See* Craig S. Smith, *Europeans Try to Stem Anti-U.S. Anger,* N.Y. TIMES, Jan. 24, 2003.

64   *See* President George W. Bush, Press Conference Remarks, Prague (Nov. 20, 2002).

65   *See* Pact of Paris, Aug. 27, 1928, 46 Stat. 2343, T.S. No. 796, 94 L.N.T.S. 57.

66   U.N. Charter art. 51.

67   For more on this point, see GEORGE P. FLETCHER & JENS DAVID OHLIN, DEFENDING HUMANITY: WHEN FORCE IS JUSTIFIED AND WHY 83 (2008).

68   U.N. Charter art. 42.

69   *See, e.g.,* Saira Mohamed, *From Keeping Peace to Building Peace: A Proposal for a Revitalized United Nations Trusteeship Council,* 105 COLUMBIA LAW REVIEW 809, 822 (2005) (discussing limitations of the Security Council).

70   *See* Ambassador Samantha Power, U.S. Permanent Representative to the United Nations, Remarks at the Security Council Stakeout Following Consultations on Syria, New York (Sept. 26, 2013) (answering press question regarding institutional viability of Security Council in the face of Russian obstruction).

71   *See, e.g.,* Krista Nelson, *The Significance of Chemical Weapons Use Under International Law,* OPINIO JURIS (Sept. 6, 2013, 1:30 PM), *available at* http://opiniojuris.org/2013/09/06/syria-insta-symposium-significance-chemical-weapons-use-international-law/ (noting that the Chemical Weapons Convention triggers its own framework for noncompliance as opposed to triggering a unilateral right of intervention).

72   *See* Michael Abramowitz, *Does the United States Have a "Responsibility to Protect" the Syrian People?,* WASHINGTON POST, Sept. 6, 2013 ("However unpopular or unknown R2P might be in the United States, it has emerged as a preferred vehicle in other parts of the world for mobilizing support for action against potential mass atrocities.").

73   John Kerry, U.S. Secretary of State, Remarks Delivered at the State Department, Washington, D.C. (Aug. 30, 2013) ("And because of the guaranteed Russian obstructionism of any action through the U.N. Security Council, the U.N. cannot galvanize the world to act as it should. So let me be clear. We will continue talking to the Congress, talking to our allies, and most importantly, talking to the American people . . . . But fatigue does not

absolve us of our responsibility. Just longing for peace does not necessarily bring it about. And history would judge us all extraordinarily harshly if we turned a blind eye to a dictator's wanton use of weapons of mass destruction against all warnings, against all common understanding of decency, these things we do know.").

74 *See* Paul H. Robinson & Adil Ahmad Haque, *Advantaging Aggressors: Justice & Deterrence in International Law*, 3 HARVARD NATIONAL SECURITY JOURNAL 143 (2011).

75 *Id.* at 155–56.

76 Legal Consequences of the Construction of a Wall in the Occupied Palestinian Territory, 43 I.L.M. 1009 (2004) (I.C.J. Advisory Opinion of July 9, 2004).

77 U.N. Security Council Res. 1368 (Sept. 12, 2001); U.N. Security Council Res. 1373 (Sept. 28, 2001); U.N. Security Council Res. 1377 (Nov. 12, 2001). *See also* JAN KITTRICH, THE RIGHT OF INDIVIDUAL SELF-DEFENSE IN PUBLIC INTERNATIONAL LAW 123 (2008).

78 *See, e.g.,* YORAM DINSTEIN, WAR, AGGRESSION, & SELF-DEFENCE 182 (2005).

79 *See* ALAN M. DERSHOWITZ, PREEMPTION: A KNIFE THAT CUTS BOTH WAYS (2007).

80 DINSTEIN, *supra* note 78, at 183.

81 Robert J. Delahunty & John Yoo, *The "Bush Doctrine": Can Preventive War be Justified?*, 32 HARVARD JOURNAL OF LAW & PUBLIC POLICY 843, 846 (2009).

82 *See* Jules Lobel, *Preventive War and the Lessons of History*, 68 UNIVERSITY OF PITTSBURGH LAW REVIEW 307, 321 (2006).

83 *See* FLETCHER & OHLIN, *supra* note 67, at 156–63.

84 *Id.* at 164–65.

85 Discussing and evaluating the evidentiary view of the imminence requirement, see Russell Christopher, *Imminence in Justified Targeted Killing, in* TARGETED KILLINGS: LAW AND MORALITY IN AN ASYMMETRICAL WORLD 253, 268 (Claire Finkelstein, Jens David Ohlin & Andrew Altman eds., 2012).

86 *See* Geoffrey Marston, *The London Committee and the Statute of the International Court of Justice, in* FIFTY YEARS OF THE INTERNATIONAL COURT OF JUSTICE 40, 54 (Vaughan Lowe & Malgosia Fitzmaurice eds., 2007).

87 *See* David Bederman, *The Hague Peace Conferences of 1899 and 1907, in* INTERNATIONAL COURTS FOR THE TWENTY-FIRST CENTURY 9, 11 (Mark W. Janis ed., 1992).

88 *See* Sean D. Murphy, *The United States and the International Court of Justice: Coping with Antinomies, in* THE SWORD AND THE SCALES: THE UNITED STATES AND INTERNATIONAL COURTS AND TRIBUNALS 46, 70 (Cesare P.R. Romano ed., 2009).

89 *Id.* at 52.

90   Military and Paramilitary Activities in and Against Nicaragua (Nic.
v. U.S.), 1986 I.C.J. 14, 101 (June 27).

91   *Id.*

92   Murphy, *supra* note 88, at 67.

93   Statute of the International Court of Justice, art. 26.

94   Murphy, *supra* note 88, at 65.

95   Convention on the Prevention and Punishment of the Crime of Genocide,
opened for signature Dec 9, 1948, 78 U.N.T.S. 277 (entered into force
Jan. 12, 1951), art. 9; Application of the Convention on the Prevention and
Punishment of the Crime of Genocide (Bosnia & Herzegovina v. Serbia &
Montenegro) (Feb. 26, 2007).

96   Legality of the Use of Force (Yug. v. U.S.), 1999 I.C.J. 916 (June 2); Murphy,
supra note 88, at 63.

97   *Id.* at 82.

98   *See* McLaurin, *supra* note 1, at 1942–50.

99   John Bolton, Under-Secretary of State for Arms Control and International
Security, Letter to U.N. Secretary General Kofi Annan (May 6, 2002). See
also McLaurin, *supra* note 1, at 1941.

100 American Service-Members' Protection Act (ASPA), 22 U.S.C. §§ 7421 et
seq. (2002). *See* Megan A. Fairlie, *The United States and the International
Criminal Court Post-Bush: A Beautiful Courtship but an Unlikely Marriage,*
29 BERKELEY JOURNAL OF INTERNATIONAL LAW 528, 539 n.63 (2011).

101 *See* Rome Statute, art. 5(2).

102 *See* Rome Statute, art. 8*bis*, art. 15*bis* ("Where the Prosecutor concludes
that there is a reasonable basis to proceed with an investigation in respect
of a crime of aggression, he or she shall first ascertain whether the Security
Council has made a determination of an act of aggression committed by
the State concerned. The Prosecutor shall notify the Secretary-General of
the United Nations of the situation before the Court, including any relevant information and documents.").

103 Article 15*bis* also allows state parties to the Rome Statute to exempt themselves from jurisdiction over the crime of aggression: "The Court may, in
accordance with article 12, exercise jurisdiction over a crime of aggression,
arising from an act of aggression committed by a State Party, unless that
State Party has previously declared that it does not accept such jurisdiction by lodging a declaration with the Registrar. The withdrawal of such
a declaration may be effected at any time and shall be considered by the
State Party within three years."

104 *See* Security Council Res. 1593 (Mar. 31, 2005). Algeria, Brazil, and China
also abstained.

105 *See* Elizabeth Rubin, *If Not Peace, Then Justice,* N.Y. TIMES, Apr. 2, 2006.

106 Security Council Res. 1970 (Feb. 26, 2011).

107 Ambassador Samantha Power, U.S. Permanent Representative to the United Nations, Remarks on Syria, Center for American Progress, Washington, D.C. (Sept. 6, 2013) ("Russia, often backed by China, has blocked every relevant action in the Security Council, even mild condemnations of the use of chemical weapons that did not ascribe blame to any particular party.").

108 Eric Posner, *The Absurd International Criminal Court*, WALL STREET JOURNAL, June 10, 2012.

109 *Id. See also* Eric Posner, *Assad and the Death of the International Criminal Court*, Slate.com (Sept 19, 2013); Eric Posner, *All Justice, Too, Is Local*, N.Y. TIMES, Dec. 30, 2004.

110 John Yoo, *Prosecuting the Peace*, WALL STREET JOURNAL, Jan. 6, 2012.

111 *See* Jens David Ohlin, *A Meta-Theory of International Criminal Procedure: Vindicating the Rule of Law*, 14 UCLA JOURNAL OF INTERNATIONAL LAW & FOREIGN AFFAIRS 77 (2009) (discussing anti-impunity norm); Max Pensky, *Amnesty on Trial: Impunity, Accountability, and the Norms of International Law*, 1 ETHICS & GLOBAL POLITICS 40 (2008).

112 The cornerstone of the ICC's anti-impunity regime is its complementary jurisdiction. The court can only exercise jurisdiction if domestic states are unable or unwilling to prosecute a particular defendant. Rome Statute, art. 17(1)(a).

113 Julian Ku & Jide Nzelibe, *Do International Criminal Tribunals Deter or Exacerbate Humanitarian Atrocities?*, 84 WASHINGTON UNIVERSITY LAW REVIEW 777 (2007); Mark Drumbl, *Collective Violence and Individual Punishment: The Criminality of Mass Atrocity*, 99 NORTHWESTERN UNIVERSITY LAW REVIEW 539, 590 (2005) (no evidence of deterrent effect during atrocities and international conflicts).

114 *See* Jens David Ohlin, *Towards a Unique Theory of International Criminal Sentencing, in* INTERNATIONAL CRIMINAL PROCEDURE: TOWARDS A COHERENT BODY OF LAW 373, 384–86 (Goran Sluiter & Sergey Vasiliev eds., 2009).

115 *See* M. Bergsmo, *Article 16, Deferral of an Investigation or Prosecution, in* COMMENTARY ON THE ROME STATUTE OF THE INTERNATIONAL CRIMINAL COURT 373 (Otto Triffterer ed., 2008).

116 The U.S. understanding of article 98 is not without academic or diplomatic controversy. Some argue that the provision was designed to privilege prior agreements, not license future agreements to shield a state's nationals from ICC prosecution. For a discussion, see William A. Schabas, THE INTERNATIONAL CRIMINAL COURT: A COMMENTARY ON THE ROME STATUTE 1042 (2010); David Scheffer, *Article 98(2) of the Rome Statute: America's Original Intent*, 3 JOURNAL OF INTERNATIONAL CRIMINAL JUSTICE 333, 340–41 (2005) ("The original US negotiating intent was to provide for a

means within the Rome Statute to negotiate future international agreements for non-surrender of US personnel. This was intended to include, in addition to then-existing SOFAs and SOMAs, stand-alone Article 98(2) agreements when necessary and future SOFAs and SOMAs that either would be of amended character or new agreements negotiated from scratch.").

117   Rome Statute, art. 98.

INDEX